150 best ebelskiver recipes

Camilla V. Saulsbury

Robert
ROSE

150 Best Ebelskiver Recipes

For complete cataloguing information, see page 247.

Disclaimer
The recipes in this book have been carefully tested by our kitchen and our tasters. To the best of our knowledge, they are safe and nutritious for ordinary use and users. For those people with food or other allergies, or who have special food requirements or health issues, please read the suggested contents of each recipe carefully and determine whether or not they may create a problem for you. All recipes are used at the risk of the consumer.

We cannot be responsible for any hazards, loss or damage that may occur as a result of any recipe use.

For those with special needs, allergies, requirements or health problems, in the event of any doubt, please contact your medical adviser prior to the use of any recipe.

Design and production: Daniella Zanchetta/PageWave Graphics Inc.
Editor: Sue Sumeraj
Recipe editor: Jennifer MacKenzie
Proofreader: Sheila Wawanash
Indexer: Gillian Watts
Recipe photographer: Colin Erricson
Associate recipe photographer: Matt Johannsson
Recipe food stylist: Kathryn Robertson
Recipe prop stylist: Charlene Erricson
Techniques photographer: David Shaughnessy
Techniques stylist: Anne Fisher
Techniques hand model: Shannon Knopke

Cover image: Raspberry Blintz Ebelskivers (page 78), Blackberry Mint Puffs (page 112) and Lemon Poppy Seed Ebelskivers with Lemon Cream (page 124).

We acknowledge the financial support of the Government of Canada through the Book Publishing Industry Development Program (BPIDP) for our publishing activities.

Published by Robert Rose Inc.
120 Eglinton Avenue East, Suite 800, Toronto, Ontario, Canada M4P 1E2
Tel: (416) 322-6552 Fax: (416) 322-6936
www.robertrose.ca

Printed and bound in Canada

1 2 3 4 5 6 7 8 9 MI 21 20 19 18 17 16 15 14 13

Contents

Introduction

Life is filled with countless little pleasures, and the light, puffy filled pancakes known as ebelskivers are one of them. Ebelskivers (pronounced "able-skeevers") are traditional Danish pancakes served as a sweet treat on special occasions. About the size of a racquetball, they taste like a hybrid of a doughnut, a popover and a pancake. They are cooked entirely on the stovetop — in a few short minutes — in a seven-well ebelskiver pan. Although the name translates as "sliced apples," referring to a traditional spiced apple filling, modern Danes typically stuff ebelskivers with raspberry jam, dust them with confectioners' (icing) sugar and serve at them Christmastime, accompanied by a mug of glögg (warm spiced wine).

Because they are made from pantry staples — flour, milk, eggs and butter — ebelskivers are in a class of their own when it comes to simplicity and style. But what makes them so exciting is their incredible variability and versatility. With one old-fashioned pan, you can make an array of modern, simple, convenient and incredibly delicious puffs. Ebelskivers are in essence quick breads, and just like muffins, scones and biscuits, the possibilities for variation are vast, from classic ebelskivers to modern breakfast options (sit-down and to-go), sophisticated make-ahead appetizers, sweet and savory snacks for the family, decadent desserts and more. They are truly stovetop wonders: snacks, mini breads and desserts that can be made in minutes, *without turning on the oven.*

In the pages that follow, you will find 150 recipes celebrating ebelskivers. All are centered on ease of preparation, with flavors ranging from subtle to bold and everywhere in between, with plenty of innovative interpretations as well as tried and true classics.

The first two chapters offer a suite of sweets: faintly sweet breakfast and brunch options followed by seriously decadent desserts. The third chapter offers savory options aplenty that will inspire your lunches and dinners, wow guests at your next party and charm children of all ages. Last up are global puffs, including puffed and/or stuffed pancakes from Asia, Europe and Africa that are made in pans similar to the ebelskiver pan, as well as contemporary renditions of breads and pancakes from around the world, recast into puffy pancake form.

I hope you will enjoy the charm of ebelskivers as much as I do and that these recipes will make their way into your repertoire for every meal (and snack!) of the day. With a few short steps and one amazing pan, Denmark's delightful puffs can be yours.

Ebelskiver History: Beyond the Borders of Denmark

The origins of ebelskivers are murky, but a common legend of their creation persists. As the story goes, ebelskivers were created by Vikings following a long day of (very unsuccessful) battle. As the weary men gathered around the evening fire, someone mixed up a batter for pancakes. But alas, the griddle had been misplaced! A quick-thinking member of their throng decided his much-dented shield would do and placed it on the fire to heat. As the batter was poured onto the hot shield, it settled into the dents. The result was the inaugural batch of ebelskivers.

While the legend is amusing, an alternative and far more plausible history of ebelskivers comes from Asia. Denmark maintained a significant amount of trade with East and Southeast Asia from the 17th to the 19th century, including the maintenance of small colonies and trading posts in the Indian subcontinent. Throughout these regions, a variety of pancake puffs and breads are made in pans that are similar or nearly identical to ebelskiver pans. In Japan, the *takoyaki* pan is used to make *takoyaki*, a wildly popular savory puffed pancake ball with cooked pieces of octopus (*tako*) stuffed into the center. In China, a larger pan with smaller wells, reminiscent of a waffle maker, is used to make the equally popular, lightly sweetened puffed pancake bites called *gai daan jai*, or Hong Kong egg cakes. In Thailand, the *kanom krok* pan is used to make the quintessentially Thai street food snack *kanom krok*. And in India, the *paniyaram* pan is used to make tender puffed rice flour breads called *kuzhi paniyaram*.

More than likely, versions of the Asian pans were brought back to Denmark and used by home cooks to make distinctive — and now traditional — Danish treats. The Dutch, too, have a version of the ebelskiver pan, the *poffertje* pan. Given Holland's extensive levels of trade throughout Asia from the 17th to the 19th century, the origins of the *poffertje* pan are quite likely identical to those of the ebelskiver pan.

Essential Equipment

Ebelskivers require a special pan, but everything else you need is likely already in your kitchen. Nevertheless, I love to make lists, and this one will ensure that you have the essential tools on hand for making ebelskivers.

The Ebelskiver Pan

Traditional ebelskiver pans, also known as "monk pans," were made of copper or cast iron, but modern versions are made of cast iron or cast aluminum, both of which heat quickly and evenly. The choice of pan is a matter of preference, but also depends on your stovetop. A cast-iron pan may not be suitable for some glass- or porcelain-top stoves, while a cast-aluminum pan may be unsuitable for some gas stoves. Check the manual for your stovetop, or consult the stove manufacturer if necessary.

Modern ebelskiver pans are typically 9 to 10 inches (23 to 25 cm) in diameter and feature a long handle and seven deep, round wells. They are readily available in cooking stores, housewares stores and superstores, as well as through online and mail-order sources. They are also very reasonably priced.

If you opt for a cast-iron pan, choose one that comes pre-seasoned, as they are ready to use immediately and, with proper care, will maintain their nonstick properties over time. It goes without saying that cast-iron pans have a long life, and there is no need to worry about scratching the surface of the wells. If cast aluminum is your choice, select a good-quality, heavy pan that features a nonstick coating to allow for easy flipping and removal of the ebelskivers.

Electric Ebelskiver Makers

One of the most recent additions to ebelskiver-making is the electric ebelskiver maker, which can be found at specialty cooking stores and through online and mail-order sources. These rectangular machines are made of cast aluminum with a nonstick finish and feature nine wells instead of the typical seven. The heat settings match those for a stovetop burner, so adjust to low, medium, medium-high, and so on as directed in the recipe. The makers are easy to use, easy to clean and are very reasonably priced.

Wooden Skewers

Wooden skewers are used to flip the ebelskivers midway through cooking, as well as to remove them from the pan. No skewers? No problem. Chopsticks, heatproof knitting needles, narrow icing spatulas or fondue forks all work swimmingly — just be careful not to scratch the pan.

Spring-Loaded Scoop

While a spring-loaded cookie or ice cream scoop is by no means an essential piece of equipment for making ebelskivers, it is worth singling out because it makes filling the ebelskiver wells a breeze. Further, the scoop allows for accurate measurement of batter, ensuring evenly sized puffs that cook at the same rate. Choose a small scoop that holds 1 or 2 tbsp (15 or 30 mL).

Making Ebelskivers

One of the many joys of making ebelskivers is their quick and straightforward preparation. The primary method can be broken down into a short list of simple steps:

Prepare the Batter

1. **Whisk the dry ingredients.** Whisking the dry ingredients distributes the baking powder, baking soda, salt and spices in the flour. If the leavening is not evenly distributed, the ebelskivers may have a bitter taste.

2. **Whisk the wet ingredients.** Whisk the wet ingredients, such as milk, eggs, oil and melted butter, until thoroughly combined. Sugar is sometimes also whisked in with the wet ingredients.

3. **Combine the dry and wet ingredients.** Add the wet ingredients to the dry ingredients all at once. *Stir just until the dry ingredients are moistened and the batter is combined.* A few lumps are okay. Overmixing the batter develops the gluten in the flour, causing the ebelskivers to be tough, gummy or both.

4. **Add any extra ingredients.** Gently stir or fold in any extra ingredients, such as berries or chocolate chips. As in step 3, the goal is to avoid overmixing.

5. **Beat the egg whites.** Select a squeaky-clean, medium-size bowl. Using an electric mixer, beat the egg whites on medium-high speed until frothy. Increase the speed to high and beat the whites until stiff, but not dry, peaks form.

6. **Gently mix in one-third of the egg whites.** Add one-third of the egg whites to the bowl of batter. Using a rubber spatula, gently mix in the whites, lifting the batter up from the sides and bottom of bowl, to incorporate into and lighten the batter.

7. **Fold in the remaining egg whites.** Add the remaining egg whites to the bowl of batter. Using the rubber spatula, slice through the egg whites and batter, then pull the spatula up and out along the side of the bowl. Take your time and be methodical to avoid deflating the batter, rotating the bowl a quarter turn at a time. Continue until no white streaks are visible in the batter. Use the batter immediately.

Cook the Ebelskivers

1. **Grease the wells.** Although many recipes call for melted butter to grease the wells, I prefer to use neutral vegetable oil because the pan gets very hot and butter can quickly burn. Use a pastry brush or a piece of paper towel dipped in oil to brush or rub each well with a thin, even coat of oil.

2. **Warm the pan.** Place the pan on one of the stove burners and turn the heat to medium. Let the pan and oil heat for 2 to 3 minutes (the oil should be hot but not smoking).

3. **Fill the wells with batter.** When the oil begins to sizzle, scoop the specified amount of batter into each well (typically 1 tbsp/15 mL for filled ebelskivers and 2 tbsp/30 mL for unfilled ebelskivers). Work quickly and efficiently, beginning with the center well, then proceeding clockwise from the top with the remaining wells.

4. **Add the filling.** If making filled ebelskivers, quickly add the filling or fillings specified in the recipe (typically 1 tsp/5 mL of filling) in the center of the batter.

5. **Cover the filling.** For filled ebelskivers, add the remaining batter specified in the recipe to each well (typically 1 tbsp/15 mL), covering the filling.

6. **Cook the first side.** Cook ebelskivers for 2 to 4 minutes, until a few bubbles rise to the surface (the batter will still be quite runny at the center). Shift one of the ebelskivers slightly with a wooden skewer to check that the bottom is golden brown.

7. **Flip the ebelskivers.** Using two wooden skewers, one on either side of an ebelskiver, gently lift and flip the ebelskiver so the cooked side is on top. The uncooked batter will flow out into the well. Repeat with remaining ebelskivers.

8. **Cook the second side.** Continue cooking the ebelskivers for 2 to 3 minutes, until they are golden brown on the second side. To test for interior doneness, insert a toothpick into the center of the ebelskiver. Toothpicks inserted into unfilled ebelskivers should come out with a few moist crumbs attached; with filled ebelskivers, they should come out with a bit of the filling and moist crumbs attached, but not wet batter.

9. **Remove the ebelskivers from the pan.** Using the skewers, lift each ebelskiver from the pan and transfer it to a plate.

10. **Wipe and grease the wells between batches.** After each round of ebelskivers, let the pan cool slightly, then use a damp paper towel to wipe out any crumbs or residue, to avoid burnt pieces and sticking. Grease the wells again before reheating the pan and adding more batter.

The Ebelskiver Pantry

Although ebelskivers require a special pan, they do not require special ingredients. If you have all-purpose flour, baking powder, salt, sugar, butter or oil, milk and eggs, you have what you need to make classic ebelskivers. From there, the simple puffs can be accessorized with an endless array of mix-ins, fillings, sauces and sprinkles. On the following pages, you'll find information on the key ingredients to keep on hand for a wealth of ebelskiver recipes.

Flours, Grains and Nuts

All-Purpose Flour

Made from a blend of high-gluten hard wheat and low-gluten soft wheat, all-purpose flour is fine-textured flour milled from the inner part of the wheat kernel and contains neither the germ nor the bran. All-purpose flour comes either bleached or unbleached; they can be used interchangeably.

Whole Wheat Flour

Whole wheat flour is milled from hard red wheat. It has a fuller flavor and is far more nutritious than all-purpose flour because it contains the wheat bran and sometimes the germ. Because of its higher fat content, it should be stored in the refrigerator to prevent rancidity.

Cake Flour

This finely ground, soft white flour is low in protein, which means it will develop less gluten during mixing and will yield particularly tender baked goods. For a quick substitute for cake flour, replace 2 tbsp (30 mL) of each cup (250 mL) of all-purpose flour with cornstarch.

Rice Flour

Rice flour is used in several of the recipes in "Global Puffs." It is milled from white rice and is gluten-free. It is important to choose rice flour with a fine, powdery texture. Rub the flour between your fingers: it should feel powdery, not gritty. If you use a grittier rice flour, the results will have a gritty texture; not terrible, but not ideal.

Cornmeal

Cornmeal is simply ground dried corn kernels. There are two methods of grinding. The first is the modern method, in which milling is done by huge steel rollers, which remove the husk and germ almost entirely; this creates the most common variety of cornmeal found in supermarkets. The second is the stone-ground method, in which some of the hull and germ of the corn is retained; this type of cornmeal is available at health food stores and in the health food sections of most supermarkets. The two varieties can be used interchangeably in most of the recipes in this collection, but I recommend sticking with the stone-ground variety where specified, as it has a much deeper corn flavor and is far more nutritious.

Rolled Oats

Two types of rolled oats are called for in these recipes: large-flake (old-fashioned) rolled oats are oat groats (hulled and cleaned whole oats) that have been steamed and flattened with huge rollers; quick-cooking rolled oats are groats that have been cut into several pieces before being steamed and rolled into thinner flakes. For the best results, it is important to use the type of rolled oats specified in the recipe.

Ground Flax Seeds (Flaxseed Meal)

Flax seeds are highly nutritious, tiny seeds from the flax plant. They have gained tremendous popularity in recent years thanks to their high levels of omega-3 fatty acids. However, to reap the most benefits from the seeds, they must be ground into meal. Look for packages of ready-ground flax seeds, which may be labeled "flaxseed meal," or grind whole flax seeds in a spice or coffee grinder to a very fine meal. The meal adds a warm, nutty flavor to a wide range of ebelskivers throughout the collection. Store the ground flax seeds in an airtight bag in the refrigerator for 4 to 5 months, or in the freezer for up to 8 months.

Nuts

I've used a wide variety of nuts in this collection, including walnuts, pecans, almonds, pine nuts and pistachios. Many of the recipes call for the nuts to be toasted

Toasting Nuts

Spread the amount of nuts needed for the recipe on a rimmed baking sheet. Bake in a preheated 350°F (180°C) oven for 8 to 10 minutes or until golden and fragrant. Alternatively, toast the nuts in a dry skillet over low heat, stirring constantly for 2 to 4 minutes or until golden and fragrant.

before they are added to the ebelskiver batter. Toasting nuts deepens their flavor and makes them crisp.

Sweeteners
Granulated Sugar

Granulated sugar (also called white sugar) is refined cane or beet sugar, and is the most common sweetener used in this book. Once opened, store granulated sugar in an airtight container in a cool, dry place.

Brown Sugar

Brown sugar is granulated sugar with some molasses added to it. The molasses gives the sugar a soft texture. Light brown sugar (also known as golden yellow sugar) has less molasses and a more delicate flavor than dark brown sugar. Once opened, store brown sugar in an airtight container or a resealable plastic food bag, to prevent clumping.

Confectioners' (Icing) Sugar

Confectioners' (icing) sugar (also called powdered sugar) is granulated sugar that has been ground to a fine powder. Cornstarch is added to prevent the sugar from clumping together. It is used in recipes where regular sugar would be too grainy.

Turbinado Sugar

Turbinado sugar is raw sugar that has been steam-cleaned. The coarse crystals are blond in color and have a delicate molasses flavor. They are typically used for decoration and texture atop baked goods.

Honey

Honey is plant nectar that has been gathered and concentrated by honeybees. Any variety of honey may be used in the recipes in this collection. Unopened containers of honey may be stored at room temperature. After opening, store honey in the refrigerator to protect against mold. Honey will keep indefinitely when stored properly.

Maple Syrup

Maple syrup is a thick liquid sweetener made by boiling the sap from maple trees. It has a strong, pure maple flavor. Maple-flavored pancake syrup is just corn syrup with coloring and artificial maple flavoring added, and it is not recommended as a substitute for pure maple syrup. Unopened containers of maple syrup may be stored at room temperature. After opening, store maple syrup in the refrigerator to protect against mold. Maple syrup will keep indefinitely when stored properly.

Molasses

Molasses is made from the juice of sugar cane or sugar beets, which is boiled until a syrupy mixture remains. The recipes in this collection were tested using dark (cooking) molasses, but you can substitute light (fancy) molasses if you prefer. Blackstrap molasses is thick and very dark, and it has a bitter flavor; it is not recommended for the recipes in this collection. Unopened containers of molasses may be stored at room temperature. After opening, store molasses in the refrigerator to protect against mold. Molasses will keep indefinitely when stored properly.

Fats and Oils
Butter

Fresh butter has a delicate cream flavor and a pale yellow color, and adds tremendous flavor to a wide range of recipes. Although margarine is an acceptable substitute for butter in ebelskiver recipes, I don't recommended using it, as it lacks the nuanced flavor of butter.

Butter quickly picks up off-flavors during storage and when exposed to oxygen; once the carton or wrap is opened, place it in a zipper-top plastic food bag or an airtight container. Store it away from foods with strong odors, especially items such as onions or garlic.

Melting Butter

Cut the specified amount into small pieces, place in a small saucepan and melt over the lowest heat setting. Once the butter has melted, remove the pan from the heat and let cool. Alternatively, arrange the small pieces of butter in a medium-size, microwave-safe dish (it will splatter if crowded into a small dish). Loosely cover with a paper towel and microwave on High for 5- to 10-second intervals, until just melted. To speed the cooling, pour the melted butter into a small bowl or liquid measuring cup.

Vegetable Oil

"Vegetable oil" is a generic term used to describe any neutral, plant-based oil that is liquid at room temperature. You can use a vegetable oil blend, canola oil, light olive oil, grapeseed oil, safflower oil, sunflower oil, peanut oil or corn oil.

Olive Oil

Olive oil is monounsaturated oil that is prized for a wide range of cooking preparations. Plain olive oil (the products are simply labeled "olive oil") contains a combination of refined olive oil and virgin or extra virgin oil. It has a mild flavor and is significantly less expensive than extra virgin olive oil. Extra virgin olive oil is the cold-pressed result of the first pressing of the olives and is considered the finest and fruitiest of the olive oils.

I prefer to use extra virgin olive oil in the recipes that call for olive oil. Since ebelskivers cook for just a brief amount of time, the fruity and spicy nuances of the oil still shine through. However, you are welcome to use any variety of olive oil you prefer.

Toasted Sesame Oil

Toasted sesame oil has a dark brown color and a rich, nutty flavor. It is used sparingly, most often in Asian recipes.

Eggs and Dairy
Eggs

All of the recipes in this book were tested with large eggs. Select clean, fresh eggs that have been handled properly and refrigerated. Do not use dirty, cracked or leaking eggs, or eggs that have a bad odor or unnatural color when cracked open. They may have become contaminated with harmful bacteria, such as salmonella.

Separating Eggs

It is easiest to separate eggs when they are very cold. I like to separate them before I do anything else, then allow them to come to room temperature as I gather my remaining ingredients and equipment.

Milk

Both lower-fat and whole milk are used in a wide range of recipes in this book. Be sure to note when whole milk is specified — the extra fat is needed in the recipe, so lower-fat milk should not be substituted. If the recipe does not specify the type of milk, then either lower-fat or whole milk may be used. Nonfat (skim) milk is not recommended, as the decreased fat will lead to tough ebelskivers.

Sour Cream

Commercial sour cream contains 14% to 20% fat and has been treated with a lactic acid culture to add its characteristic tang. For best results, do not use reduced-fat sour cream in the recipes, as the lower amount of fat can lead to somewhat tough ebelskivers.

Refrigerate sour cream in its container for up to a week after the date stamped on the bottom. If any mold forms on the surface of the cream, discard the entire container immediately.

Buttermilk

Commercially prepared buttermilk is made by culturing nonfat (skim) or lower-fat milk with bacteria. It has a distinctive tang and, when added to baked goods, yields a tender, moist result and a slightly buttery flavor.

Making a Buttermilk Substitute

If you don't have buttermilk, it's easy to make a substitute. Mix 1 tbsp (15 mL) lemon juice or white vinegar into 1 cup (250 mL) whole or lower-fat milk. Let stand for at least 15 minutes before using, to allow the milk to curdle. Any extra can be stored in the refrigerator for the same amount of time as the milk from which it was made.

Yogurt

Yogurt, like buttermilk, is acidic and tenderizes baked goods. It makes an excellent substitution for sour cream in a wide range of recipes. Always use plain (unflavored) yogurt in these recipes. If the recipe does not specify lower-fat or whole-milk yogurt, then either may be used. Nonfat yogurt is not recommended, as the decreased fat will lead to tough ebelskivers.

Cream Cheese

Two varieties of cream cheese are called for in the recipes in this book. Unless otherwise specified, use brick-style cream cheese, typically sold in 8-oz (250 g) rectangular packages. Whipped cream cheese, which is usually sold in tubs, is cream cheese that has been whipped until fluffy and smooth.

It does not require softening. Brick-style cream cheese and whipped cream cheese are not interchangeable, so be sure to use the variety specified in the recipe.

For best results, do not use reduced-fat cream cheese in the recipes. The lower amount of fat and increased amount of water in these products can lead to dry, somewhat tough ebelskivers.

Softening Brick-Style Cream Cheese

Unwrap the cream cheese and cut it into chunks with a sharp knife. Let it stand at room temperature for 30 to 45 minutes, until softened. To speed the softening, place the chunks of cream cheese on a microwave-safe plate or in a microwave-safe bowl and microwave on High for 15 seconds. If necessary, microwave for 5 or 10 seconds longer.

Ricotta Cheese

Ricotta is a rich, fresh cheese with a texture that is slightly grainy but still far smoother than cottage cheese. It is white and moist and has a slightly sweet flavor. For best results, do not use reduced-fat ricotta cheese in ebelskiver recipes. The lower amount of fat can lead to dry, somewhat tough ebelskivers.

Cottage Cheese

Cottage cheese makes a great addition to both sweet and savory ebelskivers, lending richness, moistness and a tender crumb. For best results, use the type of cottage cheese (small-curd, large-curd, etc.) specified in the recipe. Avoid reduced-fat cottage cheese, as the lower amount of fat and increased amount of water in these products can lead to deflated, somewhat gummy ebelskivers.

Mascarpone Cheese

Mascarpone is a buttery, ultra-rich Italian-style double- or triple-cream cheese made from cow's milk. It has a velvety texture and a slightly buttery flavor.

Leaveners

Leaveners lighten batters, causing them to rise. The three leaveners used in the baking recipes in this collection are baking powder, baking soda and yeast.

Baking Powder

Baking powder is a chemical leavening agent made from a blend of alkali (sodium bicarbonate, known commonly as baking soda) and acid (most commonly calcium acid phosphate, sodium aluminum sulfate or cream of tartar), plus some form of starch to absorb any moisture so a reaction does not take place until a liquid is added.

Baking Soda

Baking soda is a chemical leavener consisting of bicarbonate of soda. It is alkaline in nature and, when combined with an acidic ingredient, such as buttermilk, yogurt, citrus juice, honey or molasses, it creates carbon dioxide bubbles, giving baked goods a dramatic rise.

Quick-Rising (Instant) Dry Yeast

Quick-rising (instant) dry yeast is a variety of baker's yeast used to leaven breads and batters. It comes in the form of small, dehydrated granules. For best results, store the yeast in a cool, dry place or in the refrigerator.

Chocolate and Cocoa

With so many chocolates on the market these days, choosing a good one for the perfect batch of ebelskivers may seem daunting. But it's quite simple. Choose a chocolate with 50% to 70% cocoa solids in the ingredient list, and avoid vegetable fat and artificial flavors. Look for cocoa butter instead. A high percentage of sugar is an indicator of lower quality.

Unsweetened Baking Chocolate

Unsweetened chocolate should list one ingredient on the package: chocolate. It is composed of more than 50% cocoa butter, the remainder being cocoa solids.

Semisweet and Bittersweet Baking Chocolate

Semisweet chocolate is a dark chocolate with a low (typically half) sugar content. If you prefer darker, more assertively flavored chocolate, choose bittersweet chocolate, which has even less sugar and a greater percentage of cocoa solids.

Milk Chocolate

Milk chocolate has milk powder, liquid milk or condensed milk added, and therefore has a milder flavor than semisweet and bittersweet chocolate.

White Chocolate

White chocolate is primarily composed of cocoa butter. The ingredients listed on a package of white chocolate should be sugar, cocoa butter, milk, soy lecithin (an emulsifier) and vanilla extract. Avoid any white chocolate that lists palm kernel oil or any other vegetable fat, as these are used by the manufacturer as cheap substitutes for some of the cocoa butter.

Chocolate Chips

Chocolate chips are small chunks of chocolate that are typically sold in a round, flat-bottomed teardrop shape. They are available in numerous sizes, from large to miniature, but are usually around $\frac{1}{2}$ inch (1 cm) in diameter.

Cocoa Powder

Select natural cocoa powder rather than Dutch process for the recipes in this collection. Natural cocoa powder has a deep, true chocolate flavor. The packaging should state whether it is Dutch process or not, but you can also tell the difference by sight: if it is dark to almost black, it is Dutch process; natural cocoa powder is much lighter and is typically brownish-red in color.

Flavorings
Fresh Herbs

Fresh herbs add depth of flavor and freshness to a wide variety of ebelskivers. Flat-leaf (Italian) parsley, cilantro and chives are readily available and inexpensive, and they store well in the produce bin of the refrigerator, so keep them on hand year-round. Basil, mint and thyme are best in the spring and summer, when they are in season in your own garden or at the farmers' market.

Spices

All of the recipes in this collection use ground spices (as opposed to whole spices). With ground spices, freshness is everything. To determine whether a ground spice is fresh, open the container and sniff. A strong fragrance means the spice is still acceptable for use.

Salt

Unless otherwise specified, the recipes in this collection were tested with ordinary table salt. Salt connoisseurs often prefer to use kosher salt, which is all-natural and additive-free; you are welcome to substitute it (the fine kosher salt, not the coarse) for the table salt.

Black Pepper

Black pepper is made by grinding black peppercorns, which have been picked when the berry is not quite ripe, then dried until it shrivels and the skin turns dark brown to black. Black pepper has a strong, slightly hot flavor, with a hint of sweetness.

Vanilla Extract

Vanilla extract adds a sweet, fragrant flavor to countless varieties of ebelskivers; it is particularly good for enhancing the flavors of chocolate and fresh fruit. It is produced by combining an extraction from dried vanilla beans with an alcohol and water mixture. It is then aged for several months. The three most common types of vanilla beans used to make vanilla extract are Bourbon-Madagascar, Mexican and Tahitian.

Almond Extract

Almond extract is a flavoring manufactured by combining bitter almond oil with ethyl alcohol. It is used in much the same way as vanilla extract. Almond extract has a highly concentrated, intense flavor, so measure with care.

Citrus Zest

Zest is the name for the colored outer layer of citrus peel. The oils in zest are intense in flavor. Use a zester, a Microplane-style grater or the small holes of a box grater to grate zest. Avoid grating the white layer (pith) just below the zest; it is very bitter.

Instant Espresso Powder

Stronger than regular coffee powder, a small amount of espresso powder can dramatically flavor a wide variety of ebelskiver batters. It is available where coffee is shelved in most supermarkets and at specialty stores.

Ebelskivers 101

Cinnamon Hazelnut Ebelskivers

Just a few years ago, finding shelled hazelnuts required a special trip to the health food store. Now they are increasingly available — shelled and chopped — in the baking aisle of all my local supermarkets. Here, they find harmony with sweet cinnamon.

Tip

An equal amount of chopped toasted walnuts, pecans or almonds may be used in place of the hazelnuts.

● **7-well ebelskiver pan**

1¼ cups	all-purpose flour	300 mL
2¼ tsp	ground cinnamon	11 mL
¾ tsp	baking powder	3 mL
¼ tsp	salt	1 mL
3 tbsp	packed dark brown sugar	45 mL
2	large eggs, separated	2
1 cup	milk	250 mL
2 tbsp	unsalted butter, melted	30 mL
1 tsp	vanilla extract	5 mL
⅔ cup	chopped toasted hazelnuts	150 mL
	Vegetable oil	

1. In a large bowl, whisk together flour, cinnamon, baking powder and salt.

2. In a medium bowl, whisk together brown sugar, egg yolks, milk, butter and vanilla until well blended.

3. Add the egg yolk mixture to the flour mixture and stir until just blended (the batter will appear slightly lumpy). Gently stir in hazelnuts.

4. In a medium bowl, using an electric mixer on medium-high speed, beat egg whites until frothy. Increase speed to high and beat until stiff, but not dry, peaks form. Using a rubber spatula, gently mix one-third of the egg whites into the batter. Gently fold in the remaining whites.

5. Brush wells of pan lightly with oil. Set pan over medium heat. When oil begins to sizzle, add 2 tbsp (30 mL) batter to each well. Cook for 2 to 4 minutes or until bottoms are golden brown. Using two skewers, flip the puffs over. Cook for 2 to 3 minutes or until bottoms are golden brown and a toothpick inserted in the center comes out with a few moist crumbs attached. Remove pan from heat and transfer puffs to a plate. Let pan cool slightly.

6. Repeat with the remaining batter, brushing wells with oil and reheating pan before each batch. Serve warm or at room temperature.

See the step-by-step photographs on photo page A. ▶

Tips

It is easiest to separate eggs when they are very cold.

If you crack an egg on the rim of a bowl, it will be easier to get the egg to crack right in the middle; however, you are more likely to get pieces of egg shell in the egg whites.

In addition to sanitary reasons, it is crucial to wash your hands before separating eggs to remove any natural body oil. Any fat or oil (from the egg yolk or your hands) will interfere with the egg white's ability to whip up properly.

Separating Eggs

1. Wash your hands thoroughly.

2. Set out two deep, medium bowls. Crack one egg by gently tapping it on a flat surface or the rim of a bowl, as close to the middle of the egg as possible.

3. Working over one of the bowls, use your thumbs to gently pry the egg shell halves apart.

4. Let the yolk settle in one egg shell half while the egg white runs off the sides of the shell into the bowl.

5. Gently transfer the egg yolk back and forth between the egg shell halves, letting as much egg white as possible drip into the bowl below. Be careful not to break the egg yolk.

6. Place the egg yolk in the other bowl. Repeat with remaining egg(s).

Apple Compote Ebelskivers

It's easy to understand why everyone goes crazy over these ebelskivers: they pack all the flavor and fragrance of traditional apple pie underneath a carapace of buttery vanilla batter. Adding cinnamon to the compote evokes a familiar fall nostalgia that makes every calorie worthwhile.

Variation

Apple Cheese Ebelskivers: Omit the nutmeg. Stir 1 cup (250 mL) shredded extra-sharp (extra-old) Cheddar cheese into the batter at the end of step 4.

- 7-well ebelskiver pan

Apple Compote

2 tbsp	unsalted butter	30 mL
3 tbsp	granulated sugar	45 mL
1/2 tsp	ground cinnamon	2 mL
2	medium-large tart-sweet apples (such as Braeburn or Gala), peeled and chopped	2

Ebelskivers

1 1/4 cups	all-purpose flour	300 mL
3/4 tsp	baking powder	3 mL
1/4 tsp	salt	1 mL
1/4 tsp	ground nutmeg	1 mL
1 tbsp	granulated sugar	15 mL
2	large eggs, separated	2
1 cup	milk	250 mL
2 tbsp	unsalted butter, melted	30 mL
1 tsp	vanilla extract	5 mL
	Vegetable oil	
	Confectioners' (icing) sugar	

1. *Compote:* In a medium saucepan, melt butter over medium-high heat. Add sugar and cinnamon; cook, stirring, until sugar is dissolved. Add apples, reduce heat to medium-low and cook, stirring, for about 10 minutes or until apples are very tender. Remove from heat and let cool completely.

2. *Ebelskivers:* In a large bowl, whisk together flour, baking powder, salt and nutmeg.

3. In a medium bowl, whisk together sugar, egg yolks, milk, butter and vanilla until well blended.

4. Add the egg yolk mixture to the flour mixture and stir until just blended (the batter will appear slightly lumpy).

5. In a medium bowl, using an electric mixer on medium-high speed, beat egg whites until frothy. Increase speed to high and beat until stiff, but not dry, peaks form. Using a rubber spatula, gently mix one-third of the egg whites into the batter. Gently fold in the remaining whites.

6. Brush wells of pan lightly with oil. Set pan over medium heat. When oil begins to sizzle, add 1 tbsp (15 mL) batter to each well. Place 1 tsp (5 mL) compote in the center of each well and top with 1 tbsp (15 mL) batter. Cook for

2 to 4 minutes or until bottoms are golden brown. Using two skewers, flip the puffs over. Cook for 2 to 3 minutes or until bottoms are golden brown and a toothpick inserted in the center comes out with a bit of filling and moist crumbs attached. Remove pan from heat and transfer puffs to a plate. Let pan cool slightly.

7. Repeat with the remaining batter and compote, brushing wells with oil and reheating pan before each batch.

8. Dust the ebelskivers with confectioners' sugar. Serve warm or at room temperature.

See the step-by-step photographs on photo page B. ▶

Tips

As noted on page 17, it's best to separate eggs while they're cold, so start with cold eggs out of the fridge, separate them, then let the whites warm up.

The fresher the eggs, the better they will whip up into peaks.

Whipping Egg Whites

1. Check for any traces of yolk or shells in the whites. Remove any stray shell pieces with a spoon. If any egg yolk is visible, save the whites for another use and separate more eggs.

2. For maximum volume, let the egg whites warm to room temperature for 30 minutes, or place the bowl of egg whites in a larger bowl of lukewarm water for 4 to 5 minutes.

3. Prepare your mixer (either a handheld or a stand mixer), making sure the beaters are very clean.

4. Start the mixer on medium-high speed, beating the egg whites for 30 to 45 seconds, until whites are frothy with lots of medium-size bubbles.

5. Increase speed to high and beat for 45 to 60 seconds longer, until stiff, but not dry, peaks form. You've reached the stiff peak stage when the egg whites are smooth, moist and shiny, and peaks stand straight up when the beaters are lifted from the bowl.

6. Avoid overbeating. You will know you have overbeaten the whites if little granules begin to form on the side of the bowl and the volume of the whites starts to decrease. Further beating will result in egg whites that appear dry and curdled. If this occurs, it is best to start over with fresh egg whites.

Classic Ebelskivers

Makes about 21 puffs

If you're looking for the quintessential ebelskiver recipe, this is it. Any variety of jam, jelly or preserves makes a terrific filling, so pick your fancy. Or try lemon curd, apple butter, marmalade, chocolate-hazelnut spread... you get the idea.

Variations

Whole Wheat Ebelskivers: Replace ¾ cup (175 mL) of the all-purpose flour with whole wheat flour. Alternatively, replace all of the all-purpose flour with white whole wheat flour or whole wheat pastry flour.

Gluten-Free Ebelskivers: Use a gluten-free all-purpose flour blend in place of the all-purpose flour. Use gluten-free vanilla, gluten-free baking powder and gluten-free confectioners' (icing) sugar.

Buttermilk Ebelskivers: Use an equal amount of buttermilk in place of the milk. Decrease the baking powder to ½ tsp (2 mL) and add ½ tsp (2 mL) baking soda in step 1.

● **7-well ebelskiver pan**

1¼ cups	all-purpose flour	300 mL
¾ tsp	baking powder	3 mL
¼ tsp	salt	1 mL
1 tbsp	granulated sugar	15 mL
2	large eggs, separated	2
1 cup	milk	250 mL
2 tbsp	unsalted butter, melted	30 mL
1 tsp	vanilla extract	5 mL
	Vegetable oil	
½ cup	jam, jelly or preserves of choice	125 mL
	Confectioners' (icing) sugar	

1. In a large bowl, whisk together flour, baking powder and salt.

2. In a medium bowl, whisk together sugar, egg yolks, milk, butter and vanilla until well blended.

3. Add the egg yolk mixture to the flour mixture and stir until just blended (the batter will appear slightly lumpy).

4. In a medium bowl, using an electric mixer on medium-high speed, beat egg whites until frothy. Increase speed to high and beat until stiff, but not dry, peaks form. Using a rubber spatula, gently mix one-third of the egg whites into the batter. Gently fold in the remaining whites.

5. Brush wells of pan lightly with oil. Set pan over medium heat. When oil begins to sizzle, add 1 tbsp (15 mL) batter to each well. Place 1 tsp (5 mL) jam in the center of each well and top with 1 tbsp (15 mL) batter. Cook for 2 to 4 minutes or until bottoms are golden brown. Using two skewers, flip the puffs over. Cook for 2 to 3 minutes or until bottoms are golden brown and a toothpick inserted in the center comes out with a bit of filling and moist crumbs attached. Remove pan from heat and transfer puffs to a plate. Let pan cool slightly.

6. Repeat with the remaining batter and jam, brushing wells with oil and reheating pan before each batch.

7. Dust the ebelskivers with confectioners' sugar. Serve warm or at room temperature.

See the step-by-step photographs on photo page C. ▶

Tips

While folding the egg whites into the batter, take care to avoid deflating the batter.

Don't worry if your finished batter is less than perfect: the batter is quite forgiving and will puff up from both the egg whites and the chemical leaveners (baking powder and/or baking soda).

Preparing Traditional Ebelskiver Batter

1. In a large bowl, whisk together flour, baking powder and salt. (See Classic Ebelskivers, opposite, for ingredient amounts.)

2. In a medium bowl, whisk together sugar, egg yolks, milk, butter and vanilla until well blended. It is fine if the mixture appears somewhat curdled.

3. Add the egg yolk mixture to the flour mixture and stir until just blended. Do not overmix at this point, as too much mixing will lead to tough ebelskivers. The batter should appear slightly lumpy.

4. In a medium bowl, using an electric mixer on medium-high speed, beat egg whites until frothy. Increase speed to high and beat until stiff, but not dry, peaks form (see complete step-by-step instructions on page 19).

5. Using a rubber spatula, gently mix one-third of the egg whites into the batter. White streaks will still be visible.

6. Add the remaining egg whites to the bowl of batter. Using the rubber spatula, fold in the whites by slicing through the center of the egg whites and batter, then pulling the spatula up along the side of the bowl and over the top to combine the two mixtures. Rotate the bowl a quarter turn and repeat the folding action. Continue turning the bowl and folding until the egg whites have been incorporated into the batter and no white streaks remain.

Mediterranean Ebelskivers

Sun-dried tomatoes, olives, feta and herbs turn simple ebelskivers into something extraordinary. They are perfect mid-winter, just as you are dreaming of sun-drenched summer days.

Tips

You can use 2 tbsp (30 mL) of the drained sun-dried tomato oil in place of the olive oil.

Either green or black brine-cured olives may be used in this recipe.

Other fresh herbs, such as an equal amount of flat-leaf (Italian) parsley or chives, or 1½ tsp (7 mL) chopped fresh rosemary or oregano, may be used in place of the basil.

- **7-well ebelskiver pan**

1¼ cups	all-purpose flour	300 mL
¾ tsp	baking powder	3 mL
¼ tsp	salt	1 mL
1 tsp	granulated sugar	5 mL
2	large eggs, separated	2
1 cup	milk	250 mL
2 tbsp	extra virgin olive oil	30 mL
½ cup	crumbled feta cheese	125 mL
⅓ cup	chopped drained oil-packed sun-dried tomatoes	75 mL
¼ cup	chopped pitted brine-cured olives	60 mL
3 tbsp	chopped fresh basil	45 mL
	Olive oil or vegetable oil	

1. In a large bowl, whisk together flour, baking powder and salt.

2. In a medium bowl, whisk together sugar, egg yolks, milk and oil until well blended.

3. Add the egg yolk mixture to the flour mixture and stir until just blended (the batter will appear slightly lumpy). Gently stir in cheese, tomatoes, olives and basil.

4. In a medium bowl, using an electric mixer on medium-high speed, beat egg whites until frothy. Increase speed to high and beat until stiff, but not dry, peaks form. Using a rubber spatula, gently mix one-third of the egg whites into the batter. Gently fold in the remaining whites.

5. Brush wells of pan lightly with oil. Set pan over medium heat. When oil begins to sizzle, add 2 tbsp (30 mL) batter to each well. Cook for 2 to 4 minutes or until bottoms are golden brown. Using two skewers, flip the puffs over. Cook for 2 to 3 minutes or until bottoms are golden brown and a toothpick inserted in the center comes out with a few moist crumbs attached. Remove pan from heat and transfer puffs to a plate. Let pan cool slightly.

6. Repeat with the remaining batter, brushing wells with oil and reheating pan before each batch. Serve warm or at room temperature.

See the step-by-step photographs on photo page D. ▶

Tips

Although many recipes call for melted butter to grease the wells, I prefer to use neutral vegetable oil because the pan gets very hot and butter can quickly burn.

The oil in the wells should be sizzling when the batter is added. If the ebelskivers stick, it is most likely because the pan was not hot enough when the batter was added.

Preparing the Pan and Filling Wells

1a. Using a pastry brush dipped in vegetable oil, brush each well of the ebelskiver pan with a thin, even coat of oil.

1b. Alternatively, use a paper towel dipped in vegetable oil to rub each well of the ebelskiver pan with a thin, even coat of oil.

2. Place the pan on a stovetop burner and turn the heat to medium.

3. Let the pan and oil heat for 2 to 3 minutes or until the oil begins to sizzle. (The oil should be hot but not smoking.)

4. Scoop the specified amount of batter into each well (typically 2 tbsp/30 mL for unfilled ebelskivers). Work quickly and efficiently, beginning with the center well.

5. Continue to fill wells, proceeding clockwise from the top with the remaining wells.

Fresh Herb Ebelskivers

If you think ebelskivers are merely sweet treats, let this recipe rise to the top of your must-try list. Perfect for dinner alongside soups, stews or salads, they are a wonderful way to make homemade, savory mini breads with little time and effort — and no oven!

Tips

While these are smashing when made with a mix of herbs, they may also be made with a single herb variety.

An equal amount of grated Romano, Asiago or Manchego cheese can be used in place of the Parmesan.

- **7-well ebelskiver pan**

1¼ cups	all-purpose flour	300 mL
¾ tsp	baking powder	3 mL
¼ tsp	salt	1 mL
⅛ tsp	freshly cracked black pepper	0.5 mL
1 tsp	granulated sugar	5 mL
2	large eggs, separated	2
1 cup	milk	250 mL
2 tbsp	unsalted butter, melted	30 mL
⅓ cup	freshly grated Parmesan cheese	75 mL
3 tbsp	chopped assorted fresh herbs (such as chives, basil, tarragon and dill)	45 mL
	Vegetable oil	

1. In a large bowl, whisk together flour, baking powder, salt and black pepper.

2. In a medium bowl, whisk together sugar, egg yolks, milk and butter until well blended.

3. Add the egg yolk mixture to the flour mixture and stir until just blended (the batter will appear slightly lumpy). Gently stir in cheese and herbs.

4. In a medium bowl, using an electric mixer on medium-high speed, beat egg whites until frothy. Increase speed to high and beat until stiff, but not dry, peaks form. Using a rubber spatula, gently mix one-third of the egg whites into the batter. Gently fold in the remaining whites.

5. Brush wells of pan lightly with oil. Set pan over medium heat. When oil begins to sizzle, add 2 tbsp (30 mL) batter to each well. Cook for 2 to 4 minutes or until bottoms are golden brown. Using two skewers, flip the puffs over. Cook for 2 to 3 minutes or until bottoms are golden brown and a toothpick inserted in the center comes out with a few moist crumbs attached. Remove pan from heat and transfer puffs to a plate. Let pan cool slightly.

6. Repeat with the remaining batter, brushing wells with oil and reheating pan before each batch. Serve warm or at room temperature.

See the step-by-step photographs on photo page E. ▶

Tip

Avoid the temptation of trying to cook ebelskivers more quickly by increasing the heat. If the heat is too high, the outside of the ebelskivers will be done long before the batter inside is set. If you know that your stove runs hot, set the heat to medium-low instead of medium.

Cooking Ebelskivers

1. Prepare the pan and fill wells with ebelskiver batter as directed on page 23.

2. Cook the ebelskivers for 2 to 4 minutes, until a few bubbles rise to the surface (the batter will still be quite runny at the center).

3. Using a wooden skewer, shift one of the ebelskivers slightly so you can check that the bottom is golden brown.

4. Using two wooden skewers, one on either side of an ebelskiver, gently lift and flip the ebelskiver so the cooked side is on top. The uncooked batter will flow out into the well. Repeat with the remaining ebelskivers.

5. Continue cooking the ebelskivers for 2 to 3 minutes or until bottoms are golden brown and a toothpick inserted in the center comes out with a few moist crumbs attached.

6. Using the skewers, lift each ebelskiver from the pan and transfer it to a plate.

Cornmeal Ebelskivers with Cherry Jam

These ebelskivers are mildly sweet, with a rich corn flavor. I love the contrast between the delicate crunch of the cornmeal and the bright burst of cherry jam in the center — it sings of summer.

Tip

An equal amount of other varieties of fruit jam, jelly or preserves may be used in place of the cherry jam.

● **7-well ebelskiver pan**

⅔ cup	all-purpose flour	150 mL
⅔ cup	yellow cornmeal (preferably stone-ground)	150 mL
¾ tsp	baking powder	3 mL
¼ tsp	salt	1 mL
1 tbsp	granulated sugar	15 mL
2	large eggs, separated	2
1 cup	milk	250 mL
3 tbsp	unsalted butter, melted	45 mL
	Vegetable oil	
½ cup	cherry jam or preserves	125 mL

1. In a large bowl, whisk together flour, cornmeal, baking powder and salt.

2. In a medium bowl, whisk together sugar, egg yolks, milk and butter until well blended.

3. Add the egg yolk mixture to the flour mixture and stir until just blended (the batter will appear slightly lumpy).

4. In a medium bowl, using an electric mixer on medium-high speed, beat egg whites until frothy. Increase speed to high and beat until stiff, but not dry, peaks form. Using a rubber spatula, gently mix one-third of the egg whites into the batter. Gently fold in the remaining whites.

5. Brush wells of pan lightly with oil. Set pan over medium heat. When oil begins to sizzle, add 1 tbsp (15 mL) batter to each well. Place 1 tsp (5 mL) jam in the center of each well and top with 1 tbsp (15 mL) batter. Cook for 2 to 4 minutes or until bottoms are golden brown. Using two skewers, flip the puffs over. Cook for 2 to 3 minutes or until bottoms are golden brown and a toothpick inserted in the center comes out with a bit of filling and moist crumbs attached. Remove pan from heat and transfer puffs to a plate. Let pan cool slightly.

6. Repeat with the remaining batter and jam, brushing wells with oil and reheating pan before each batch. Serve warm or at room temperature.

See the step-by-step photographs on photo page F. ▶

Tips

Try to keep sweet fillings away from the edges of the wells, to avoid burning.

Cover the filling entirely with the second half of the batter to prevent the filling from leaking out and burning.

Making Filled Ebelskivers

1. Oil the pan wells and preheat the pan as directed on page 23 (steps 1 to 3).

2. When the oil begins to sizzle, scoop 1 tbsp (15 mL) of batter into each well. Work quickly and efficiently, beginning with the center well, then proceeding clockwise from the top with the remaining wells.

3. Working quickly and efficiently, add the filling to the center of the batter. Work in the same clockwise motion as used to fill the wells with batter, beginning with the center well, then proceeding clockwise from the top with the remaining wells.

4. Cover the filling by adding an additional 1 tbsp (15 mL) batter to each well. Work in the same clockwise motion, beginning with the center well, then proceeding clockwise from the top with the remaining wells.

5. Cook ebelskivers for 2 to 4 minutes, until a few bubbles rise to the surface (the batter will still be quite runny at the center). Shift one of the ebelskivers slightly with a wooden skewer to check that the bottom is golden brown. Flip the ebelskivers with wooden skewers (see page 25 for detailed instructions).

6. Continue cooking the ebelskivers for 2 to 3 minutes or until bottoms are golden brown and a toothpick inserted in the center comes out with a bit of filling and a few moist crumbs attached.

Bacon, Chive and Cheddar Puffs

Equally at home as part of a weekend brunch, breakfast on the run or an innovative appetizer, these addictive puffs are guaranteed to please one and all.

Tips

To save on time and cleanup, look for precooked and crumbled real bacon pieces in the salad dressing section of the supermarket.

An equal amount of minced green onions (green parts only) can be used in place of the chives.

● **7-well ebelskiver pan**

1¼ cups	all-purpose flour	300 mL
½ tsp	baking soda	2 mL
¼ tsp	baking powder	1 mL
¼ tsp	salt	1 mL
1 tsp	granulated sugar	5 mL
2	large eggs, separated	2
1 cup	buttermilk	250 mL
2 tbsp	unsalted butter, melted	30 mL
⅔ cup	crumbled cooked bacon	150 mL
3 tbsp	minced fresh chives	45 mL
	Vegetable oil	
3 oz	sharp (old) Cheddar cheese, cut into ½-inch (1 cm) cubes	90 g

1. In a large bowl, whisk together flour, baking soda, baking powder and salt.

2. In a medium bowl, whisk together sugar, egg yolks, buttermilk and butter until well blended.

3. Add the egg yolk mixture to the flour mixture and stir until just blended (the batter will appear slightly lumpy). Gently stir in bacon and chives.

4. In a medium bowl, using an electric mixer on medium-high speed, beat egg whites until frothy. Increase speed to high and beat until stiff, but not dry, peaks form. Using a rubber spatula, gently mix one-third of the egg whites into the batter. Gently fold in the remaining whites.

5. Brush wells of pan lightly with oil. Set pan over medium heat. When oil begins to sizzle, add 1 tbsp (15 mL) batter to each well. Place 1 cheese cube in the center of each well and top with 1 tbsp (15 mL) batter. Cook for 2 to 4 minutes or until bottoms are golden brown. Using two skewers, flip the puffs over. Cook for 2 to 3 minutes or until bottoms are golden brown and a toothpick inserted in the center comes out with a bit of cheese and a few moist crumbs attached. Remove pan from heat and transfer puffs to a plate. Let pan cool slightly.

6. Repeat with the remaining batter and cheese cubes, brushing wells with oil and reheating pan before each batch. Serve warm or at room temperature.

See the step-by-step photographs on photo page G. ▶

Tip

Ebelskivers may be cooked up to 1 day in advance and reheated. Let the ebelskivers cool completely on a wire rack, then store them in an airtight container in the refrigerator. Reheat in a 200°F (100°C) oven on an ovenproof platter or plate, loosely covered with foil, for 15 to 20 minutes or until warmed through.

Prepping the Pan Between Batches

1. Preheat the oven to 200°F (100°C) before preparing the batter and making the first batch of 7 ebelskivers.

2. Remove the ebelskiver pan from the heat and, using two skewers, transfer the ebelskivers to an ovenproof platter or plate.

3. Loosely cover the platter or plate with foil and place it in the oven to keep the ebelskivers warm.

4. Let the ebelskiver pan cool slightly, then use a damp paper towel to wipe out any crumbs or residue from the wells and on the top of the pan, to avoid burnt pieces and sticking.

5. Oil the pan again and reheat it over medium heat, then cook another batch of ebelskivers.

6. Repeat steps 2 to 5 until all of the batter is used. In the last batch, it's fine if some of the wells remain empty. Continue adding the cooked ebelskivers to the platter or plate in the oven, and keep warm until ready to serve.

Candied Ginger Ebelskivers with Rhubarb Compote

The bright, lush flavor of rhubarb compote is the perfect counterpoint to the peppery-sweet heat of candied ginger in these ebelskivers.

Tip

Rhubarb is one of spring's first treasures — look for it at the market between April and September — but you can also find it cut and frozen year-round in the frozen foods section of the supermarket.

- **7-well ebelskiver pan**

Rhubarb Compote

2 cups	chopped rhubarb (about 12 oz/375 g, cut into $\frac{1}{2}$-inch/1 cm pieces)	500 mL
$\frac{3}{4}$ cup	granulated sugar	175 mL
1 tbsp	freshly squeezed lemon juice	15 mL

Ebelskivers

1$\frac{1}{4}$ cups	all-purpose flour	300 mL
$\frac{3}{4}$ tsp	baking powder	3 mL
$\frac{1}{4}$ tsp	salt	1 mL
2 tbsp	granulated sugar	30 mL
2	large eggs, separated	2
1 cup	milk	250 mL
2 tbsp	unsalted butter, melted	30 mL
1 tsp	vanilla extract	5 mL
$\frac{1}{3}$ cup	finely chopped candied ginger	75 mL
	Vegetable oil	
	Confectioners' (icing) sugar	

1. *Compote:* In a medium saucepan, combine rhubarb, sugar and lemon juice. Cook over medium heat, stirring, for 4 to 5 minutes, until sugar is dissolved. Reduce heat to medium-low, cover and simmer, stirring occasionally, for 6 to 8 minutes or until rhubarb is tender. Transfer to a small bowl and let cool.

2. *Ebelskivers:* In a large bowl, whisk together flour, baking powder and salt.

3. In a medium bowl, whisk together sugar, egg yolks, milk, butter and vanilla until well blended.

4. Add the egg yolk mixture to the flour mixture and stir until just blended (the batter will appear slightly lumpy). Gently stir in ginger.

5. In a medium bowl, using an electric mixer on medium-high speed, beat egg whites until frothy. Increase speed to high and beat until stiff, but not dry, peaks form. Using a rubber spatula, gently mix one-third of the egg whites into the batter. Gently fold in the remaining whites.

6. Brush wells of pan lightly with oil. Set pan over medium heat. When oil begins to sizzle, add 2 tbsp (30 mL) batter to each well. Cook for 2 to 4 minutes or until bottoms are golden brown. Using two skewers, flip the puffs over. Cook for 2 to 3 minutes or until bottoms are golden brown and a toothpick inserted in the center comes out with a few moist crumbs attached. Remove pan from heat and transfer puffs to a plate. Let pan cool slightly.

7. Repeat with the remaining batter, brushing wells with oil and reheating pan before each batch.

8. Dust the ebelskivers with confectioners' sugar. Serve warm, with the rhubarb compote.

See the step-by-step photographs on photo page H. ▶

Tips

You can prepare the sauce up to 1 day ahead. Store it in an airtight container in the refrigerator, then bring it to room temperature before serving.

A sifter may be used in place of the mesh sieve.

Decorating and Serving Ebelskivers

1. Prepare a sauce (such as Rhubarb Compote, opposite) and set aside to cool while preparing the ebelskivers.

2. Prepare all batches of the ebelskivers, then place 2 or 3 ebelskivers on each plate.

3. Place 2 to 3 tbsp (30 to 45 mL) confectioners' (icing) sugar in a small mesh sieve.

4. With one hand, hold the sieve about 6 inches (15 cm) directly above the ebelskivers. With the flat of the other hand, gently tap the side of the sieve three to four times, until the ebelskivers are lightly coated in sugar.

5a. Spoon some of the sauce alongside the ebelskivers

5b. Alternatively, spoon some of the sauce on top of the ebelskivers.

Ebelskiver Tips

Part of the fun of sharing ebelskivers with friends and family is that they look so special but are in fact very easy to make. Still, it helps to have a few tips and techniques in your back pocket to ensure perfectly puffed pancakes time after time.

- **Practice making two or three ebelskivers first.** Your first ebelskivers may be lopsided, messy, lumpy or all of the above. There, I said it. I could have left this part out, but I wish someone had told me this when I prepared my first batch of ebelskivers. I didn't preheat the pan long enough, I worked too slowly, I added far too much jam filling (what could go wrong?), and I waited too long to make my initial flip so that, while one side of the ebelskivers was a perfect golden brown, the other resembled charcoal briquettes. Hence, I strongly suggest filling just two or three wells, as opposed to all seven, on the first round of your inaugural batch. All of my recipes make at least 21 pancakes, so if the first two or three are less than perfect, no problem. After that, you will surprise yourself with how easy it is to make perfect puffs.

- **Preheat your pan!** My directions instruct you to do this, but it is worth reiterating (as well as adding an exclamation point). The fat (oil or butter) in the wells should be sizzling when the batter is added. If the ebelskivers stick, it is most likely because the pan was not hot enough when the batter was added.

- **Keep the heat at medium.** Avoid the temptation of trying to cook ebelskivers more quickly by increasing the heat. If the heat is too high, the outside of the ebelskivers will be done long before the batter inside is set. If you know that your stove runs hot, set the heat to medium-low instead of medium.

- **Work methodically.** I can never remember which well I filled first unless I work in a methodical manner when filling and flipping. Start by filling the center well with batter, then work clockwise from the top to fill the remaining wells. If you're filling the pancakes, follow the same pattern to add the fillings and remaining batter. Follow the same pattern again when flipping the ebelskivers. This will ensure the ebelskivers are evenly cooked.

- **Look for bubbles before flipping.** The ebelskivers are ready to flip when a few small bubbles rise to the surface of the batter. The middle of the ebelskivers will not be set. As you flip the ebelskivers, the uncooked batter will run into the wells to cook. This is what leads to the pancakes' spherical shape.

- **Let filled pancakes cool slightly before eating.** Be sure to let filled pancakes cool for a few minutes before serving them. Jam and jellies will be particularly hot straight from the pan, so take caution to avoid burned mouths. Be especially careful when feeding children, but let all of your family or guests know to take care as they tuck in.

- **Keep the pancakes warm as you go.** You may want to eat the pancakes as they come out of the pan, but if you prefer to keep each batch warm as you go, simply preheat the oven to 200°F (100°C) before you begin. Transfer each batch of cooked ebelskivers to an ovenproof platter or plate as you work and place it in the oven to keep warm.

Separating Eggs

(see page 17 for detailed step-by-step instructions)

1

Wash your hands thoroughly.

2

Crack an egg on a flat surface (or bowl rim).

3

Working over a bowl, pry egg shell apart into two halves.

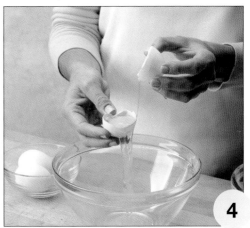

4

Let yolk settle in one shell half while white runs off into the bowl.

5

Transfer egg yolk back and forth between shell halves.

6

Place egg yolk in a second bowl.

A.

Whipping Egg Whites

(see page 19 for detailed step-by-step instructions)

Use a spoon to remove stray shell pieces from whites.

Bring egg whites to room temperature.

Make sure beaters are very clean.

Beat egg whites on medium-high speed until frothy.

Beat egg whites on high speed until stiff peaks form.

Avoid overbeating whites.

B.

Preparing Traditional Ebelskiver Batter (see page 21 for detailed step-by-step instructions)

Whisk together the dry ingredients.

Whisk together sugar and wet ingredients until well blended.

Stir wet ingredients into dry ingredients until just blended.

Beat egg whites until stiff peaks form.

Gently mix one-third of whites into batter.

Fold remaining whites into batter.

C.

Preparing the Pan and Filling Wells

(see page 23 for detailed step-by-step instructions)

Brush each well of the pan with oil.

Or use a paper towel to rub each well with oil.

Place pan on burner and set heat to medium.

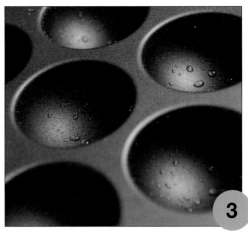

Heat pan until oil sizzles.

Scoop batter into wells, beginning with center well.

Continue to fill wells, proceeding clockwise from the top.

D.

Cooking Ebelskivers

(see page 25 for detailed step-by-step instructions)

1

Prepare pan and fill wells with batter.

2

Cook for 2 to 4 minutes, until bubbles rise to surface.

3

Shift ebelskiver with skewer to check that bottom is golden brown.

4

Using two skewers, lift and flip the ebelskivers.

5

Cook ebelskivers until a toothpick comes out with moist crumbs attached.

6

Using skewers, lift ebelskivers from pan to a plate.

E.

Making Filled Ebelskivers

(see page 27 for detailed step-by-step instructions)

Oil and preheat the pan.

Fill each well with 1 tbsp (15 mL) batter.

Add filling to the center of each well of batter.

Cover filling in each well with 1 tbsp (15 mL) batter.

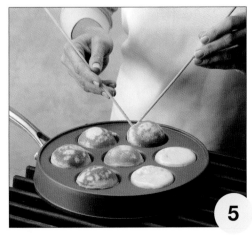

Cook first side of ebelskivers, then flip.

F.

Cook until a toothpick comes out with a bit of filling and moist crumbs attached.

Prepping the Pan Between Batches

(see page 29 for detailed step-by-step instructions)

Preheat oven to 200°F (100°C), then make first batch of ebelskivers.

Remove pan from heat and transfer ebelskivers to a platter or plate.

Loosely cover platter with foil and place in oven.

Let pan cool slightly, then wipe off residue or crumbs.

Oil pan again, reheat, then cook another batch.

Repeat steps 2 to 5 until all of the batter is used.

Decorating and Serving Ebelskivers

(see page 31 for detailed step-by-step instructions)

1

Prepare a sauce and let it cool.

2

Place 2 to 3 ebelskivers on each plate.

3

Place confectioners' (icing) sugar in a mesh sieve.

4

Sprinkle sugar over ebelskivers.

5a

Spoon sauce alongside ebelskivers.

5b

Or spoon sauce on top of ebelskivers.

H.

Lightly Sweet Puffs for Breakfast and Brunch

continued...

Simplified Ebelskivers

Longing for ebelskivers but crunched for time? Then this recipe, which skips the step of separating the eggs and beating the egg whites, is your solution. And if you have a favorite pancake mix, see the variation below — you can use it, too!

Variation

Pancake Mix Ebelskivers: Omit the baking powder and salt and replace the flour with an equal amount of pancake mix (any variety of mix that calls for the addition of eggs and milk).

• 7-well ebelskiver pan

1¼ cups	all-purpose flour	300 mL
¾ tsp	baking powder	3 mL
¼ tsp	salt	1 mL
1 tbsp	granulated sugar	15 mL
3	large eggs	3
¾ cup	milk	175 mL
1 tbsp	unsalted butter, melted	15 mL
1 tsp	vanilla extract	5 mL
	Vegetable oil	
½ cup	jam, jelly or preserves of choice	125 mL
	Confectioners' (icing) sugar	

1. In a large bowl, whisk together flour, baking powder and salt.

2. In a medium bowl, whisk together sugar, eggs, milk, butter and vanilla until well blended.

3. Add the egg mixture to the flour mixture and stir until just blended (the batter will appear slightly lumpy).

4. Brush wells of pan lightly with oil. Set pan over medium heat. When oil begins to sizzle, add 1 tbsp (15 mL) batter to each well. Place 1 tsp (5 mL) jam in the center of each well and top with 1 tbsp (15 mL) batter. Cook for 2 to 4 minutes or until bottoms are golden brown. Using two skewers, flip the puffs over. Cook for 2 to 3 minutes or until bottoms are golden brown and a toothpick inserted in the center comes out with a bit of filling and moist crumbs attached. Remove pan from heat and transfer puffs to a plate. Let pan cool slightly.

5. Repeat with the remaining batter and jam, brushing wells with oil and reheating pan before each batch.

6. Dust the ebelskivers with confectioners' sugar. Serve warm or at room temperature.

Buttery Beignet Puffs

Each bite of these incredibly tender golden puffs is like a warm and tasty trip to Café du Monde in New Orleans — without the travel or the deep fryer. Bite into one and be rewarded with the aroma of sweet butter and vanilla, as well as a shower of confectioners' sugar.

Variation

Jelly Doughnut Puffs: You will need ½ cup (125 mL) jelly, jam or preserves of choice. Prepare batter as directed. In step 6, instead of adding 2 tbsp (30 mL) batter to each well, first add 1 tbsp (15 mL) batter to each well. Place 1 tsp (5 mL) jelly in the center of each well and top with 1 tbsp (15 mL) batter. Cook as directed and proceed with step 7.

● **7-well ebelskiver pan**

2 cups	confectioners' (icing) sugar	500 mL
1¼ cups	all-purpose flour	300 mL
¾ tsp	baking powder	3 mL
¼ tsp	salt	1 mL
2 tbsp	granulated sugar	30 mL
2	large eggs, separated	2
¾ cup	milk	175 mL
¼ cup	unsalted butter, melted	60 mL
1½ tsp	vanilla extract	7 mL
	Unsalted butter, melted	

1. Sift the confectioners' sugar into a medium bowl. Set aside.

2. In a large bowl, whisk together flour, baking powder and salt.

3. In a medium bowl, whisk together granulated sugar, egg yolks, milk, ¼ cup (60 mL) butter and vanilla until well blended.

4. Add the egg yolk mixture to the flour mixture and stir until just blended (the batter will appear slightly lumpy).

5. In a medium bowl, using an electric mixer on medium-high speed, beat egg whites until frothy. Increase speed to high and beat until stiff, but not dry, peaks form. Using a rubber spatula, gently mix one-third of the egg whites into the batter. Gently fold in the remaining whites.

6. Brush wells of pan lightly with butter. Set pan over medium heat. When oil begins to sizzle, add 2 tbsp (30 mL) batter to each well. Cook for 2 to 4 minutes or until bottoms are golden brown. Using two skewers, flip the puffs over. Cook for 2 to 3 minutes or until bottoms are golden brown and a toothpick inserted in the center comes out with a few moist crumbs attached.

7. Remove pan from heat and transfer puffs to the bowl of confectioners' sugar, turning to coat. Transfer to a plate. Let pan cool slightly.

8. Repeat steps 6 and 7 with the remaining batter and confectioners' sugar, brushing wells with butter and reheating pan before each batch. Serve warm.

Toasted Wheat Germ Ebelskivers

It's not a mistake: these incredibly delicious ebelskivers are made mostly from wheat germ. Toasted wheat germ has a delectable, nutty flavor and is also very nutritious — high in folate, fiber, B vitamins, potassium and more.

Tip

You can either use pre-toasted wheat germ in this recipe or toast raw wheat germ yourself: spread wheat germ on a large rimmed baking sheet and bake in a 350°F (180°C) oven for 5 to 8 minutes, stirring once, until golden and fragrant. Let cool completely before using.

● **7-well ebelskiver pan**

¾ cup	toasted wheat germ (see tip, at left)	175 mL
½ cup	all-purpose flour	125 mL
¾ tsp	baking powder	3 mL
¼ tsp	salt	1 mL
1 tbsp	packed light brown sugar	15 mL
2	large eggs, separated	2
1 cup	milk	250 mL
2 tbsp	unsalted butter, melted	30 mL
½ tsp	almond extract	2 mL
	Vegetable oil	
½ cup	jam, jelly or preserves of choice	125 mL
	Confectioners' (icing) sugar	

1. In a large bowl, whisk together wheat germ, flour, baking powder and salt.

2. In a medium bowl, whisk together brown sugar, egg yolks, milk, butter and almond extract until well blended.

3. Add the egg yolk mixture to the flour mixture and stir until just blended (the batter will appear slightly lumpy).

4. In a medium bowl, using an electric mixer on medium-high speed, beat egg whites until frothy. Increase speed to high and beat until stiff, but not dry, peaks form. Using a rubber spatula, gently mix one-third of the egg whites into the batter. Gently fold in the remaining whites.

5. Brush wells of pan lightly with oil. Set pan over medium heat. When oil begins to sizzle, add 1 tbsp (15 mL) batter to each well. Place 1 tsp (5 mL) jam in the center of each well and top with 1 tbsp (15 mL) batter. Cook for 2 to 4 minutes or until bottoms are golden brown. Using two skewers, flip the puffs over. Cook for 2 to 3 minutes or until bottoms are golden brown and a toothpick inserted in the center comes out with a bit of filling and moist crumbs attached. Remove pan from heat and transfer puffs to a plate. Let pan cool slightly.

6. Repeat with the remaining batter and jam, brushing wells with oil and reheating pan before each batch.

7. Dust the ebelskivers with confectioners' sugar. Serve warm or at room temperature.

Quinoa Ebelskivers

Botanically speaking, quinoa is an herb, but it's used as a grain and we should all be eating it by the heaping bowlful — or, perhaps, puff-full. It is loaded with all of the essential amino acids, as well as vitamins and minerals. It's also delicious and produces ebelskivers with a mildly nutty flavor and addictively nubby texture that you will likely make one of your new standard breakfasts.

● **7-well ebelskiver pan**

¼ cup	quinoa, rinsed	60 mL
⅓ cup	water	75 mL
¾ cup	all-purpose flour	175 mL
½ cup	whole wheat flour	125 mL
¾ tsp	baking powder	3 mL
¾ tsp	ground cinnamon	3 mL
¼ tsp	salt	1 mL
2	large eggs, separated	2
1 cup	milk	250 mL
2 tbsp	unsalted butter, melted	30 mL
1 tbsp	agave nectar or liquid honey	15 mL
1 tsp	vanilla extract	5 mL
	Vegetable oil	
½ cup	jam, jelly or preserves of choice	125 mL
	Confectioners' (icing) sugar	

1. In a small saucepan, combine quinoa and water. Bring to a boil over medium-high heat. Reduce heat to low, cover and simmer for 10 to 12 minutes or until water is absorbed. Fluff with a fork and let cool completely.

2. In a large bowl, whisk together all-purpose flour, whole wheat flour, baking powder, cinnamon and salt.

3. In a medium bowl, whisk together egg yolks, milk, butter, agave nectar and vanilla until well blended. Gently stir in quinoa.

4. Add the egg yolk mixture to the flour mixture and stir until just blended (the batter will appear slightly lumpy).

5. In a medium bowl, using an electric mixer on medium-high speed, beat egg whites until frothy. Increase speed to high and beat until stiff, but not dry, peaks form. Using a rubber spatula, gently mix one-third of the egg whites into the batter. Gently fold in the remaining whites.

Tips

Use any color of quinoa — white, red, black or multicolored — for these puffs.

Make sure to rinse the quinoa thoroughly before use. Quinoa has a natural protective coating, called saponin, that has a strong bitter taste; even though the majority of the saponin has been removed from almost all of the quinoa available in stores, a small amount of saponin residue may remain after processing. Place the quinoa in a fine-mesh strainer and rinse thoroughly under cold water for 30 to 60 seconds.

For ¾ cup (175 mL) cooked quinoa, you'll need ¼ cup (60 mL) raw quinoa. Feel free to substitute leftover plain cooked quinoa for the quinoa in step 1.

6. Brush wells of pan lightly with oil. Set pan over medium heat. When oil begins to sizzle, add 1 tbsp (15 mL) batter to each well. Place 1 tsp (5 mL) jam in the center of each well and top with 1 tbsp (15 mL) batter. Cook for 2 to 4 minutes or until bottoms are golden brown. Using two skewers, flip the puffs over. Cook for 2 to 3 minutes or until bottoms are golden brown and a toothpick inserted in the center comes out with a bit of filling and moist crumbs attached. Remove pan from heat and transfer puffs to a plate. Let pan cool slightly.

7. Repeat with the remaining batter and jam, brushing wells with oil and reheating pan before each batch.

8. Dust the ebelskivers with confectioners' sugar. Serve warm or at room temperature.

Toasted Millet Ebelskivers

Millet may look familiar if you've ever filled a bird feeder: it is a primary ingredient in most bird seed mixes. But it is extremely nutritious and delicious for humans, too, and is a staple food across Africa and the Far East. Easily digested because it is alkaline (most grains are acidic), millet adds great crunch and nutty flavor to all sorts of baked goods and is a wonderful — and inexpensive — substitute for nuts.

● **7-well ebelskiver pan**

1/3 cup	millet	75 mL
1 1/4 cups	all-purpose flour	300 mL
1/2 tsp	baking powder	2 mL
1/4 tsp	baking soda	1 mL
1/4 tsp	salt	1 mL
1 tbsp	packed dark brown sugar	15 mL
2	large eggs, separated	2
1 cup	buttermilk	250 mL
2 tbsp	unsalted butter, melted	30 mL
1 tsp	vanilla extract	5 mL
	Vegetable oil	
	Pure maple syrup	

1. Heat a large skillet over medium-high heat. Toast millet, stirring, for 3 to 4 minutes or until golden brown and just beginning to pop. Transfer to a plate and let cool completely.

2. In a large bowl, whisk together flour, baking powder, baking soda and salt.

3. In a medium bowl, whisk together brown sugar, egg yolks, buttermilk, butter and vanilla until well blended.

4. Add the egg yolk mixture to the flour mixture and stir until just blended (the batter will appear slightly lumpy). Gently stir in millet.

5. In a medium bowl, using an electric mixer on medium-high speed, beat egg whites until frothy. Increase speed to high and beat until stiff, but not dry, peaks form. Using a rubber spatula, gently mix one-third of the egg whites into the batter. Gently fold in the remaining whites.

6. Brush wells of pan lightly with oil. Set pan over medium heat. When oil begins to sizzle, add 2 tbsp (30 mL) batter to each well. Cook for 2 to 4 minutes or until bottoms are golden brown. Using two skewers, flip the puffs over. Cook for 2 to 3 minutes or until bottoms are golden brown and a toothpick inserted in the center comes out with a few moist crumbs attached. Remove pan from heat and transfer puffs to a plate. Let pan cool slightly.

7. Repeat with the remaining batter, brushing wells with oil and reheating pan before each batch.

8. Serve the ebelskivers warm or at room temperature, with maple syrup.

Oat Bran Ebelskivers

**Makes about
21 puffs**

Oat bran is the outer layer of the oat grain. It is normally discarded during the milling process, which is unfortunate, since it contains the bulk of the dietary fiber of the grain, along with a large amount of useful minerals. Moreover, it makes fantastic ebelskivers. While they are rich with whole-grain goodness, these puffs have a light texture that both children and adults love.

● **7-well ebelskiver pan**

½ cup	all-purpose flour	125 mL
½ cup	oat bran	125 mL
¼ cup	whole wheat flour	60 mL
¾ tsp	baking powder	3 mL
½ tsp	ground cinnamon	2 mL
¼ tsp	salt	1 mL
1 tbsp	packed light brown sugar	15 mL
2	large eggs, separated	2
1 cup	milk	250 mL
	Vegetable oil	
1 tsp	vanilla extract	5 mL
½ cup	jam, jelly or preserves of choice	125 mL
	Confectioners' (icing) sugar	

1. In a large bowl, whisk together all-purpose flour, oat bran, whole wheat flour, baking powder, cinnamon and salt.

2. In a medium bowl, whisk together brown sugar, egg yolks, milk, 2 tbsp (30 mL) oil and vanilla until well blended.

3. Add the egg yolk mixture to the flour mixture and stir until just blended (the batter will appear slightly lumpy).

4. In a medium bowl, using an electric mixer on medium-high speed, beat egg whites until frothy. Increase speed to high and beat until stiff, but not dry, peaks form. Using a rubber spatula, gently mix one-third of the egg whites into the batter. Gently fold in the remaining whites.

5. Brush wells of pan lightly with oil. Set pan over medium heat. When oil begins to sizzle, add 1 tbsp (15 mL) batter to each well. Place 1 tsp (5 mL) jam in the center of each well and top with 1 tbsp (15 mL) batter. Cook for 2 to 4 minutes or until bottoms are golden brown. Using two skewers, flip the puffs over. Cook for 2 to 3 minutes or until bottoms are golden brown and a toothpick inserted in the center comes out with a bit of filling and moist crumbs attached. Remove pan from heat and transfer puffs to a plate. Let pan cool slightly.

6. Repeat with the remaining batter and jam, brushing wells with oil and reheating pan before each batch.

7. Dust the ebelskivers with confectioners' sugar. Serve warm or at room temperature.

Oats and Honey Ebelskivers

If you're thinking that the addition of oats will make these ebelskivers heavy, think again: these pancakes have a delicate texture and a toasty flavor that pairs ever so well with honey.

Tip

If you prefer, ½ tsp (2 mL) pure orange extract may be used in place of the grated orange zest.

Variation

Replace the orange zest with 1 tsp (5 mL) vanilla extract.

● **7-well ebelskiver pan**

¾ cup	all-purpose flour	175 mL
½ cup	quick-cooking rolled oats	125 mL
¼ tsp	baking soda	1 mL
½ tsp	baking powder	2 mL
¼ tsp	salt	1 mL
¼ tsp	ground nutmeg	1 mL
2	large eggs, separated	2
1 cup	milk	250 mL
½ cup	liquid honey, divided	125 mL
2 tbsp	unsalted butter, melted	30 mL
1 tsp	finely grated orange zest	5 mL

1. In a large bowl, whisk together flour, oats, baking soda, baking powder, salt and nutmeg.

2. In a medium bowl, whisk together egg yolks, milk, 1 tbsp (15 mL) honey, butter and orange zest until well blended.

3. Add the egg yolk mixture to the flour mixture and stir until just blended (the batter will appear slightly lumpy).

4. In a medium bowl, using an electric mixer on medium-high speed, beat egg whites until frothy. Increase speed to high and beat until stiff, but not dry, peaks form. Using a rubber spatula, gently mix one-third of the egg whites into the batter. Gently fold in the remaining whites.

5. Brush wells of pan lightly with oil. Set pan over medium heat. When oil begins to sizzle, add 2 tbsp (30 mL) batter to each well. Cook for 2 to 4 minutes or until bottoms are golden brown. Using two skewers, flip the puffs over. Cook for 2 to 3 minutes or until bottoms are golden brown and a toothpick inserted in the center comes out with a few moist crumbs attached. Remove pan from heat and transfer puffs to a plate. Let pan cool slightly.

6. Repeat with the remaining batter, brushing wells with oil and reheating pan before each batch.

7. Drizzle ebelskivers with the remaining honey. Serve warm or at room temperature.

Flax and Molasses Ebelskivers

Dark and delicious, these homey ebelskivers have the aromatic nuances of cloves and notes of caramel from the molasses. Rounding out the batter are ground flax seeds, which are rich in nutrients that protect against heart disease and cancer.

Variation

For a milder flavor, use an equal amount of pure maple syrup or liquid honey in place of the molasses.

● **7-well ebelskiver pan**

1/3 cup	all-purpose flour	75 mL
1/3 cup	whole wheat flour	75 mL
1/3 cup	ground flax seeds (flaxseed meal)	75 mL
3/4 tsp	baking powder	3 mL
1/4 tsp	salt	1 mL
1/4 tsp	ground cloves	1 mL
2	large eggs, separated	2
1 cup	milk	250 mL
	Vegetable oil	
2 tbsp	dark (cooking) molasses	30 mL
1 tsp	vanilla extract	5 mL
	Confectioners' (icing) sugar	

1. In a large bowl, whisk together all-purpose flour, whole wheat flour, flax seeds, baking powder, salt and cloves.

2. In a medium bowl, whisk together egg yolks, milk, 1 tbsp (15 mL) oil, molasses and vanilla until well blended.

3. Add the egg yolk mixture to the flour mixture and stir until just blended (the batter will appear slightly lumpy).

4. In a medium bowl, using an electric mixer on medium-high speed, beat egg whites until frothy. Increase speed to high and beat until stiff, but not dry, peaks form. Using a rubber spatula, gently mix one-third of the egg whites into the batter. Gently fold in the remaining whites.

5. Brush wells of pan lightly with oil. Set pan over medium heat. When oil begins to sizzle, add 2 tbsp (30 mL) batter to each well. Cook for 2 to 4 minutes or until bottoms are firm to the touch. Using two skewers, flip the puffs over. Cook for 2 to 3 minutes or until puffs are firm to the touch and a toothpick inserted in the center comes out with a few moist crumbs attached. Remove pan from heat and transfer puffs to a plate. Let pan cool slightly.

6. Repeat with the remaining batter, brushing wells with oil and reheating pan before each batch.

7. Dust the ebelskivers with confectioners' sugar. Serve warm or at room temperature.

Eight-Grain Maple Ebelskivers

Looking to incorporate more whole grains into your diet? Here's my quick, easy, portable and oh-so-delicious solution.

Tip

There are many multigrain hot cereals available, such as Bob's Red Mill, Hodgson Mill, Quaker or Red River. Just be sure not to use an instant variety.

● **7-well ebelskiver pan**

⅔ cup	8-grain or other multigrain hot cereal	150 mL
1 cup	milk	250 mL
⅔ cup	whole wheat flour	150 mL
¾ tsp	baking powder	3 mL
¼ tsp	salt	1 mL
¼ tsp	ground cinnamon	1 mL
2	large eggs, separated	2
¾ cup	pure maple syrup, divided	175 mL
2 tbsp	unsalted butter, melted	30 mL
1 tsp	vanilla extract	5 mL
	Vegetable oil	

1. In a medium bowl, combine cereal and milk. Let stand for 20 minutes.

2. In a large bowl, whisk together flour, baking powder, salt and cinnamon.

3. Whisk egg yolks, 2 tbsp (30 mL) of the maple syrup, butter and vanilla into the cereal mixture until well blended.

4. Add the egg yolk mixture to the flour mixture and stir until just blended (the batter will appear slightly lumpy).

5. In a medium bowl, using an electric mixer on medium-high speed, beat egg whites until frothy. Increase speed to high and beat until stiff, but not dry, peaks form. Using a rubber spatula, gently mix one-third of the egg whites into the batter. Gently fold in the remaining whites.

6. Brush wells of pan lightly with oil. Set pan over medium heat. When oil begins to sizzle, add 2 tbsp (30 mL) batter to each well. Cook for 2 to 4 minutes or until bottoms are golden brown. Using two skewers, flip the puffs over. Cook for 2 to 3 minutes or until bottoms are golden brown and a toothpick inserted in the center comes out with a few moist crumbs attached. Remove pan from heat and transfer puffs to a plate. Let pan cool slightly.

7. Repeat with the remaining batter, brushing wells with oil and reheating pan before each batch.

8. Serve the ebelskivers warm, with the remaining maple syrup.

Cottage Cheese and Jam Ebelskivers

Cottage cheese is the stealth ingredient here, adding tenderness and moisture to these vanilla-scented ebelskivers. It also packs in some good-for-you protein, meaning just a few ebelskivers will help sustain you through a busy morning.

Tip

For best results, do not use nonfat cottage cheese.

● **7-well ebelskiver pan**

1⅓ cups	all-purpose flour	325 mL
¾ tsp	baking powder	3 mL
¼ tsp	salt	1 mL
1½ tbsp	granulated sugar	22 mL
2	large eggs, separated	2
1 cup	small-curd cottage cheese	250 mL
½ cup	milk	125 mL
2 tbsp	unsalted butter, melted	30 mL
1 tsp	vanilla extract	5 mL
	Vegetable oil	
⅔ cup	jam, jelly or preserves of choice	150 mL
	Confectioners' (icing) sugar	

1. In a large bowl, whisk together flour, baking powder and salt.

2. In a medium bowl, whisk together sugar, egg yolks, cottage cheese, milk, butter and vanilla until well blended.

3. Add the egg yolk mixture to the flour mixture and stir until just blended (the batter will appear slightly lumpy).

4. In a medium bowl, using an electric mixer on medium-high speed, beat egg whites until frothy. Increase speed to high and beat until stiff, but not dry, peaks form. Using a rubber spatula, gently mix one-third of the egg whites into the batter. Gently fold in the remaining whites.

5. Brush wells of pan lightly with oil. Set pan over medium heat. When oil begins to sizzle, add 1 tbsp (15 mL) batter to each well. Place 1 tsp (5 mL) jam in the center of each well and top with 1 tbsp (15 mL) batter. Cook for 2 to 4 minutes or until bottoms are golden brown. Using two skewers, flip the puffs over. Cook for 2 to 3 minutes or until bottoms are golden brown and a toothpick inserted in the center comes out with a bit of filling and moist crumbs attached. Remove pan from heat and transfer puffs to a plate. Let pan cool slightly.

6. Repeat with the remaining batter and jam, brushing wells with oil and reheating pan before each batch.

7. Dust the ebelskivers with confectioners' sugar. Serve warm.

Cinnamon Roll Ebelskivers

This simplified, puffed-up rendition of a morning classic is supremely satisfying. There's something about homemade cinnamon anything that exerts a primordial pull, and a cream cheese icing makes for ebelskivers that are somehow both nostalgic and sophisticated.

● **7-well ebelskiver pan**

Cinnamon Filling

½ cup	packed light brown sugar	125 mL
2 tbsp	all-purpose flour	30 mL
1½ tbsp	ground cinnamon	22 mL
¼ tsp	salt	1 mL
¼ cup	unsalted butter, softened	60 mL

Cream Cheese Icing

1½ cups	confectioners' (icing) sugar	375 mL
3 oz	cream cheese, softened	90 g
¼ cup	unsalted butter, softened	60 mL
3 tbsp	milk	45 mL

Ebelskivers

1¾ cups	all-purpose flour	425 mL
1¼ tsp	baking powder	6 mL
¼ tsp	salt	1 mL
1 tbsp	granulated sugar	15 mL
3	large eggs, separated	3
1⅓ cups	milk	325 mL
3 tbsp	unsalted butter, melted	45 mL
1 tsp	vanilla extract	5 mL
	Vegetable oil	

1. *Filling:* In a small bowl, stir together brown sugar, flour, cinnamon and salt. Add butter and stir until mixture forms a paste. Set aside.

2. *Icing:* In a medium bowl, using an electric mixer on medium-high speed, beat confectioners' sugar, cream cheese and butter until fluffy. Add milk and beat on low speed until just blended. Set icing aside. Clean the beaters.

3. *Ebelskivers:* In a large bowl, whisk together flour, baking powder and salt.

4. In a medium bowl, whisk together sugar, egg yolks, milk, butter and vanilla until well blended.

5. Add the egg yolk mixture to the flour mixture and stir until just blended (the batter will appear slightly lumpy).

Tip

If you do not have cream cheese on hand, make a simple confectioners' sugar frosting to replace the cream cheese icing. In a small bowl, whisk together 2¼ cups (550 mL) confectioners' (icing) sugar, 3 tbsp (45 mL) unsalted butter, melted and slightly cooled, 3 tbsp (45 mL) milk and 1 tsp (5 mL) vanilla extract until blended and smooth.

Variation

Cinnamon-Pecan Roll Ebelskivers: Add ¾ cup (175 mL) chopped toasted pecans to the batter at the end of step 5.

6. In a medium bowl, using an electric mixer on medium-high speed, beat egg whites until frothy. Increase speed to high and beat until stiff, but not dry, peaks form. Using a rubber spatula, gently mix one-third of the egg whites into the batter. Gently fold in the remaining whites.

7. Brush wells of pan lightly with oil. Set pan over medium heat. When oil begins to sizzle, add 1 tbsp (15 mL) batter to each well. Place 1 tsp (5 mL) filling in the center of each well and top with 1 tbsp (15 mL) batter. Cook for 2 to 4 minutes or until bottoms are golden brown. Using two skewers, flip the puffs over. Cook for 2 to 3 minutes or until bottoms are golden brown and a toothpick inserted in the center comes out with a bit of filling and moist crumbs attached. Remove pan from heat and transfer puffs to a plate. Let pan cool slightly.

8. Repeat with the remaining batter and filling, brushing wells with oil and reheating pan before each batch.

9. Drizzle the ebelskivers with the cream cheese icing. Serve warm or at room temperature.

Bear Claw Ebelskivers

My childhood breakfasts were healthy fare: sugar-free cereals, fresh fruit, homemade granola, whole wheat pancakes and waffles, and multigrain muffins. But once in a rare while, my mother would throw caution to the wind and surprise us with bear claws (one of her favorite breakfast pastries of all time). With buttery pastry, brown sugar filling and icing, they were worth the wait. These bear claw–inspired ebelskivers are a close second, plus they receive bonus points for being so easy to make.

● **7-well ebelskiver pan**

Filling

1 cup	plain (unseasoned) dry bread crumbs	250 mL
2½ tbsp	packed dark brown sugar	37 mL
½ cup	milk	125 mL
3 tbsp	unsalted butter, melted	45 mL
2 tsp	almond extract	10 mL

Ebelskivers

1¾ cups	all-purpose flour	425 mL
1 tsp	baking powder	5 mL
¼ tsp	salt	1 mL
1 tbsp	granulated sugar	15 mL
3	large eggs, separated	3
2 tbsp	unsalted butter, melted	30 mL
1 tsp	vanilla extract	5 mL
1⅓ cups	milk	325 mL
	Vegetable oil	

Icing

1½ cups	confectioners' (icing) sugar	375 mL
1½ tbsp	milk	22 mL

1. *Filling:* In a small bowl, stir together bread crumbs, brown sugar, milk, butter and almond extract until blended.

2. *Ebelskivers:* In a large bowl, whisk together flour, baking powder and salt.

3. In a medium bowl, whisk together sugar, egg yolks, butter and vanilla. Whisk in milk until well blended.

4. Add the egg yolk mixture to the flour mixture and stir until just blended (the batter will appear slightly lumpy).

5. In a medium bowl, using an electric mixer on medium-high speed, beat egg whites until frothy. Increase speed to high and beat until stiff, but not dry, peaks form. Using a rubber spatula, gently mix one-third of the egg whites into the batter. Gently fold in the remaining whites.

6. Brush wells of pan lightly with oil. Set pan over medium heat. When oil begins to sizzle, add 1 tbsp (15 mL) batter to each well. Place 1 tsp (5 mL) filling in the center of each well and top with 1 tbsp (15 mL) batter. Cook for 2 to 4 minutes or until bottoms are golden brown. Using two skewers, flip the puffs over. Cook for 2 to 3 minutes or until bottoms are golden brown and a toothpick inserted in the center comes out with a bit of filling and moist crumbs attached. Remove pan from heat and transfer puffs to a plate. Let pan cool slightly.

7. Repeat with the remaining batter and filling, brushing wells with oil and reheating pan before each batch.

8. *Icing:* In a small bowl, stir together confectioners' sugar and milk until smooth.

9. Drizzle the ebelskivers with the icing. Serve warm or at room temperature.

Crumb Coffeecake Ebelskivers

Some dessert icons, such as New York–style crumb coffeecake, are so exceptional that they are exempt from any new interpretations. But I think even the most diehard aficionados of the coffeehouse favorite will be delighted by this ebelskiver adaptation.

Tip

Be sure to fill the ebelskiver wells with batter very quickly after adding the topping to avoid scorching the sugar in the topping.

- **7-well ebelskiver pan**

Crumb Topping

1/3 cup	finely chopped toasted walnuts or pecans	75 mL
1/3 cup	all-purpose flour	75 mL
1/3 cup	packed dark brown sugar	75 mL
1 tsp	ground cinnamon	5 mL
1/8 tsp	salt	0.5 mL
3 tbsp	unsalted butter, melted	45 mL

Ebelskivers

1 1/4 cups	all-purpose flour	300 mL
3/4 tsp	baking powder	3 mL
1/4 tsp	salt	1 mL
1 1/2 tbsp	granulated sugar	22 mL
2	large eggs, separated	2
1 cup	milk	250 mL
2 tbsp	unsalted butter, melted	30 mL
1 tsp	vanilla extract	5 mL
	Vegetable oil	
	Confectioners' (icing) sugar	

1. *Topping:* In a small bowl, stir together walnuts, flour, brown sugar, cinnamon and salt until blended. Add butter and stir until blended. Set aside.

2. *Ebelskivers:* In a large bowl, whisk together flour, baking powder and salt.

3. In a medium bowl, whisk together sugar, egg yolks, milk, butter and vanilla until well blended.

4. Add the egg yolk mixture to the flour mixture and stir until just blended (the batter will appear slightly lumpy).

5. In a medium bowl, using an electric mixer on medium-high speed, beat egg whites until frothy. Increase speed to high and beat until stiff, but not dry, peaks form. Using a rubber spatula, gently mix one-third of the egg whites into the batter. Gently fold in the remaining whites.

Variations

For an extra-decadent treat, frost the finished ebelskivers with Cream Cheese Icing (page 46).

The walnuts can be omitted from the topping. Increase the flour and brown sugar to ½ cup (125 mL) each, and increase the butter to 3½ tbsp (52 mL).

6. Brush wells of pan lightly with oil. Set pan over medium heat. When oil begins to sizzle, add 1 tsp (5 mL) topping to each well, then immediately top with 2 tbsp (30 mL) batter. Cook for 2 to 4 minutes or until bottoms are golden brown. Using two skewers, flip the puffs over. Cook for 2 to 3 minutes or until bottoms are golden brown and a toothpick inserted in the center comes out with a few moist crumbs attached. Remove pan from heat and transfer puffs to a plate. Let pan cool slightly.

7. Repeat with the remaining topping and batter, brushing wells with oil and reheating pan before each batch.

8. Dust the ebelskivers with confectioners' sugar. Serve warm or at room temperature.

Stuffed French Toast Ebelskivers

Perfumed with nutmeg and vanilla, stuffed with a cheesecake-like filling and puffed into an eggy, custardy cloak, this take on French toast is one of those magical dishes that works just as well for dessert as it does for breakfast.

● **7-well ebelskiver pan**

Filling

8 oz	cream cheese, softened	250 g
2 tbsp	granulated sugar	30 mL
1 tsp	vanilla extract	5 mL

Ebelskivers

1¾ cups	all-purpose flour	425 mL
1 tsp	baking powder	5 mL
¾ tsp	baking soda	3 mL
½ tsp	ground nutmeg	2 mL
¼ tsp	salt	1 mL
1 tbsp	granulated sugar	15 mL
3	large eggs, separated	3
2 tbsp	unsalted butter, melted	30 mL
1 tsp	vanilla extract	5 mL
1⅓ cups	buttermilk	325 mL
	Vegetable oil	
	Confectioners' (icing) sugar	

1. *Filling:* In a medium bowl, using an electric mixer on medium-high speed, beat cream cheese, sugar and vanilla until smooth and creamy. Cover and refrigerate while preparing the batter. Clean the beaters.

2. *Ebelskivers:* In a large bowl, whisk together flour, baking powder, baking soda, nutmeg and salt.

3. In a medium bowl, whisk together sugar, egg yolks, butter and vanilla. Whisk in buttermilk until well blended.

4. Add the egg yolk mixture to the flour mixture and stir until just blended (the batter will appear slightly lumpy).

5. In a medium bowl, using an electric mixer on medium-high speed, beat egg whites until frothy. Increase speed to high and beat until stiff, but not dry, peaks form. Using a rubber spatula, gently mix one-third of the egg whites into the batter. Gently fold in the remaining whites.

Tips

Softened ricotta or mascarpone cheese may be used in place of the cream cheese in the filling.

You can replace the nutmeg with 1 tsp (5 mL) ground cinnamon.

No buttermilk? No problem. For every 1 cup (250 mL) of buttermilk, mix 1 tbsp (15 mL) lemon juice or white vinegar into 1 cup (250 mL) whole, lower-fat or skim milk. Let stand for at least 15 minutes before using.

6. Brush wells of pan lightly with oil. Set pan over medium heat. When oil begins to sizzle, add 1 tbsp (15 mL) batter to each well. Place 1 tsp (5 mL) filling in the center of each well and top with 1 tbsp (15 mL) batter. Cook for 2 to 4 minutes or until bottoms are golden brown. Using two skewers, flip the puffs over. Cook for 2 to 3 minutes or until bottoms are golden brown and a toothpick inserted in the center comes out with a bit of filling and moist crumbs attached. Remove pan from heat and transfer puffs to a plate. Let pan cool slightly.

7. Repeat with the remaining batter and filling, brushing wells with oil and reheating pan before each batch.

8. Dust the ebelskivers with confectioners' sugar. Serve warm.

Brown Sugar Bacon Ebelskivers

Improving the rich, smoky flavor of bacon is no easy feat, but I've done it: crisp bacon encased in brown sugar puffs with a hint of cayenne makes one addictive breakfast.

Tips

You can streamline this recipe by omitting step 1 and substituting ⅔ cup (150 mL) packaged real bacon pieces for the bacon and 2 tbsp (30 mL) unsalted butter, melted, for the bacon drippings.

No buttermilk? No problem. For every 1 cup (250 mL) of buttermilk, mix 1 tbsp (15 mL) lemon juice or white vinegar into 1 cup (250 mL) whole, lower-fat or skim milk. Let stand for at least 15 minutes before using.

For a deeper molasses-like flavor, use an equal amount of dark brown sugar in place of the light brown sugar.

● **7-well ebelskiver pan**

6 oz	bacon, chopped	175 g
1¼ cups	all-purpose flour	300 mL
½ tsp	baking soda	2 mL
½ tsp	baking powder	2 mL
¼ tsp	salt	1 mL
¼ tsp	cayenne pepper	1 mL
3 tbsp	packed light brown sugar	45 mL
2	large eggs, separated	2
1 cup	buttermilk	250 mL
1 tsp	vanilla extract	5 mL
	Vegetable oil	
	Confectioners' (icing) sugar	

1. In a large skillet, cook bacon over medium-high heat, stirring, until crisp. Using a slotted spoon, transfer bacon to a plate lined with paper towels to drain and cool. Reserve 2 tbsp (30 mL) bacon drippings.

2. In a large bowl, whisk together flour, baking soda, baking powder, salt and cayenne.

3. In a medium bowl, whisk together brown sugar, reserved bacon drippings, egg yolks, buttermilk and vanilla until well blended.

4. Add the egg yolk mixture to the flour mixture and stir until just blended (the batter will appear slightly lumpy). Gently stir in cooled bacon.

5. In a medium bowl, using an electric mixer on medium-high speed, beat egg whites until frothy. Increase speed to high and beat until stiff, but not dry, peaks form. Using a rubber spatula, gently mix one-third of the egg whites into the batter. Gently fold in the remaining whites.

Variation

Brown Sugar Pecan Puffs:
Omit the bacon and replace
the bacon drippings with
2 tbsp (30 mL) unsalted
butter, melted. Add ⅔ cup
(150 mL) finely chopped
toasted pecans at the end
of step 3.

6. Brush wells of pan lightly with oil. Set pan over medium heat. When oil begins to sizzle, add 2 tbsp (30 mL) batter to each well. Cook for 2 to 4 minutes or until bottoms are golden brown. Using two skewers, flip the puffs over. Cook for 2 to 3 minutes or until bottoms are golden brown and a toothpick inserted in the center comes out with a few moist crumbs attached. Remove pan from heat and transfer puffs to a plate. Let pan cool slightly.

7. Repeat with the remaining batter, brushing wells with oil and reheating pan before each batch.

8. Dust the ebelskivers with confectioners' sugar. Serve warm or at room temperature.

Fresh Ginger Ebelskivers

Golden brown and graced
with two of my favorite
ingredients — ginger
and lemon — a plateful
of these ebelskivers is
always a cheery sight.

Variation

*Lemon Curd–Filled Ginger
Ebelskivers:* You will need
½ cup (125 mL) lemon curd.
Prepare batter as directed.
In step 6, instead of adding
2 tbsp (30 mL) batter, first
add 1 tbsp (15 mL) batter to
each well, then place 1 tsp
(5 mL) lemon curd in the
center of each well and top
with 1 tbsp (15 mL) batter.
Cook as directed.

● **7-well ebelskiver pan**

2 tbsp	coarsely chopped gingerroot	30 mL
2 tbsp	granulated sugar	30 mL
1 cup	milk, divided	250 mL
1¼ cups	all-purpose flour	300 mL
¾ tsp	baking powder	3 mL
¼ tsp	salt	1 mL
2	large eggs, separated	2
2 tbsp	unsalted butter, melted	30 mL
1½ tsp	finely grated lemon zest	7 mL
	Vegetable oil	
	Confectioners' (icing) sugar	

1. In a small saucepan, combine ginger, sugar and ⅓ cup (75 mL) of the milk. Cook over medium-high heat, stirring, for 3 to 4 minutes or until sugar is dissolved. Scrape into a medium bowl and whisk in the remaining milk. Let cool completely.

2. In a large bowl, whisk together flour, baking powder and salt.

3. Whisk the egg yolks, butter and lemon zest into the milk mixture until well blended.

4. Add the milk mixture to the flour mixture and stir until just blended (the batter will appear slightly lumpy).

5. In a medium bowl, using an electric mixer on medium-high speed, beat egg whites until frothy. Increase speed to high and beat until stiff, but not dry, peaks form. Using a rubber spatula, gently mix one-third of the egg whites into the batter. Gently fold in the remaining whites.

6. Brush wells of pan lightly with oil. Set pan over medium heat. When oil begins to sizzle, add 2 tbsp (30 mL) batter to each well. Cook for 2 to 4 minutes or until bottoms are golden brown. Using two skewers, flip the puffs over. Cook for 2 to 3 minutes or until bottoms are golden brown and a toothpick inserted in the center comes out with a few moist crumbs attached. Remove pan from heat and transfer puffs to a plate. Let pan cool slightly.

7. Repeat with the remaining batter, brushing wells with oil and reheating pan before each batch.

8. Dust the ebelskivers with confectioners' sugar. Serve warm or at room temperature.

Multi-Seed Ebelskivers

Who knew that a mix of seeds could be so delicious? Okay, I knew. Here they star in faintly sweet whole wheat ebelskivers that are smashing for breakfast, snacks and any other time of night or day when hunger strikes.

Tip

To toast the sesame seeds and anise seeds, place both in a dry skillet set over medium heat. Cook, shaking the pan every few seconds, for 30 to 90 seconds, until the seeds are golden and aromatic, and the sesame seeds begin to make a popping sound. Immediately transfer to a bowl and let cool.

● **7-well ebelskiver pan**

¾ cup	all-purpose flour	175 mL
½ cup	whole wheat flour	125 mL
½ tsp	baking soda	2 mL
¼ tsp	baking powder	1 mL
¼ tsp	salt	1 mL
2 tbsp	packed dark brown sugar	30 mL
2	large eggs, separated	2
1 cup	plain yogurt	250 mL
2 tbsp	unsalted butter, melted	30 mL
2 tbsp	sesame seeds, toasted (see tip, at left)	30 mL
1 tbsp	anise or fennel seeds, toasted	15 mL
1 tbsp	poppy seeds	15 mL
	Vegetable oil	
	Pure maple syrup or liquid honey (optional)	

1. In a large bowl, whisk together all-purpose flour, whole wheat flour, baking soda, baking powder and salt.

2. In a medium bowl, whisk together brown sugar, egg yolks, yogurt and butter until well blended.

3. Add the egg yolk mixture to the flour mixture and stir until just blended (the batter will appear slightly lumpy). Gently stir in sesame seeds, anise seeds and poppy seeds.

4. In a medium bowl, using an electric mixer on medium-high speed, beat egg whites until frothy. Increase speed to high and beat until stiff, but not dry, peaks form. Using a rubber spatula, gently mix one-third of the egg whites into the batter. Gently fold in the remaining whites.

5. Brush wells of pan lightly with oil. Set pan over medium heat. When oil begins to sizzle, add 2 tbsp (30 mL) batter to each well. Cook for 2 to 4 minutes or until bottoms are golden brown. Using two skewers, flip the puffs over. Cook for 2 to 3 minutes or until bottoms are golden brown and a toothpick inserted in the center comes out with a few moist crumbs attached. Remove pan from heat and transfer puffs to a plate. Let pan cool slightly.

6. Repeat with the remaining batter, brushing wells with oil and reheating pan before each batch.

7. Drizzle the ebelskivers with maple syrup, if using. Serve warm or at room temperature.

Citrus and Olive Oil Ebelskivers

Extra virgin olive oil is the (not so) secret ingredient in these moist, citrus-scented ebelskivers. They're perfect as an afternoon snack, or for breakfast with a café au lait.

● **7-well ebelskiver pan**

Ebelskivers

1¼ cups	all-purpose flour	300 mL
¾ tsp	baking powder	3 mL
¼ tsp	salt	1 mL
1 tbsp	granulated sugar	15 mL
2	large eggs, separated	2
1 cup	milk	250 mL
2 tbsp	extra virgin olive oil	30 mL
1½ tsp	finely grated lemon zest	7 mL
	Vegetable oil	
½ cup	orange marmalade	125 mL

Lemon Icing

1½ cups	confectioners' (icing) sugar, sifted	375 mL
1½ tbsp	freshly squeezed lemon juice	22 mL

1. *Ebelskivers:* In a large bowl, whisk together flour, baking powder and salt.

2. In a medium bowl, whisk together sugar, egg yolks, milk, olive oil and lemon zest until well blended.

3. Add the egg yolk mixture to the flour mixture and stir until just blended (the batter will appear slightly lumpy).

4. In a medium bowl, using an electric mixer on medium-high speed, beat egg whites until frothy. Increase speed to high and beat until stiff, but not dry, peaks form. Using a rubber spatula, gently mix one-third of the egg whites into the batter. Gently fold in the remaining whites.

Tips

For a simpler presentation, omit the icing and dust the finished ebelskivers with confectioners' (icing) sugar.

For a milder flavor, use an equal amount of unsalted butter, melted, or vegetable oil in place of the olive oil.

5. Brush wells of pan lightly with vegetable oil. Set pan over medium heat. When oil begins to sizzle, add 1 tbsp (15 mL) batter to each well. Place 1 tsp (5 mL) marmalade in the center of each well and top with 1 tbsp (15 mL) batter. Cook for 2 to 4 minutes or until bottoms are golden brown. Using two skewers, flip the puffs over. Cook for 2 to 3 minutes or until bottoms are golden brown and a toothpick inserted in the center comes out with a bit of filling and moist crumbs attached. Remove pan from heat and transfer puffs to a plate. Let pan cool slightly.

6. Repeat with the remaining batter and marmalade, brushing wells with oil and reheating pan before each batch.

7. *Icing:* Stir together confectioners' sugar and lemon juice until smooth.

8. Drizzle the ebelskivers with the lemon icing. Serve warm or at room temperature.

PB&J Ebelskivers

This whimsical interpretation of peanut butter and jelly is irresistible to kids of all ages.

Tips

If serving the ebelskivers at room temperature, wait until ready to serve before drizzling them with peanut butter sauce.

An equal amount of other smooth nut or seed butters (such as almond, cashew or sunflower seed butter) may be used in place of the peanut butter.

● **7-well ebelskiver pan**

1 1/4 cups	all-purpose flour	300 mL
3/4 tsp	baking powder	3 mL
1/4 tsp	salt	1 mL
1 tbsp	packed dark brown sugar	15 mL
2	large eggs, separated	2
1 cup	milk	250 mL
2 tbsp	unsalted butter, melted	30 mL
1 tsp	vanilla extract	5 mL
	Vegetable oil	
1/2 cup	raspberry or strawberry jam or preserves	125 mL
2/3 cup	creamy peanut butter	150 mL
1/3 cup	canned sweetened condensed milk	75 mL

1. In a large bowl, whisk together flour, baking powder and salt.

2. In a medium bowl, whisk together brown sugar, egg yolks, milk, butter and vanilla until well blended.

3. Add the egg yolk mixture to the flour mixture and stir until just blended (the batter will appear slightly lumpy).

4. In a medium bowl, using an electric mixer on medium-high speed, beat egg whites until frothy. Increase speed to high and beat until stiff, but not dry, peaks form. Using a rubber spatula, gently mix one-third of the egg whites into the batter. Gently fold in the remaining whites.

5. Brush wells of pan lightly with oil. Set pan over medium heat. When oil begins to sizzle, add 1 tbsp (15 mL) batter to each well. Place 1 tsp (5 mL) jam in the center of each well and top with 1 tbsp (15 mL) batter. Cook for 2 to 4 minutes or until bottoms are golden brown. Using two skewers, flip the puffs over. Cook for 2 to 3 minutes or until bottoms are golden brown and a toothpick inserted in the center comes out with a bit of filling and moist crumbs attached. Remove pan from heat and transfer puffs to a plate. Let pan cool slightly.

6. Repeat with the remaining batter and jam, brushing wells with oil and reheating pan before each batch.

7. In a small saucepan, combine peanut butter and condensed milk. Heat over low heat, stirring, until melted and warmed through.

8. Drizzle the ebelskivers with peanut butter sauce. Serve warm or at room temperature.

Raisin Bran Puffs

Can raisin bran be exciting and new? Absolutely, and here it is.

Tips

If the raisins are especially large, give them a coarse chop so they will be more evenly distributed throughout the batter.

Look for bran cereal that has a minimal amount of sugar added (or no sugar added). If it has added sugar, consider omitting the granulated sugar.

Variation

For extra-healthy ebelskivers, replace the all-purpose flour with white whole wheat flour or whole wheat pastry flour, and replace the butter with 1 tbsp (15 mL) extra virgin olive oil or vegetable oil.

- **7-well ebelskiver pan**

2 cups	bran flakes cereal, crushed	500 mL
3	large eggs, separated	3
1 cup	milk	250 mL
1 cup	all-purpose flour	250 mL
¾ tsp	baking powder	3 mL
¼ tsp	salt	1 mL
1 tbsp	granulated sugar	15 mL
2 tbsp	unsalted butter, melted	30 mL
1 tsp	vanilla extract	5 mL
⅔ cup	raisins	150 mL
	Vegetable oil	

1. In a large bowl, stir together cereal, egg yolks and milk. Let stand for 10 minutes.

2. In another large bowl, whisk together flour, baking powder and salt.

3. Stir sugar, butter and vanilla into the cereal mixture until well blended.

4. Add the egg yolk mixture to the flour mixture and stir until just blended (the batter will appear slightly lumpy). Gently stir in raisins.

5. In a medium bowl, using an electric mixer on medium-high speed, beat egg whites until frothy. Increase speed to high and beat until stiff, but not dry, peaks form. Using a rubber spatula, gently mix one-third of the egg whites into the batter. Gently fold in the remaining whites.

6. Brush wells of pan lightly with oil. Set pan over medium heat. When oil begins to sizzle, add 2 tbsp (30 mL) batter to each well. Cook for 2 to 4 minutes or until bottoms are golden brown. Using two skewers, flip the puffs over. Cook for 2 to 3 minutes or until bottoms are golden brown and a toothpick inserted in the center comes out with a few moist crumbs attached. Remove pan from heat and transfer puffs to a plate. Let pan cool slightly.

7. Repeat with the remaining batter, brushing wells with oil and reheating pan before each batch. Serve warm or at room temperature.

Golden Raisin and Rosemary Ebelskivers

Rosemary lends an unexpected nuance to these sophisticated ebelskivers. The golden raisins offer a bright, citrusy contrast that is further accentuated by fresh lemon zest. In sum, they are one of my favorite accompaniments to tea.

Tips

If you don't have fresh rosemary on hand, you can substitute ¾ tsp (3 mL) dried rosemary, crushed.

If the raisins are especially large, give them a coarse chop so they will be more evenly distributed throughout the batter.

● **7-well ebelskiver pan**

1¼ cups	all-purpose flour	300 mL
¾ tsp	baking powder	3 mL
¼ tsp	salt	1 mL
1 tbsp	granulated sugar	15 mL
2	large eggs, separated	2
1 cup	milk	250 mL
2 tbsp	unsalted butter, melted	30 mL
2 tsp	finely grated lemon zest	10 mL
1½ tsp	minced fresh rosemary	7 mL
½ cup	golden raisins	125 mL
	Vegetable oil	
	Confectioners' (icing) sugar	

1. In a large bowl, whisk together flour, baking powder and salt.

2. In a medium bowl, whisk together sugar, egg yolks, milk, butter, lemon zest and rosemary until well blended.

3. Add the egg yolk mixture to the flour mixture and stir until just blended (the batter will appear slightly lumpy). Gently stir in raisins.

4. In a medium bowl, using an electric mixer on medium-high speed, beat egg whites until frothy. Increase speed to high and beat until stiff, but not dry, peaks form. Using a rubber spatula, gently mix one-third of the egg whites into the batter. Gently fold in the remaining whites.

5. Brush wells of pan lightly with oil. Set pan over medium heat. When oil begins to sizzle, add 2 tbsp (30 mL) batter to each well. Cook for 2 to 4 minutes or until bottoms are golden brown. Using two skewers, flip the puffs over. Cook for 2 to 3 minutes or until bottoms are golden brown and a toothpick inserted in the center comes out with a few moist crumbs attached. Remove pan from heat and transfer puffs to a plate. Let pan cool slightly.

6. Repeat with the remaining batter, brushing wells with oil and reheating pan before each batch.

7. Dust the ebelskivers with confectioners' sugar. Serve warm or at room temperature.

Ricotta Apricot Ebelskivers

The flavor combination of apricot and almond frames these sumptuous ebelskivers. The honey in the batter adds a delicate floral sweetness; the ricotta, a velvety texture.

● **7-well ebelskiver pan**

1½ cups	all-purpose flour	375 mL
1 tsp	baking powder	5 mL
¼ tsp	salt	1 mL
3	large eggs, separated	3
¾ cup	ricotta cheese	175 mL
½ cup	milk	125 mL
1 tbsp	liquid honey	15 mL
2 tbsp	unsalted butter, melted	30 mL
1 tsp	almond extract	5 mL
¾ cup	chopped dried apricots	175 mL
	Vegetable oil	
	Confectioners' (icing) sugar	

1. In a large bowl, whisk together flour, baking powder and salt.

2. In a medium bowl, whisk together egg yolks, ricotta, milk, honey, butter and almond extract until well blended.

3. Add the egg yolk mixture to the flour mixture and stir until just blended (the batter will appear slightly lumpy). Gently stir in apricots.

4. In a medium bowl, using an electric mixer on medium-high speed, beat egg whites until frothy. Increase speed to high and beat until stiff, but not dry, peaks form. Using a rubber spatula, gently mix one-third of the egg whites into the batter. Gently fold in the remaining whites.

5. Brush wells of pan lightly with oil. Set pan over medium heat. When oil begins to sizzle, add 2 tbsp (30 mL) batter to each well. Cook for 2 to 4 minutes or until bottoms are golden brown. Using two skewers, flip the puffs over. Cook for 2 to 3 minutes or until bottoms are golden brown and a toothpick inserted in the center comes out with a few moist crumbs attached. Remove pan from heat and transfer puffs to a plate. Let pan cool slightly.

6. Repeat with the remaining batter, brushing wells with oil and reheating pan before each batch.

7. Dust the ebelskivers with confectioners' sugar. Serve warm or at room temperature.

Cardamom Ebelskivers with Date Filling

Alluringly spiced and not too sweet, these ebelskivers are perfected with a hint of lime and a luscious date filling.

● **7-well ebelskiver pan**

Filling

½ cup	chopped dates	125 mL
3 tbsp	water	45 mL
3 tbsp	packed dark brown sugar	45 mL

Ebelskivers

1¼ cups	all-purpose flour	300 mL
¾ tsp	baking powder	3 mL
½ tsp	ground cardamom	2 mL
¼ tsp	salt	1 mL
1 tbsp	granulated sugar	15 mL
2	large eggs, separated	2
1 cup	milk	250 mL
2 tbsp	unsalted butter, melted	30 mL
1½ tsp	finely grated lime zest	7 mL
	Vegetable oil	
	Confectioners' (icing) sugar	

1. *Filling:* In a small saucepan, combine dates, water and brown sugar. Bring to a boil over medium-high heat. Reduce heat to low and cook, stirring, for 3 to 4 minutes or until mixture thickens to a paste. Remove from heat and let cool completely.

2. *Ebelskivers:* In a large bowl, whisk together flour, baking powder, cardamom and salt.

3. In a medium bowl, whisk together sugar, egg yolks, milk, butter and lime zest until well blended.

4. Add the egg yolk mixture to the flour mixture and stir until just blended (the batter will appear slightly lumpy).

5. In a medium bowl, using an electric mixer on medium-high speed, beat egg whites until frothy. Increase speed to high and beat until stiff, but not dry, peaks form. Using a rubber spatula, gently mix one-third of the egg whites into the batter. Gently fold in the remaining whites.

Tips

If desired, substitute ¼ tsp (1 mL) ground nutmeg or ½ tsp (2 mL) ground cinnamon for the cardamom.

Two ounces (60 g) of pitted whole dates will yield approximately ½ cup (125 mL) chopped dates.

6. Brush wells of pan lightly with oil. Set pan over medium heat. When oil begins to sizzle, add 1 tbsp (15 mL) batter to each well. Place 1 tsp (5 mL) filling in the center of each well and top with 1 tbsp (15 mL) batter. Cook for 2 to 4 minutes or until bottoms are golden brown. Using two skewers, flip the puffs over. Cook for 2 to 3 minutes or until bottoms are golden brown and a toothpick inserted in the center comes out with a bit of filling and moist crumbs attached. Remove pan from heat and transfer puffs to a plate. Let pan cool slightly.

7. Repeat with the remaining batter and filling, brushing wells with oil and reheating pan before each batch.

8. Dust the ebelskivers with confectioners' sugar. Serve warm or at room temperature.

Cranberry Orange Ebelskivers

The sweet-tartness of dried cranberries is perfectly balanced here by enticing hints of orange and nutmeg.

Tip

If the marmalade is particularly chunky, roughly chop the large pieces.

Variation

Lemon Currant Ebelskivers: Omit the nutmeg and replace the cranberries with dried currants (do not chop). Replace the orange zest with lemon zest and omit the marmalade. Dust the ebelskivers with confectioners' (icing) sugar just before serving.

● **7-well ebelskiver pan**

1¼ cups	all-purpose flour	300 mL
¾ tsp	baking powder	3 mL
½ tsp	ground nutmeg	2 mL
¼ tsp	salt	1 mL
1 tbsp	granulated sugar	15 mL
2	large eggs, separated	2
1 cup	milk	250 mL
2 tbsp	unsalted butter, melted	30 mL
2 tsp	finely grated orange zest	10 mL
¾ cup	dried cranberries, finely chopped	175 mL
	Vegetable oil	
⅔ cup	orange marmalade	150 mL

1. In a large bowl, whisk together flour, baking powder, nutmeg and salt.

2. In a medium bowl, whisk together sugar, egg yolks, milk, butter and orange zest until well blended.

3. Add the egg yolk mixture to the flour mixture and stir until just blended (the batter will appear slightly lumpy). Gently stir in cranberries.

4. In a medium bowl, using an electric mixer on medium-high speed, beat egg whites until frothy. Increase speed to high and beat until stiff, but not dry, peaks form. Using a rubber spatula, gently mix one-third of the egg whites into the batter. Gently fold in the remaining whites.

5. Brush wells of pan lightly with oil. Set pan over medium heat. When oil begins to sizzle, add 2 tbsp (30 mL) batter to each well. Cook for 2 to 4 minutes or until bottoms are golden brown. Using two skewers, flip the puffs over. Cook for 2 to 3 minutes or until bottoms are golden brown and a toothpick inserted in the center comes out with a few moist crumbs attached. Remove pan from heat and transfer puffs to a plate. Let pan cool slightly.

6. Repeat with the remaining batter, brushing wells with oil and reheating pan before each batch.

7. In a small saucepan set over low heat, melt the marmalade.

8. Drizzle the ebelskivers with marmalade. Serve warm.

Superpower Puffs

Loaded with a laundry list of good-for-you ingredients, these delectable ebelskivers are a perfect way to start the day.

Tip

An equal amount of liquid honey or pure maple syrup may be used in place of the agave nectar.

● **7-well ebelskiver pan**

¾ cup	whole-grain spelt flour or whole wheat flour	175 mL
½ cup	ground flax seeds (flax seed meal)	125 mL
1 tsp	baking powder	5 mL
¼ tsp	salt	1 mL
2	large eggs, separated	2
1 cup	vanilla-flavored almond milk or vanilla-flavored hemp milk	250 mL
2 tbsp	walnut oil or olive oil	30 mL
2 tbsp	agave nectar	30 mL
1 tsp	vanilla extract	5 mL
⅔ cup	dried tart cherries, chopped	150 mL
½ cup	chopped toasted walnuts	125 mL
	Vegetable oil	

1. In a large bowl, whisk together flour, flax seeds, baking powder and salt.

2. In a medium bowl, whisk together egg yolks, almond milk, oil, agave nectar and vanilla until well blended.

3. Add the egg yolk mixture to the flour mixture and stir until just blended (the batter will appear slightly lumpy). Gently stir in cherries and walnuts.

4. In a medium bowl, using an electric mixer on medium-high speed, beat egg whites until frothy. Increase speed to high and beat until stiff, but not dry, peaks form. Using a rubber spatula, gently mix one-third of the egg whites into the batter. Gently fold in the remaining whites.

5. Brush wells of pan lightly with oil. Set pan over medium heat. When oil begins to sizzle, add 2 tbsp (30 mL) batter to each well. Cook for 2 to 4 minutes or until bottoms are golden brown. Using two skewers, flip the puffs over. Cook for 2 to 3 minutes or until bottoms are golden brown and a toothpick inserted in the center comes out with a few moist crumbs attached. Remove pan from heat and transfer puffs to a plate. Let pan cool slightly.

6. Repeat with the remaining batter, brushing wells with oil and reheating pan before each batch. Serve warm or at room temperature.

Multigrain Ebelskivers with Dried Fruit

Whole grains, milk, olive oil and a smattering of dried fruit — these ebelskivers have everything you need to start the day right.

Tip

An equal amount of agave nectar or maple syrup may be used in place of the honey.

● **7-well ebelskiver pan**

¾ cup	whole wheat flour	175 mL
¼ cup	ground flax seeds (flax seed meal)	60 mL
¼ cup	quick-cooking rolled oats	60 mL
1 tsp	ground cinnamon	5 mL
¾ tsp	baking powder	3 mL
¼ tsp	salt	1 mL
2	large eggs, separated	2
1 cup	milk	250 mL
2 tbsp	olive oil or vegetable oil	30 mL
1 tbsp	liquid honey	15 mL
⅔ cup	chopped dried fruit (such as apricots, cranberries, raisins and/or cherries)	150 mL
	Vegetable oil	
	Confectioners' (icing) sugar	

1. In a large bowl, whisk together flour, flax seeds, oats, cinnamon, baking powder and salt.

2. In a medium bowl, whisk together egg yolks, milk, olive oil and honey until well blended.

3. Add the egg yolk mixture to the flour mixture and stir until just blended (the batter will appear slightly lumpy). Gently stir in dried fruit.

4. In a medium bowl, using an electric mixer on medium-high speed, beat egg whites until frothy. Increase speed to high and beat until stiff, but not dry, peaks form. Using a rubber spatula, gently mix one-third of the egg whites into the batter. Gently fold in the remaining whites.

5. Brush wells of pan lightly with vegetable oil. Set pan over medium heat. When oil begins to sizzle, add 2 tbsp (30 mL) batter to each well. Cook for 2 to 4 minutes or until bottoms are golden brown. Using two skewers, flip the puffs over. Cook for 2 to 3 minutes or until bottoms are golden brown and a toothpick inserted in the center comes out with a few moist crumbs attached. Remove pan from heat and transfer puffs to a plate. Let pan cool slightly.

6. Repeat with the remaining batter, brushing wells with oil and reheating pan before each batch.

7. Dust the ebelskivers with confectioners' sugar. Serve warm or at room temperature.

Fruit and Yogurt Ebelskivers

Feeling burnt out on the same old morning yogurt and fruit? I was too, until my love was rekindled by light and tangy ebelskivers, zesty with ginger and citrus and accompanied by fresh fruit.

Tips

For best results, use regular lower-fat (not nonfat) or whole milk yogurt (not Greek yogurt).

For richer ebelskivers, use an equal amount of sour cream in place of the yogurt.

• **7-well ebelskiver pan**

2 cups	plain yogurt, divided	500 mL
3 tbsp	liquid honey, divided	45 mL
2 tsp	finely grated orange zest	10 mL
2 tbsp	freshly squeezed orange juice	30 mL
1¼ cups	all-purpose flour	300 mL
1 tsp	ground ginger	5 mL
½ tsp	baking soda	2 mL
½ tsp	baking powder	2 mL
¼ tsp	salt	1 mL
2	large eggs, separated	2
2 tbsp	unsalted butter, melted	30 mL
	Vegetable oil	
2 cups	assorted diced fruit and berries (such as kiwifruit, peaches and/or raspberries)	500 mL

1. In a small bowl, whisk together 1 cup (250 mL) of the yogurt, 1 tbsp (15 mL) of the honey and orange juice. Cover and refrigerate while preparing the ebelskivers.

2. In a large bowl, whisk together flour, ginger, baking soda, baking powder and salt.

3. In a medium bowl, whisk together the remaining yogurt, the remaining honey, orange zest, egg yolks and butter until well blended.

4. Add the egg yolk mixture to the flour mixture and stir until just blended (the batter will appear slightly lumpy).

5. In a medium bowl, using an electric mixer on medium-high speed, beat egg whites until frothy. Increase speed to high and beat until stiff, but not dry, peaks form. Using a rubber spatula, gently mix one-third of the egg whites into the batter. Gently fold in the remaining whites.

6. Brush wells of pan lightly with oil. Set pan over medium heat. When oil begins to sizzle, add 2 tbsp (30 mL) batter to each well. Cook for 2 to 4 minutes or until bottoms are golden brown. Using two skewers, flip the puffs over. Cook for 2 to 3 minutes or until bottoms are golden brown and a toothpick inserted in the center comes out with a few moist crumbs attached. Remove pan from heat and transfer puffs to a plate. Let pan cool slightly.

7. Repeat with the remaining batter, brushing wells with oil and reheating pan before each batch.

8. Serve the ebelskivers warm or at room temperature, with the reserved yogurt mixture and fruit.

Muesli Ebelskivers

It almost goes without saying that these ebelskivers, based on the traditional Scandinavian cereal, are good for you, but they are absolutely delicious, too.

Tip

You can replace the whole wheat flour with an equal amount of all-purpose flour, if desired.

● **7-well ebelskiver pan**

2 cups	plain yogurt, divided	500 mL
2 tbsp	liquid honey, divided	30 mL
¾ cup	whole wheat flour	175 mL
½ cup	quick-cooking rolled oats	125 mL
½ tsp	baking soda	2 mL
½ tsp	baking powder	2 mL
½ tsp	ground cinnamon	2 mL
¼ tsp	salt	1 mL
2	large eggs, separated	2
2 tbsp	unsalted butter, melted	30 mL
1 tsp	vanilla extract	5 mL
⅔ cup	chopped dried fruit (such as apricots, cranberries, cherries and/or blueberries)	150 mL
½ cup	chopped toasted walnuts or pecans	125 mL
	Vegetable oil	

1. In a small bowl, whisk together 1 cup (250 mL) of the yogurt and 1 tbsp (15 mL) of the honey. Cover and refrigerate while preparing the ebelskivers.

2. In a large bowl, whisk together flour, oats, baking soda, baking powder, cinnamon and salt.

3. In a medium bowl, whisk together the remaining yogurt, the remaining honey, egg yolks, butter and vanilla until well blended.

4. Add the egg yolk mixture to the flour mixture and stir until just blended (the batter will appear slightly lumpy). Gently stir in dried fruit and walnuts.

5. In a medium bowl, using an electric mixer on medium-high speed, beat egg whites until frothy. Increase speed to high and beat until stiff, but not dry, peaks form. Using a rubber spatula, gently mix one-third of the egg whites into the batter. Gently fold in the remaining whites.

Tips

An equal amount of agave nectar or maple syrup may be used in place of the honey.

An equal amount of olive oil or vegetable oil may be used in place of the butter.

6. Brush wells of pan lightly with oil. Set pan over medium heat. When oil begins to sizzle, add 2 tbsp (30 mL) batter to each well. Cook for 2 to 4 minutes or until bottoms are golden brown. Using two skewers, flip the puffs over. Cook for 2 to 3 minutes or until bottoms are golden brown and a toothpick inserted in the center comes out with a few moist crumbs attached. Remove pan from heat and transfer puffs to a plate. Let pan cool slightly.

7. Repeat with the remaining batter, brushing wells with oil and reheating pan before each batch.

8. Serve the ebelskivers warm or at room temperature, with the honey-sweetened yogurt.

Fall Fruit Ebelskivers

Cranberries, walnuts and pumpkin pie spice form an irresistible autumn trinity inside a delicate brown sugar batter. Buttery pear compote sweetens the deal.

● **7-well ebelskiver pan**

Pear Compote

2 tbsp	unsalted butter	30 mL
3 tbsp	packed light brown sugar	45 mL
½ tsp	pumpkin pie spice or ground cinnamon	2 mL
2	medium-large pears, peeled and chopped	2

Ebelskivers

1¼ cups	all-purpose flour	300 mL
¾ tsp	baking powder	3 mL
½ tsp	pumpkin pie spice or ground cinnamon	2 mL
¼ tsp	salt	1 mL
1 tbsp	packed light brown sugar	15 mL
2	large eggs, separated	2
1 cup	milk	250 mL
2 tbsp	unsalted butter, melted	30 mL
1 tsp	vanilla extract	5 mL
½ cup	dried cranberries, chopped	125 mL
½ cup	chopped toasted walnuts or pecans	125 mL
	Vegetable oil	
	Confectioners' (icing) sugar	

1. *Compote:* In a medium saucepan, melt butter over medium-high heat. Add brown sugar and pumpkin pie spice; cook, stirring, until sugar is dissolved. Add pears, reduce heat to medium and cook, stirring occasionally, for 3 to 4 minutes or until pears are tender. Remove from heat and let cool completely.

2. *Ebelskivers:* In a large bowl, whisk together flour, baking powder, pumpkin pie spice and salt.

3. In a medium bowl, whisk together brown sugar, egg yolks, milk, butter and vanilla until well blended.

4. Add the egg yolk mixture to the flour mixture and stir until just blended (the batter will appear slightly lumpy). Gently stir in cranberries and walnuts.

5. In a medium bowl, using an electric mixer on medium-high speed, beat egg whites until frothy. Increase speed to high and beat until stiff, but not dry, peaks form. Using a rubber spatula, gently mix one-third of the egg whites into the batter. Gently fold in the remaining whites.

6. Brush wells of pan lightly with oil. Set pan over medium heat. When oil begins to sizzle, add 1 tbsp (15 mL) batter to each well. Place 1 tsp (5 mL) compote in the center of each well and top with 1 tbsp (15 mL) batter. Cook for 2 to 4 minutes or until bottoms are golden brown. Using two skewers, flip the puffs over. Cook for 2 to 3 minutes or until bottoms are golden brown and a toothpick inserted in the center comes out with a bit of filling and moist crumbs attached. Remove pan from heat and transfer puffs to a plate. Let pan cool slightly.

7. Repeat with the remaining batter and compote, brushing wells with oil and reheating pan before each batch.

8. Dust the ebelskivers with confectioners' sugar. Serve warm or at room temperature.

Cinnamon Applesauce Ebelskivers

Cinnamon, applesauce and buttermilk — three beloved home cooking ingredients — add up to ebelskivers you'll adore.

Variation

Spiced Applesauce Ebelskivers: Use a combination of 1/2 tsp (2 mL) ground nutmeg, 1/4 tsp (1 mL) ground allspice and 1/4 tsp (1 mL) ground cloves in place of the ground cinnamon.

● **7-well ebelskiver pan**

3/4 cup	all-purpose flour	175 mL
3/4 cup	whole wheat flour	175 mL
1 tsp	ground cinnamon	5 mL
1/2 tsp	baking powder	2 mL
1/2 tsp	baking soda	2 mL
1/4 tsp	salt	1 mL
2 tbsp	packed light brown sugar	30 mL
2	large eggs, separated	2
1 cup	buttermilk	250 mL
1 cup	unsweetened applesauce	250 mL
2 tbsp	unsalted butter, melted	30 mL
1 tsp	vanilla extract	5 mL
1/2 cup	chopped toasted walnuts or pecans (optional)	125 mL
	Vegetable oil	
	Confectioners' (icing) sugar	

1. In a large bowl, whisk together all-purpose flour, whole wheat flour, cinnamon, baking powder, baking soda and salt.

2. In a medium bowl, whisk together brown sugar, egg yolks, buttermilk, applesauce, butter and vanilla until well blended.

3. Add the egg yolk mixture to the flour mixture and stir until just blended (the batter will appear slightly lumpy). Gently stir in walnuts (if using).

4. In a medium bowl, using an electric mixer on medium-high speed, beat egg whites until frothy. Increase speed to high and beat until stiff, but not dry, peaks form. Using a rubber spatula, gently mix one-third of the egg whites into the batter. Gently fold in the remaining whites.

Variation

Apple Butter–Filled Ebelskivers: You will need ⅔ cup (150 mL) apple butter. Prepare batter as directed. In step 4, instead of adding 2 tbsp (30 mL) batter to each well, first add 1 tbsp (15 mL) batter to each well, then place 1 tsp (5 mL) apple butter in the center of each well and top with 1 tbsp (15 mL) batter. Cook as directed.

5. Brush wells of pan lightly with oil. Set pan over medium heat. When oil begins to sizzle, add 2 tbsp (30 mL) batter to each well. Cook for 2 to 4 minutes or until bottoms are golden brown. Using two skewers, flip the puffs over. Cook for 2 to 3 minutes or until bottoms are golden brown and a toothpick inserted in the center comes out with a few moist crumbs attached. Remove pan from heat and transfer puffs to a plate. Let pan cool slightly.

6. Repeat with the remaining batter, brushing wells with oil and reheating pan before each batch.

7. Dust the ebelskivers with confectioners' sugar. Serve warm or at room temperature.

Maple Blueberry Ebelskivers

<table>
<tr><td colspan="3">● 7-well ebelskiver pan</td></tr>
<tr><td>1¾ cups</td><td>all-purpose flour</td><td>425 mL</td></tr>
<tr><td>1 tsp</td><td>baking powder</td><td>5 mL</td></tr>
<tr><td>¾ tsp</td><td>baking soda</td><td>3 mL</td></tr>
<tr><td>¼ tsp</td><td>salt</td><td>1 mL</td></tr>
<tr><td>3</td><td>large eggs, separated</td><td>3</td></tr>
<tr><td>¾ cup</td><td>sour cream</td><td>175 mL</td></tr>
<tr><td>½ cup</td><td>milk</td><td>125 mL</td></tr>
<tr><td>3 tbsp</td><td>unsalted butter, melted</td><td>45 mL</td></tr>
<tr><td>2 tbsp</td><td>pure maple syrup</td><td>30 mL</td></tr>
<tr><td>1 tsp</td><td>vanilla extract</td><td>5 mL</td></tr>
<tr><td></td><td>Vegetable oil</td><td></td></tr>
<tr><td>2 cups</td><td>blueberries</td><td>500 mL</td></tr>
<tr><td></td><td>Confectioners' (icing) sugar</td><td></td></tr>
<tr><td></td><td>Additional pure maple syrup</td><td></td></tr>
</table>

Makes about 35 puffs

A quick spell in the kitchen produces puffy, berry-filled pancakes everyone will fawn over. The sweet, fresh flavor of the blueberries finds perfect harmony with everyone's favorite breakfast flavor: maple.

Tips

When shopping for cultivated blueberries, look for the fattest berries you can find; they should be grayish-purple and covered with a silvery bloom. (Wild blueberries — typically unavailable fresh in supermarkets — are tiny and almost black). Scent makes no difference; unlike many other fruits, ripe blueberries have no fragrance.

The maple syrup can be replaced with an equal amount of liquid honey or granulated sugar.

1. In a large bowl, whisk together flour, baking powder, baking soda and salt.

2. In a medium bowl, whisk together egg yolks, sour cream, milk, butter, maple syrup and vanilla until well blended.

3. Add the egg yolk mixture to the flour mixture and stir until just blended (the batter will appear slightly lumpy).

4. In a medium bowl, using an electric mixer on medium-high speed, beat egg whites until frothy. Increase speed to high and beat until stiff, but not dry, peaks form. Using a rubber spatula, gently mix one-third of the egg whites into the batter. Gently fold in the remaining whites.

5. Brush wells of pan lightly with oil. Set pan over medium heat. When oil begins to sizzle, add 1 tbsp (15 mL) batter to each well. Place 4 to 6 blueberries in the center of each well and top with 1 tbsp (15 mL) batter. Cook for 2 to 4 minutes or until bottoms are golden brown. Using two skewers, flip the puffs over. Cook for 2 to 3 minutes or until bottoms are golden brown and a toothpick inserted in the center comes out with moist crumbs attached. Remove pan from heat and transfer puffs to a plate. Let pan cool slightly.

6. Repeat with the remaining batter and blueberries, brushing wells with oil and reheating pan before each batch.

7. Dust the ebelskivers with confectioners' sugar. Serve warm, with maple syrup.

Thyme and Raspberry Ebelskivers

Makes about 21 puffs

The key to combining raspberries with thyme is striking just the right balance between tart fruit and savory freshness. I think I've hit it with this rendition. And it only gets better with the complementary addition of lemon zest.

● **7-well ebelskiver pan**

1¼ cups	all-purpose flour	300 mL
¾ tsp	baking powder	3 mL
¼ tsp	salt	1 mL
1 tbsp	granulated sugar	15 mL
2	large eggs, separated	2
1 cup	milk	250 mL
2 tbsp	unsalted butter, melted	30 mL
1 tsp	minced fresh thyme	5 mL
1 tsp	finely grated lemon zest	5 mL
	Vegetable oil	
21	raspberries	21
	Confectioners' (icing) sugar	

1. In a large bowl, whisk together flour, baking powder and salt.

2. In a medium bowl, whisk together sugar, egg yolks, milk, butter, thyme and lemon zest until well blended.

3. Add the egg yolk mixture to the flour mixture and stir until just blended (the batter will appear slightly lumpy).

4. In a medium bowl, using an electric mixer on medium-high speed, beat egg whites until frothy. Increase speed to high and beat until stiff, but not dry, peaks form. Using a rubber spatula, gently mix one-third of the egg whites into the batter. Gently fold in the remaining whites.

5. Brush wells of pan lightly with oil. Set pan over medium heat. When oil begins to sizzle, add 1 tbsp (15 mL) batter to each well. Place 1 raspberry in the center of each well and top with 1 tbsp (15 mL) batter. Cook for 2 to 4 minutes or until bottoms are golden brown. Using two skewers, flip the puffs over. Cook for 2 to 3 minutes or until bottoms are golden brown and a toothpick inserted in the center comes out with moist crumbs attached. Remove pan from heat and transfer puffs to a plate. Let pan cool slightly.

6. Repeat with the remaining batter and raspberries, brushing wells with oil and reheating pan before each batch.

7. Dust the ebelskivers with confectioners' sugar. Serve warm or at room temperature.

Raspberry Blintz Ebelskivers

Makes about 21 puffs

Delivering all of the flavor of cheese blintzes, but with a fraction of the time and effort, these portable, popable ebelskivers are small bites of bliss.

Tips

For best results, do not use nonfat ricotta cheese.

Softened cream cheese or mascarpone cheese may be used in place of the ricotta cheese in the filling.

These ebelskivers are delicious with any combination of berries. Blackberries with blackberry jam, blueberries with strawberry jam — it's almost impossible to go wrong!

● **7-well ebelskiver pan**

Filling

½ cup	ricotta cheese	125 mL
1 tbsp	granulated sugar	15 mL
¼ tsp	vanilla extract, divided	1 mL

Ebelskivers

1¼ cups	all-purpose flour	300 mL
¾ tsp	baking powder	3 mL
¼ tsp	salt	1 mL
1 tbsp	granulated sugar	15 mL
2	large eggs, separated	2
1 cup	milk	250 mL
2 tbsp	unsalted butter, melted	30 mL
½ tsp	vanilla extract, divided	2 mL
	Vegetable oil	
	Confectioners' (icing) sugar	

Raspberry Sauce

½ cup	raspberry jam, at room temperature	125 mL
1 cup	fresh or thawed frozen raspberries	250 mL

1. *Filling:* In a small bowl, stir together ricotta, sugar and vanilla until blended. Cover and refrigerate while preparing the batter.

2. *Ebelskivers:* In a large bowl, whisk together flour, baking powder and salt.

3. In a medium bowl, whisk together sugar, egg yolks, milk, butter and vanilla until well blended.

4. Add the egg yolk mixture to the flour mixture and stir until just blended (the batter will appear slightly lumpy).

5. In a medium bowl, using an electric mixer on medium-high speed, beat egg whites until frothy. Increase speed to high and beat until stiff, but not dry, peaks form. Using a rubber spatula, gently mix one-third of the egg whites into the batter. Gently fold in the remaining whites.

Variation

Apricot Blintz Ebelskivers:
Substitute apricot jam
for the raspberry jam
and ¾ cup (175 mL)
packed dried apricots,
finely chopped, for the
raspberries.

6. Brush wells of pan lightly with oil. Set pan over medium heat. When oil begins to sizzle, add 1 tbsp (15 mL) batter to each well. Place 1 tsp (5 mL) filling in the center of each well and top with 1 tbsp (15 mL) batter. Cook for 2 to 4 minutes or until bottoms are golden brown. Using two skewers, flip the puffs over. Cook for 2 to 3 minutes or until bottoms are golden brown and a toothpick inserted in the center comes out with a bit of filling and moist crumbs attached. Remove pan from heat and transfer puffs to a plate. Let pan cool slightly.

7. Repeat with the remaining batter and filling, brushing wells with oil and reheating pan before each batch.

8. *Sauce:* In a small bowl, whisk jam until loosened. Add raspberries and crush with the tines of a fork, mixing them into the jam.

9. Dust the ebelskivers with confectioners' sugar. Serve warm, with the raspberry sauce.

Banana Ebelskivers

Humble bananas get
sassy in these butter-rich
ebelskivers. I'm partial
to pecans stirred into
the batter, but you can
substitute the nut of your
choice or leave them out
altogether.

Tip

It will take about 2 large
bananas to yield 1 cup
(250 mL) of mashed banana.

Variation

*Whole Wheat Banana
Ebelskivers:* Replace ¾ cup
(175 mL) of the all-purpose
flour with whole wheat flour.

● **7-well ebelskiver pan**

1½ cups	all-purpose flour	375 mL
¾ tsp	baking powder	3 mL
¼ tsp	baking soda	1 mL
¼ tsp	salt	1 mL
¼ tsp	ground nutmeg	1 mL
1 tbsp	granulated sugar	15 mL
2	large eggs, separated	2
1 cup	milk	250 mL
1 cup	mashed very ripe bananas	250 mL
2 tbsp	unsalted butter, melted	30 mL
½ cup	chopped toasted pecans or walnuts (optional)	125 mL
	Vegetable oil	
	Confectioners' (icing) sugar	
	Pure maple syrup (optional)	

1. In a large bowl, whisk together flour, baking powder, baking soda, salt and nutmeg.

2. In a medium bowl, whisk together sugar, egg yolks, milk, bananas and butter until well blended.

3. Add the egg yolk mixture to the flour mixture and stir until just blended (the batter will appear slightly lumpy). Gently stir in pecans (if using).

4. In a medium bowl, using an electric mixer on medium-high speed, beat egg whites until frothy. Increase speed to high and beat until stiff, but not dry, peaks form. Using a rubber spatula, gently mix one-third of the egg whites into the batter. Gently fold in the remaining whites.

5. Brush wells of pan lightly with oil. Set pan over medium heat. When oil begins to sizzle, add 2 tbsp (30 mL) batter to each well. Cook for 2 to 4 minutes or until bottoms are golden brown. Using two skewers, flip the puffs over. Cook for 2 to 3 minutes or until bottoms are golden brown and a toothpick inserted in the center comes out with a few moist crumbs attached. Remove pan from heat and transfer puffs to a plate. Let pan cool slightly.

6. Repeat with the remaining batter, brushing wells with oil and reheating pan before each batch.

7. Dust the ebelskivers with confectioners' sugar and drizzle with maple syrup, if desired. Serve warm or at room temperature.

Cocoa Banana Ebelskivers

Bananas love cocoa and cocoa loves banana, as made evident in these irresistible ebelskivers. The unsweetened cocoa powder and a smattering of miniature semisweet chocolate chips add both rich flavor and good health: cocoa powder and dark chocolate are very high in antioxidants.

Tip

It will take about 2 medium bananas to yield $2/3$ cup (150 mL) of mashed banana.

● **7-well ebelskiver pan**

$1/2$ cup	all-purpose flour	125 mL
$1/2$ cup	whole wheat flour	125 mL
$1/4$ cup	unsweetened cocoa powder (preferably not Dutch process)	60 mL
$1/2$ tsp	baking powder	2 mL
$1/2$ tsp	baking soda	2 mL
$1/4$ tsp	salt	1 mL
2 tbsp	granulated sugar	30 mL
2	large eggs, separated	2
1 cup	milk	250 mL
$2/3$ cup	mashed very ripe bananas	150 mL
2 tbsp	unsalted butter, melted	30 mL
$1/2$ cup	miniature semisweet chocolate chips	125 mL
	Vegetable oil	
	Confectioners' (icing) sugar	

1. In a large bowl, whisk together all-purpose flour, whole wheat flour, cocoa, baking powder, baking soda and salt.

2. In a medium bowl, whisk together sugar, egg yolks, milk, bananas and butter until well blended.

3. Add the egg yolk mixture to the flour mixture and stir until just blended (the batter will appear slightly lumpy). Gently stir in chocolate chips.

4. In a medium bowl, using an electric mixer on medium-high speed, beat egg whites until frothy. Increase speed to high and beat until stiff, but not dry, peaks form. Using a rubber spatula, gently mix one-third of the egg whites into the batter. Gently fold in the remaining whites.

5. Brush wells of pan lightly with oil. Set pan over medium heat. When oil begins to sizzle, add 2 tbsp (30 mL) batter to each well. Cook for 2 to 4 minutes or until bottoms are crisp-firm to the touch. Using two skewers, flip the puffs over. Cook for 2 to 3 minutes or until bottoms are crisp-firm and a toothpick inserted in the center comes out with a few moist crumbs attached. Remove pan from heat and transfer puffs to a plate. Let pan cool slightly.

6. Repeat with the remaining batter, brushing wells with oil and reheating pan before each batch.

7. Dust the ebelskivers with confectioners' sugar. Serve warm or at room temperature.

Morning Glory Ebelskivers

Move over, morning glory muffins: there's a new breakfast favorite in town. In addition to being so darn cute, these ebelskivers have all of the healthy, delicious ingredients one might expect, including pineapple, whole wheat flour, dried fruit and carrots.

Tip

If you do not have whole wheat flour on hand, feel free to replace it with an equal amount of all-purpose flour (for a total of 1⅔ cups/400 mL all-purpose flour).

● **7-well ebelskiver pan**

1 cup	all-purpose flour	250 mL
⅔ cup	whole wheat flour	150 mL
1 tsp	ground cinnamon	5 mL
1 tsp	baking powder	5 mL
¾ tsp	salt	3 mL
¼ tsp	baking soda	1 mL
1 tbsp	granulated sugar	15 mL
3	large eggs, separated	3
1	can (8 oz/227 mL) crushed pineapple, drained	1
1 cup	milk	250 mL
	Vegetable oil	
½ cup	raisins	125 mL
½ cup	sweetened flaked or shredded coconut	125 mL
⅓ cup	shredded carrot	75 mL
	Confectioners' (icing) sugar	

1. In a large bowl, whisk together all-purpose flour, whole wheat flour, cinnamon, baking powder, salt and baking soda.

2. In a medium bowl, whisk together sugar, egg yolks, pineapple, milk and 2 tbsp (30 mL) oil until well blended.

3. Add the egg yolk mixture to the flour mixture and stir until just blended (the batter will appear slightly lumpy). Gently stir in raisins, coconut and carrot.

4. In a medium bowl, using an electric mixer on medium-high speed, beat egg whites until frothy. Increase speed to high and beat until stiff, but not dry, peaks form. Using a rubber spatula, gently mix one-third of the egg whites into the batter. Gently fold in the remaining whites.

Tips

Drain the crushed pineapple until it appears fairly dry. If too much liquid remains, it will throw off the balance of wet to dry ingredients in the batter.

An equal amount of dried currants, cherries, cranberries or blueberries may be used in place of the raisins.

The coconut can be replaced with an equal amount of chopped toasted nuts or roasted seeds. Try walnuts, pistachios, green pumpkin seeds (pepitas) or sunflower seeds.

5. Brush wells of pan lightly with oil. Set pan over medium heat. When oil begins to sizzle, add 2 tbsp (30 mL) batter to each well. Cook for 2 to 4 minutes or until bottoms are golden brown. Using two skewers, flip the puffs over. Cook for 2 to 3 minutes or until bottoms are golden brown and a toothpick inserted in the center comes out with a few moist crumbs attached. Remove pan from heat and transfer puffs to a plate. Let pan cool slightly.

6. Repeat with the remaining batter, brushing wells with oil and reheating pan before each batch.

7. Dust the ebelskivers with confectioners' sugar. Serve warm or at room temperature.

Spiced Carrot Ebelskivers

**Makes about
28 puffs**

These moist, healthy, delicious carrot ebelskivers, studded with currants and spiced with Chinese five-spice powder, will garner compliments from one and all.

Tip

Use the coarse side of a box cheese grater to shred the carrots.

● **7-well ebelskiver pan**

¾ cup	all-purpose flour	175 mL
⅔ cup	whole wheat flour	150 mL
1 tsp	baking powder	5 mL
1¼ tsp	Chinese five-spice powder or pumpkin pie spice	6 mL
¼ tsp	salt	1 mL
2 tbsp	granulated sugar	30 mL
3	large eggs, separated	3
1 cup	milk	250 mL
3 tbsp	unsalted butter, melted	45 mL
1 tsp	vanilla extract	5 mL
1 cup	shredded carrots	250 mL
½ cup	dried currants	125 mL
	Vegetable oil	
	Confectioners' (icing) sugar	

1. In a large bowl, whisk together all-purpose flour, whole wheat flour, baking powder, five-spice powder and salt.

2. In a medium bowl, whisk together sugar, egg yolks, milk, butter and vanilla until well blended.

3. Add the egg yolk mixture to the flour mixture and stir until just blended (the batter will appear slightly lumpy). Gently stir in carrots and currants.

4. In a medium bowl, using an electric mixer on medium-high speed, beat egg whites until frothy. Increase speed to high and beat until stiff, but not dry, peaks form. Using a rubber spatula, gently mix one-third of the egg whites into the batter. Gently fold in the remaining whites.

Variations

Cream Cheese–Filled Carrot Ebelskivers: In a medium bowl, using an electric mixer on medium-high speed, beat 2 tbsp (30 mL) sugar, 8 oz (250 g) softened cream cheese and 1 tsp (5 mL) vanilla until smooth and creamy. Cover and refrigerate while preparing the batter as directed at right. In step 4, instead of adding 2 tbsp (30 mL) batter to wells, first add 1 tbsp (15 mL) batter to each well, then place 1 tsp (5 mL) cream cheese filling in the center of each well and top with 1 tbsp (15 mL) batter. Cook as directed.

Spiced Zucchini Ebelskivers: Use an equal amount of shredded zucchini, pressed dry between paper towels, in place of the carrots.

5. Brush wells of pan lightly with oil. Set pan over medium heat. When oil begins to sizzle, add 2 tbsp (30 mL) batter to each well. Cook for 2 to 4 minutes or until bottoms are golden brown. Using two skewers, flip the puffs over. Cook for 2 to 3 minutes or until bottoms are golden brown and a toothpick inserted in the center comes out with a few moist crumbs attached. Remove pan from heat and transfer puffs to a plate. Let pan cool slightly.

6. Repeat with the remaining batter, brushing wells with oil and reheating pan before each batch.

7. Dust the ebelskivers with confectioners' sugar. Serve warm.

Pumpkin Spice Ebelskivers

	Makes about 28 puffs	

Moist and tender, with just the right balance of spices, these ebelskivers are too delicious to reserve for the holidays. Instead, serve them up whenever you're feeling festive.

● **7-well ebelskiver pan**

1½ cups	all-purpose flour	375 mL
2 tsp	pumpkin pie spice	10 mL
1½ tsp	baking powder	7 mL
¾ tsp	salt	3 mL
¼ cup	granulated sugar	60 mL
2	large eggs, separated	2
1 cup	milk	250 mL
1 cup	pumpkin purée (not pie filling)	250 mL
2 tbsp	unsalted butter, melted	30 mL
1½ tsp	vanilla extract	7 mL
	Vegetable oil	
	Confectioners' (icing) sugar	

1. In a large bowl, whisk together flour, pumpkin pie spice, baking powder and salt.

2. In a medium bowl, whisk together sugar, egg yolks, milk, pumpkin, butter and vanilla until well blended.

3. Add the egg yolk mixture to the flour mixture and stir until just blended (the batter will appear slightly lumpy).

4. In a medium bowl, using an electric mixer on medium-high speed, beat egg whites until frothy. Increase speed to high and beat until stiff, but not dry, peaks form. Using a rubber spatula, gently mix one-third of the egg whites into the batter. Gently fold in the remaining whites.

5. Brush wells of pan lightly with oil. Set pan over medium heat. When oil begins to sizzle, add 2 tbsp (30 mL) batter to each well. Cook for 2 to 4 minutes or until bottoms are golden brown. Using two skewers, flip the puffs over. Cook for 2 to 3 minutes or until bottoms are golden brown and a toothpick inserted in the center comes out with a few moist crumbs attached. Remove pan from heat and transfer puffs to a plate. Let pan cool slightly.

6. Repeat with the remaining batter, brushing wells with oil and reheating pan before each batch.

7. Dust the ebelskivers with confectioners' sugar. Serve warm or at room temperature.

Sweet Treats

continued...

Chocolate Chip Ebelskivers

Children will love to help make these delectable ebelskivers. They make a delicious change of pace from chocolate chip cookies.

Tip

An equal amount of regular semisweet chocolate chips may be used in place of the miniature chocolate chips. Coarsely chop the chips for more even distribution of the chocolate throughout the ebelskivers.

Variations

Mint Chip Ebelskivers: Replace the vanilla extract with an equal amount of pure peppermint extract.

Mocha Chip Ebelskivers: Dissolve 1 tbsp (15 mL) instant espresso powder in 1 tbsp (15 mL) hot water and add with the milk in step 2.

• 7-well ebelskiver pan

1¼ cups	all-purpose flour	300 mL
¾ tsp	baking powder	3 mL
¼ tsp	salt	1 mL
2 tbsp	packed light brown sugar	30 mL
2	large eggs, separated	2
1 cup	milk	250 mL
2 tbsp	unsalted butter, melted	30 mL
1 tsp	vanilla extract	5 mL
⅔ cup	miniature semisweet chocolate chips	150 mL
	Vegetable oil	

1. In a large bowl, whisk together flour, baking powder and salt.

2. In a medium bowl, whisk together brown sugar, egg yolks, milk, butter and vanilla until well blended.

3. Add the egg yolk mixture to the flour mixture and stir until just blended (the batter will appear slightly lumpy). Gently stir in chocolate chips.

4. In a medium bowl, using an electric mixer on medium-high speed, beat egg whites until frothy. Increase speed to high and beat until stiff, but not dry, peaks form. Using a rubber spatula, gently mix one-third of the egg whites into the batter. Gently fold in the remaining whites.

5. Brush wells of pan lightly with oil. Set pan over medium heat. When oil begins to sizzle, add 2 tbsp (30 mL) batter to each well. Cook for 2 to 4 minutes or until bottoms are golden brown. Using two skewers, flip the puffs over. Cook for 2 to 3 minutes or until bottoms are golden brown and a toothpick inserted in the center comes out with a few moist crumbs attached. Remove pan from heat and transfer puffs to a plate. Let pan cool slightly.

6. Repeat with the remaining batter, brushing wells with oil and reheating pan before each batch. Serve warm or at room temperature.

Triple-Chocolate Ebelskivers

A triple dose of decadent chocolate renders these ebelskivers irresistible. As heavenly as they are with the chocolate sauce, consider pairing them with the peanut butter sauce from PB&J Ebelskivers (page 60), Marshmallow Sauce (page 94) or melted raspberry jam.

● **7-well ebelskiver pan**

Chocolate Sauce

1 cup	miniature semisweet chocolate chips	250 mL
⅔ cup	heavy or whipping (35%) cream	150 mL

Ebelskivers

1 cup	all-purpose flour	250 mL
¼ cup	unsweetened cocoa powder (not Dutch process)	60 mL
1 tsp	instant espresso powder (optional)	5 mL
½ tsp	baking soda	2 mL
½ tsp	baking powder	2 mL
¼ tsp	salt	1 mL
2 tbsp	granulated sugar	30 mL
2	large eggs, separated	2
1 cup	milk	250 mL
2 tbsp	unsalted butter, melted	30 mL
1 tsp	vanilla extract	5 mL
¾ cup	miniature semisweet chocolate chips	175 mL
	Vegetable oil	

1. *Sauce:* In a small saucepan, combine chocolate chips and cream. Heat over low heat, whisking until melted and smooth. Remove from heat and let cool while preparing the ebelskivers.

2. *Ebelskivers:* In a large bowl, whisk together flour, cocoa powder, espresso powder (if using), baking soda, baking powder and salt.

3. In a medium bowl, whisk together sugar, egg yolks, milk, butter and vanilla until well blended.

4. Add the egg yolk mixture to the flour mixture and stir until just blended (the batter will appear slightly lumpy). Gently stir in chocolate chips.

5. In a medium bowl, using an electric mixer on medium-high speed, beat egg whites until frothy. Increase speed to high and beat until stiff, but not dry, peaks form. Using a rubber spatula, gently mix one-third of the egg whites into the batter. Gently fold in the remaining whites.

Tips

An equal amount of regular semisweet chocolate chips may be used in place of the miniature chocolate chips. Coarsely chop the chips for the batter, for more even distribution of the chocolate throughout the ebelskivers.

If you don't have espresso powder on hand, you can use 2 tsp (10 mL) instant coffee powder instead.

6. Brush wells of pan lightly with oil. Set pan over medium heat. When oil begins to sizzle, add 2 tbsp (30 mL) batter to each well. Cook for 2 to 4 minutes or until bottoms are crisp-firm to the touch. Using two skewers, flip the puffs over. Cook for 2 to 3 minutes or until bottoms are crisp-firm and a toothpick inserted in the center comes out with a few moist crumbs attached. Remove pan from heat and transfer puffs to a plate. Let pan cool slightly.

7. Repeat with the remaining batter, brushing wells with oil and reheating pan before each batch.

8. Serve the ebelskivers warm, with the chocolate sauce.

Caramel Chocolate Pecan Ebelskivers

Ready, set, indulge! Here, caramel, chocolate and pecans coalesce for an exceptionally delicious (and easy!) dessert.

Tip

An equal amount of regular semisweet chocolate chips may be used in place of the miniature chocolate chips. Coarsely chop the chips for more even distribution of the chocolate throughout the ebelskivers.

● **7-well ebelskiver pan**

1¼ cups	all-purpose flour	300 mL
¾ tsp	baking powder	3 mL
¼ tsp	salt	1 mL
1 tbsp	packed light brown sugar	15 mL
2	large eggs, separated	2
1 cup	milk	250 mL
2 tbsp	unsalted butter, melted	30 mL
1 tsp	vanilla extract	5 mL
½ cup	chopped toasted pecan halves	125 mL
½ cup	miniature semisweet chocolate chips	125 mL
	Vegetable oil	
14	individually wrapped soft caramel candies, unwrapped and cut in half	14
	Confectioners' (icing) sugar	

1. In a large bowl, whisk together flour, baking powder and salt.

2. In a medium bowl, whisk together brown sugar, egg yolks, milk, butter and vanilla until well blended.

3. Add the egg yolk mixture to the flour mixture and stir until just blended (the batter will appear slightly lumpy). Gently stir in pecans and chocolate chips.

4. In a medium bowl, using an electric mixer on medium-high speed, beat egg whites until frothy. Increase speed to high and beat until stiff, but not dry, peaks form. Using a rubber spatula, gently mix one-third of the egg whites into the batter. Gently fold in the remaining whites.

Tip

An equal amount of chocolate-covered caramel candies, unwrapped and halved, may be used in place of the caramels.

5. Brush wells of pan lightly with oil. Set pan over medium heat. When oil begins to sizzle, add 1 tbsp (15 mL) batter to each well. Place 1 caramel candy half in the center of each well and top with 1 tbsp (15 mL) batter. Cook for 2 to 4 minutes or until bottoms are golden brown. Using two skewers, flip the puffs over. Cook for 2 to 3 minutes or until bottoms are golden brown and the puffs are firm to the touch. Remove pan from heat and transfer puffs to a plate. Let pan cool slightly.

6. Repeat with the remaining batter and caramels, brushing wells with oil and reheating pan before each batch.

7. Dust the ebelskivers with confectioners' sugar. Serve warm or at room temperature.

Fluffernut Puffs

These crowd-pleasing
puffs take their cue from
fluffernutters, those
whimsical sandwiches
smeared thick with a dual
filling of peanut butter
and marshmallow crème.
Here the peanut butter
stars in the filling and a
luscious marshmallow
sauce is spooned on top.

● **7-well ebelskiver pan**

Marshmallow Sauce

1½ cups	marshmallow crème	375 mL
3 tbsp	milk	45 mL

Puffs

1¼ cups	all-purpose flour	300 mL
¾ tsp	baking powder	3 mL
¼ tsp	salt	1 mL
1½ tbsp	packed light brown sugar	22 mL
2	large eggs, separated	2
1 cup	milk	250 mL
2 tbsp	unsalted butter, melted	30 mL
1 tsp	vanilla extract	5 mL
	Vegetable oil	
½ cup	creamy peanut butter	125 mL

1. *Sauce:* In a small saucepan, combine marshmallow crème and milk. Heat over low heat for 3 to 5 minutes, stirring constantly, until melted and smooth. Remove from heat and let cool while preparing the ebelskivers.

2. *Puffs:* In a large bowl, whisk together flour, baking powder and salt.

3. In a medium bowl, whisk together brown sugar, egg yolks, milk, butter and vanilla until well blended.

4. Add the egg yolk mixture to the flour mixture and stir until just blended (the batter will appear slightly lumpy).

5. In a medium bowl, using an electric mixer on medium-high speed, beat egg whites until frothy. Increase speed to high and beat until stiff, but not dry, peaks form. Using a rubber spatula, gently mix one-third of the egg whites into the batter. Gently fold in the remaining whites.

Any other variety of nut or seed butter — smooth, chunky or all-natural varieties — may be used in place of the peanut butter.

6. Brush wells of pan lightly with oil. Set pan over medium heat. When oil begins to sizzle, add 1 tbsp (15 mL) batter to each well. Place 1 tsp (5 mL) peanut butter in the center of each well and top with 1 tbsp (15 mL) batter. Cook for 2 to 4 minutes or until bottoms are golden brown. Using two skewers, flip the puffs over. Cook for 2 to 3 minutes or until bottoms are golden brown and a toothpick inserted in the center comes out with a bit of filling and a few moist crumbs attached. Remove pan from heat and transfer puffs to a plate. Let pan cool slightly.

7. Repeat with the remaining batter and peanut butter, brushing wells with oil and reheating pan before each batch.

8. Serve the puffs warm, with the marshmallow sauce.

Campfire S'mores Puffs

Who doesn't love s'mores? It's near impossible to go wrong with the classic campfire trinity of graham crackers, marshmallow and chocolate, and this puffed interpretation won't fail to please.

Tip

An equal amount of regular-size semisweet chocolate chips may be used in place of the miniature chips. Measure, then coarsely chop the chips (so that the pieces are smaller and distribute more evenly in the puffs).

● **7-well ebelskiver pan**

1 cup	graham cracker crumbs	250 mL
¾ cup	all-purpose flour	175 mL
1¼ tsp	baking powder	6 mL
¼ tsp	salt	1 mL
2 tbsp	packed light brown sugar	30 mL
3	large eggs, separated	3
3 tbsp	unsalted butter, melted	45 mL
1 tsp	vanilla extract	5 mL
1⅓ cups	milk	325 mL
¾ cup	miniature semisweet chocolate chips	175 mL
	Vegetable oil	
	Marshmallow Sauce (page 94)	

1. In a large bowl, whisk together graham cracker crumbs, flour, baking powder and salt.

2. In a medium bowl, whisk together brown sugar, egg yolks, butter and vanilla. Whisk in milk until well blended.

3. Add the egg yolk mixture to the flour mixture and stir until just blended (the batter will appear slightly lumpy). Gently stir in chocolate chips.

4. In a medium bowl, using an electric mixer on medium-high speed, beat egg whites until frothy. Increase speed to high and beat until stiff, but not dry, peaks form. Using a rubber spatula, gently mix one-third of the egg whites into the batter. Gently fold in the remaining whites.

5. Brush wells of pan lightly with oil. Set pan over medium heat. When oil begins to sizzle, add 2 tbsp (30 mL) batter to each well. Cook for 2 to 4 minutes or until bottoms are golden brown. Using two skewers, flip the puffs over. Cook for 2 to 3 minutes or until bottoms are golden brown and a toothpick inserted in the center comes out with a few moist crumbs attached. Remove pan from heat and transfer puffs to a plate. Let pan cool slightly.

6. Repeat with the remaining batter, brushing wells with oil and reheating pan before each batch.

7. Serve the puffs warm, with the marshmallow sauce.

Multi-Seed Ebelskivers (page 57)

Raspberry Blintz Ebelskivers (page 78)

Cranberry Orange Ebelskivers (page 66) and
Citrus and Olive Oil Ebelskivers (page 58)

Cocoa Banana Ebelskivers (page 81)

Caramel Chocolate Pecan Ebelskivers (page 92)

Peach Melba Ebelskivers (page 116)

Raspberry Blintz Ebelskivers (page 78),
Blackberry Mint Puffs (page 112) and
Lemon Poppy Seed Ebelskivers with Lemon Cream (page 124)

Caramel Apple Ebelskivers (page 114)

Praline Ebelskivers

For Southern comfort with a sassy kick, these toffee-sweetened, pecan-freckled ebelskivers are hard to beat.

Tip

For an extra-decadent treat, serve the ebelskivers with Salted Caramel Sauce (page 108) or Chocolate Sauce (page 90).

Variation

Peanut Brittle Puffs: Use an equal amount of chopped lightly salted roasted peanuts in place of the pecans.

● **7-well ebelskiver pan**

1¼ cups	all-purpose flour	300 mL
¾ tsp	baking powder	3 mL
¼ tsp	salt	1 mL
1 tbsp	packed dark brown sugar	15 mL
2	large eggs, separated	2
1 cup	milk	250 mL
2 tbsp	unsalted butter, melted	30 mL
1 tsp	vanilla extract	5 mL
¾ cup	chopped toasted pecans	175 mL
½ cup	toffee baking bits	125 mL
	Vegetable oil	

1. In a large bowl, whisk together flour, baking powder and salt.

2. In a medium bowl, whisk together brown sugar, egg yolks, milk, butter and vanilla until well blended.

3. Add the egg yolk mixture to the flour mixture and stir until just blended (the batter will appear slightly lumpy). Gently stir in pecans and toffee bits.

4. In a medium bowl, using an electric mixer on medium-high speed, beat egg whites until frothy. Increase speed to high and beat until stiff, but not dry, peaks form. Using a rubber spatula, gently mix one-third of the egg whites into the batter. Gently fold in the remaining whites.

5. Brush wells of pan lightly with oil. Set pan over medium heat. When oil begins to sizzle, add 2 tbsp (30 mL) batter to each well. Cook for 2 to 4 minutes or until bottoms are golden brown. Using two skewers, flip the puffs over. Cook for 2 to 3 minutes or until bottoms are golden brown and a toothpick inserted in the center comes out with a few moist crumbs attached. Remove pan from heat and transfer puffs to a plate. Let pan cool slightly.

6. Repeat with the remaining batter, brushing wells with oil and reheating pan before each batch. Serve warm or at room temperature.

Pistachio, Raisin and Saffron Ebelskivers

Exotic saffron, sunny golden raisins and crunchy pistachios coalesce into a sophisticated take on traditional Middle Eastern sweets.

● **7-well ebelskiver pan**

¼ tsp	saffron threads	1 mL
1 tbsp	hot water	15 mL
1¼ cups	all-purpose flour	300 mL
¾ tsp	baking powder	3 mL
¼ tsp	salt	1 mL
2	large eggs, separated	2
1 cup	milk	250 mL
3 tbsp	unsalted butter, melted	45 mL
½ cup	liquid honey, divided	125 mL
⅔ cup	golden raisins	150 mL
½ cup	lightly salted roasted pistachios, chopped	125 mL

1. In a small cup, combine saffron and hot water. Let steep for 10 minutes.

2. In a large bowl, whisk together flour, baking powder and salt.

3. In a medium bowl, whisk together saffron mixture, egg yolks, milk, butter and 3 tbsp (45 mL) of the honey until well blended.

4. Add the egg yolk mixture to the flour mixture and stir until just blended (the batter will appear slightly lumpy). Gently stir in raisins and pistachios.

5. In a medium bowl, using an electric mixer on medium-high speed, beat egg whites until frothy. Increase speed to high and beat until stiff, but not dry, peaks form. Using a rubber spatula, gently mix one-third of the egg whites into the batter. Gently fold in the remaining whites.

Tips

If the raisins are especially large, coarsely chop them before adding them to the batter.

An equal amount of lightly salted roasted cashews or almonds may be used in place of the pistachios.

6. Brush wells of pan lightly with oil. Set pan over medium heat. When oil begins to sizzle, add 2 tbsp (30 mL) batter to each well. Cook for 2 to 4 minutes or until bottoms are golden brown. Using two skewers, flip the puffs over. Cook for 2 to 3 minutes or until bottoms are golden brown and a toothpick inserted in the center comes out with a few moist crumbs attached. Remove pan from heat and transfer puffs to a plate. Let pan cool slightly.

7. Repeat with the remaining batter, brushing wells with oil and reheating pan before each batch.

8. Drizzle the ebelskivers with the remaining honey. Serve warm or at room temperature.

Baklava Ebelskivers

**Makes about
21 puffs**

Heady with honey and
spices, this tempting take
on the layered flavors
of baklava has the same
sugar-and-spice walnut
filling found in the iconic
original.

- Food processor
- 7-well ebelskiver pan

Filling

¾ cup	walnut halves, toasted	175 mL
2 tbsp	packed light brown sugar	30 mL
½ tsp	ground cinnamon	2 mL
⅛ tsp	salt	0.5 mL
2 tsp	freshly squeezed lemon juice	10 mL

Ebelskivers

1¼ cups	all-purpose flour	300 mL
¾ tsp	ground cardamom	3 mL
½ tsp	baking powder	2 mL
¼ tsp	baking soda	1 mL
¼ tsp	salt	1 mL
2	large eggs, separated	2
1 cup	milk	250 mL
6 tbsp	liquid honey, divided	90 mL
2 tbsp	unsalted butter, melted	30 mL
1 tsp	vanilla extract	5 mL
	Vegetable oil	

1. *Filling:* In food processor, combine walnuts, brown sugar, cinnamon and salt; process until walnuts are finely ground. Add lemon juice and process until combined. Set aside.

2. *Ebelskivers:* In a large bowl, whisk together flour, cardamom, baking powder, baking soda and salt.

3. In a medium bowl, whisk together egg yolks, milk, 2 tbsp (30 mL) of the honey, butter and vanilla until well blended.

4. Add the egg yolk mixture to the flour mixture and stir until just blended (the batter will appear slightly lumpy).

5. In a medium bowl, using an electric mixer on medium-high speed, beat egg whites until frothy. Increase speed to high and beat until stiff, but not dry, peaks form. Using a rubber spatula, gently mix one-third of the egg whites into the batter. Gently fold in the remaining whites.

Tips

An equal amount of toasted whole almonds may be used in place of the walnuts.

The cardamom can be replaced with an equal amount of ground ginger.

6. Brush wells of pan lightly with oil. Set pan over medium heat. When oil begins to sizzle, add 1 tbsp (15 mL) batter to each well. Place 1 tsp (5 mL) filling in the center of each well and top with 1 tbsp (15 mL) batter. Cook for 2 to 4 minutes or until bottoms are golden brown. Using two skewers, flip the puffs over. Cook for 2 to 3 minutes or until bottoms are golden brown and the puffs feel firm to the touch. Remove pan from heat and transfer puffs to a plate. Let pan cool slightly.

7. Repeat with the remaining batter and filling, brushing wells with oil and reheating pan before each batch.

8. Drizzle the ebelskivers with the remaining honey. Serve warm or at room temperature.

Frangipane Ebelskivers with Plum Compote

Inspired by European confections filled with the sweet almond paste known as frangipane, these ebelskivers are sublime sophistication. The accompanying compote is terrific made with any type of stone fruit — peaches, nectarines, apricots — so feel free to substitute your summertime favorites.

● **7-well ebelskiver pan**

Plum Compote

1 lb	red plums, quartered	500 g
¼ cup	granulated sugar	60 mL
¼ tsp	freshly cracked black pepper	1 mL

Ebelskivers

1¼ cups	all-purpose flour	300 mL
½ tsp	baking powder	2 mL
¼ tsp	salt	1 mL
¼ tsp	baking soda	1 mL
2 tbsp	granulated sugar	30 mL
2	large eggs, separated	2
¾ cup	sour cream	175 mL
⅓ cup	milk	75 mL
2 tbsp	unsalted butter, melted	30 mL
1 tsp	vanilla extract	5 mL
	Vegetable oil	
½ cup	almond paste	125 mL

1. *Compote:* In a medium, heavy saucepan, combine plums, sugar and pepper. Bring to a boil over medium-high heat, stirring until sugar is dissolved. Reduce heat and simmer, stirring often, for 8 to 10 minutes or until plums are very tender. Remove from heat and let cool while preparing the ebelskivers.

2. *Ebelskivers:* In a large bowl, whisk together flour, baking powder, salt and baking soda.

3. In a medium bowl, whisk together sugar, egg yolks, sour cream, milk, butter and vanilla until well blended.

4. Add the egg yolk mixture to the flour mixture and stir until just blended (the batter will appear slightly lumpy).

An equal amount of prepared marzipan can be used in place of the almond paste.

In a pinch, 1 cup (250 mL) plum preserves or jam, melted, may be used in place of the plum compote.

5. In a medium bowl, using an electric mixer on medium-high speed, beat egg whites until frothy. Increase speed to high and beat until stiff, but not dry, peaks form. Using a rubber spatula, gently mix one-third of the egg whites into the batter. Gently fold in the remaining whites.

6. Brush wells of pan lightly with oil. Set pan over medium heat. When oil begins to sizzle, add 1 tbsp (15 mL) batter to each well. Place 1 tsp (5 mL) almond paste in the center of each well and top with 1 tbsp (15 mL) batter. Cook for 2 to 4 minutes or until bottoms are golden brown. Using two skewers, flip the puffs over. Cook for 2 to 3 minutes or until bottoms are golden brown and a toothpick inserted in the center comes out with a bit of filling and a few moist crumbs attached. Remove pan from heat and transfer puffs to a plate. Let pan cool slightly.

7. Repeat with the remaining batter and almond paste, brushing wells with oil and reheating pan before each batch.

8. Serve the ebelskivers warm, with the plum compote.

Cheesecake Ebelskivers

Makes about 35 puffs

As devastating as it would be to my hips, I would be happy making and eating these cheesecake-filled ebelskivers every day of the week. They transcend the seasons and adapt to any occasion, from dinner party to picnic to afternoon tea. Need I elaborate?

● **7-well ebelskiver pan**

Filling

3 tbsp	granulated sugar	45 mL
8 oz	cream cheese, softened	250 g
1 tsp	vanilla extract	5 mL

Ebelskivers

1 cup	all-purpose flour	250 mL
¾ cup	graham cracker crumbs	175 mL
1½ tsp	baking powder	7 mL
¼ tsp	salt	1 mL
2 tbsp	granulated sugar	30 mL
3	large eggs, separated	3
2 tbsp	unsalted butter, melted	30 mL
1 tsp	vanilla extract	5 mL
1⅓ cups	milk	325 mL
	Vegetable oil	
	Confectioners' (icing) sugar	

1. *Filling:* In a medium bowl, using an electric mixer on medium-high speed, beat sugar, cream cheese and vanilla until smooth and creamy. Cover and refrigerate while preparing the batter. Clean the beaters.

2. *Ebelskivers:* In a large bowl, whisk together flour, graham cracker crumbs, baking powder and salt.

3. In a medium bowl, whisk together sugar, egg yolks, butter and vanilla. Whisk in milk until well blended.

4. Add the egg yolk mixture to the flour mixture and stir until just blended (the batter will appear slightly lumpy).

5. In a medium bowl, using an electric mixer on medium-high speed, beat egg whites until frothy. Increase speed to high and beat until stiff, but not dry, peaks form. Using a rubber spatula, gently mix one-third of the egg whites into the batter. Gently fold in the remaining whites.

6. Brush wells of pan lightly with oil. Set pan over medium heat. When oil begins to sizzle, add 1 tbsp (15 mL) batter to each well. Place 1 tsp (5 mL) filling in the center of each well and top with 1 tbsp (15 mL) batter. Cook for 2 to 4 minutes or until bottoms are golden brown. Using two skewers, flip the puffs over. Cook for 2 to 3 minutes or until bottoms are golden brown and a toothpick inserted in the center comes out with a bit of filling and a few moist crumbs attached. Remove pan from heat and transfer puffs to a plate. Let pan cool slightly.

7. Repeat with the remaining batter and filling, brushing wells with oil and reheating pan before each batch.

8. Dust the ebelskivers with confectioners' sugar. Serve warm or at room temperature.

Anise Mascarpone Puffs

Inspired by two of my favorite Italian ingredients, these sophisticated puffs have much to offer: a buttery vanilla batter, silken mascarpone filling and the sweet licorice accent of anise.

Tip

An equal amount of brick-style cream cheese, softened, may be used in place of the mascarpone.

● **7-well ebelskiver pan**

Filling

3 tbsp	granulated sugar	45 mL
8 oz	mascarpone cheese	250 g
1 tsp	vanilla extract	5 mL

Ebelskivers

1¾ cups	all-purpose flour	425 mL
2½ tsp	anise seeds, crushed	12 mL
1½ tsp	baking powder	7 mL
¼ tsp	salt	1 mL
2 tbsp	granulated sugar	30 mL
3	large eggs, separated	3
2 tbsp	unsalted butter, melted	30 mL
1 tsp	vanilla extract	5 mL
1⅓ cups	milk	325 mL
	Vegetable oil	
	Confectioners' (icing) sugar	

1. *Filling:* In a small bowl, stir together sugar, mascarpone and vanilla until blended. Cover and refrigerate while preparing the batter.

2. *Ebelskivers:* In a large bowl, whisk together flour, anise seeds, baking powder and salt.

3. In a medium bowl, whisk together sugar, egg yolks, butter and vanilla. Whisk in milk until well blended.

4. Add the egg yolk mixture to the flour mixture and stir until just blended (the batter will appear slightly lumpy).

5. In a medium bowl, using an electric mixer on medium-high speed, beat egg whites until frothy. Increase speed to high and beat until stiff, but not dry, peaks form. Using a rubber spatula, gently mix one-third of the egg whites into the batter. Gently fold in the remaining whites.

Tips

If you prefer, you can replace the anise seeds with 1¼ tsp (6 mL) pure anise extract.

An equal amount of crushed fennel seeds may be used in place of the anise seeds.

6. Brush wells of pan lightly with oil. Set pan over medium heat. When oil begins to sizzle, add 1 tbsp (15 mL) batter to each well. Place 1 tsp (5 mL) filling in the center of each well and top with 1 tbsp (15 mL) batter. Cook for 2 to 4 minutes or until bottoms are golden brown. Using two skewers, flip the puffs over. Cook for 2 to 3 minutes or until bottoms are golden brown and a toothpick inserted in the center comes out with a bit of filling and a few moist crumbs attached. Remove pan from heat and transfer puffs to a plate. Let pan cool slightly.

7. Repeat with the remaining batter and filling, brushing wells with oil and reheating pan before each batch.

8. Dust the ebelskivers with confectioners' sugar. Serve warm or at room temperature.

Salted Caramel Ebelskivers

I am crazy about the trend of salty-sweet desserts and wanted to make a version of ebelskivers to showcase one of my favorites of the genre: salted caramel. While mere mention of this dessert will make everyone swoon, I promise that it will only get better from there.

- 7-well ebelskiver pan

Salted Caramel Sauce

1/3 cup	packed light brown sugar	75 mL
1/4 tsp	salt (preferably fine sea salt or fleur de sel)	1 mL
1/3 cup	heavy or whipping (35%) cream	75 mL
1/4 cup	unsalted butter, cut into small pieces	60 mL
1 tsp	vanilla extract	5 mL

Ebelskivers

1 1/3 cups	all-purpose flour	325 mL
3/4 tsp	baking powder	3 mL
1/2 tsp	salt (preferably fine sea salt or fleur de sel)	2 mL
2 tbsp	packed light brown sugar	30 mL
3	large eggs, separated	3
1 cup	milk	250 mL
1/4 cup	unsalted butter, melted	60 mL
1 tsp	vanilla extract	5 mL
	Vanilla ice cream and/or lightly sweetened whipped cream	

1. *Sauce:* In a medium saucepan, combine brown sugar, salt, cream and butter. Bring to a boil over medium-high heat, whisking constantly. Reduce heat and simmer, whisking, for 2 minutes, until sugar is dissolved. Remove from heat and whisk in vanilla. Let cool while preparing the ebelskivers.

2. *Ebelskivers:* In a large bowl, whisk together flour, baking powder and salt.

3. In a medium bowl, whisk together brown sugar, egg yolks, milk, butter and vanilla until well blended.

4. Add the egg yolk mixture to the flour mixture and stir until just blended (the batter will appear slightly lumpy).

5. In a medium bowl, using an electric mixer on medium-high speed, beat egg whites until frothy. Increase speed to high and beat until stiff, but not dry, peaks form. Using a rubber spatula, gently mix one-third of the egg whites into the batter. Gently fold in the remaining whites.

Tip

In a pinch, you can use 1 cup (250 mL) prepared premium caramel sauce in place of the caramel sauce recipe. Place prepared sauce in a small saucepan set over low heat. Stir in $\frac{1}{8}$ tsp (0.5 mL) sea salt and stir until just barely warm. Remove from heat.

6. Brush wells of pan lightly with oil. Set pan over medium heat. When oil begins to sizzle, add 2 tbsp (30 mL) batter to each well. Cook for 2 to 4 minutes or until bottoms are golden brown. Using two skewers, flip the puffs over. Cook for 2 to 3 minutes or until bottoms are golden brown and a toothpick inserted in the center comes out with a few moist crumbs attached. Remove pan from heat and transfer puffs to a plate. Let pan cool slightly.

7. Repeat with the remaining batter, brushing wells with oil and reheating pan before each batch.

8. Drizzle the ebelskivers with the caramel sauce. Serve warm or at room temperature, with ice cream and/or whipped cream.

Sweet Rosemary Polenta Ebelskivers

Cornmeal gives these ebelskivers crunchy texture, while fresh orange zest and rosemary enhance their Tuscan flair.

Tip

When grating orange zest, you want just the thin orange top coat of the skin. Overzealous grating will result in bitter flavors.

● **7-well ebelskiver pan**

¾ cup	all-purpose flour	175 mL
⅔ cup	yellow cornmeal (preferably stone-ground)	150 mL
¾ tsp	baking powder	3 mL
¼ tsp	salt	1 mL
3 tbsp	granulated sugar	45 mL
3	large eggs, separated	3
1 cup	milk	250 mL
3 tbsp	unsalted butter, melted	45 mL
2 tsp	finely grated orange zest	10 mL
1½ tsp	minced fresh rosemary	7 mL
1 tsp	vanilla extract	5 mL
	Vegetable oil	
	Confectioners' (icing) sugar	

1. In a large bowl, whisk together flour, cornmeal, baking powder and salt.

2. In a medium bowl, whisk together sugar, egg yolks, milk, butter, orange zest, rosemary and vanilla until well blended.

3. Add the egg yolk mixture to the flour mixture and stir until just blended (the batter will appear slightly lumpy).

4. In a medium bowl, using an electric mixer on medium-high speed, beat egg whites until frothy. Increase speed to high and beat until stiff, but not dry, peaks form. Using a rubber spatula, gently mix one-third of the egg whites into the batter. Gently fold in the remaining whites.

Tips

You can use ¾ tsp (3 mL) crushed dried rosemary in place of the fresh rosemary.

An equal amount of minced fresh thyme may be used in place of the rosemary.

5. Brush wells of pan lightly with oil. Set pan over medium heat. When oil begins to sizzle, add 2 tbsp (30 mL) batter to each well. Cook for 2 to 4 minutes or until bottoms are golden brown. Using two skewers, flip the puffs over. Cook for 2 to 3 minutes or until bottoms are golden brown and a toothpick inserted in the center comes out with a few moist crumbs attached. Remove pan from heat and transfer puffs to a plate. Let pan cool slightly.

6. Repeat with the remaining batter, brushing wells with oil and reheating pan before each batch.

7. Dust the ebelskivers with confectioners' sugar. Serve warm or at room temperature.

Blackberry Mint Puffs

Fresh mint and sweet-tart blackberries are a sublime combination in these pretty little puffs. Those who love all varieties of berries can use any seasonal berries — and matching jam or preserves — they like.

Tips

If using thawed frozen blackberries, do not drain them. Add the blackberry liquid to the remaining jam along with the remaining berries in step 7.

Fresh mint is essential for this recipe; do not be tempted to use dried mint in its place.

● **7-well ebelskiver pan**

1¼ cups	all-purpose flour	425 mL
¾ tsp	baking powder	3 mL
¼ tsp	salt	1 mL
1 tbsp	granulated sugar	15 mL
2	large eggs, separated	2
1 cup	milk	250 mL
2 tbsp	unsalted butter, melted	30 mL
1 tsp	vanilla extract	5 mL
	Vegetable oil	
¾ cup	seedless blackberry jam, divided	175 mL
2½ cups	fresh or thawed frozen blackberries, divided	625 mL
3 tbsp	minced fresh mint, divided	45 mL

1. In a large bowl, whisk together flour, baking powder and salt.

2. In a medium bowl, whisk together sugar, egg yolks, milk, butter and vanilla until well blended.

3. Add the egg yolk mixture to the flour mixture and stir until just blended (the batter will appear slightly lumpy).

4. In a medium bowl, using an electric mixer on medium-high speed, beat egg whites until frothy. Increase speed to high and beat until stiff, but not dry, peaks form. Using a rubber spatula, gently mix one-third of the egg whites into the batter. Gently fold in the remaining whites.

5. Brush wells of pan lightly with oil. Set pan over medium heat. When oil begins to sizzle, add 1 tbsp (15 mL) batter to each well. Place ½ tsp (2 mL) jam and 1 blackberry in the center of each well and top with 1 tbsp (15 mL) batter. Cook for 2 to 4 minutes or until bottoms are golden brown. Using two skewers, flip the puffs over. Cook for 2 to 3 minutes or until bottoms are golden brown and a toothpick inserted in the center comes out with a bit of filling and a few moist crumbs attached. Remove pan from heat and transfer puffs to a plate. Let pan cool slightly.

Variation

Blackberry Basil Puffs: Use an equal amount of minced fresh basil in place of the mint.

6. Repeat with the remaining batter, brushing wells with oil and reheating pan before each batch.

7. In a small glass bowl, microwave the remaining jam on High in 5-second intervals until melted. Add the remaining blackberries and crush with the tines of fork, mixing them into the jam. Stir in half the mint.

8. Drizzle the puffs with the blackberry sauce and sprinkle with the remaining mint. Serve warm.

Caramel Apple Ebelskivers

Apples are perfect ingredients on their own, but they also love to mingle with countless other flavors. Caramel is a natural partner, reminiscent of carnival treats and tarte Tatin.

● **7-well ebelskiver pan**

Caramel Apples

1 tbsp	unsalted butter, melted	15 mL
1½ cups	diced peeled tart apples (such as Granny Smith)	375 mL
¾ cup	caramel sauce (page 108 or store-bought)	175 mL

Ebelskivers

1¼ cups	all-purpose flour	300 mL
¾ tsp	baking powder	3 mL
¼ tsp	salt	1 mL
2 tsp	granulated sugar	10 mL
2	large eggs, separated	2
1 cup	milk	250 mL
2 tbsp	unsalted butter, melted	30 mL
½ tsp	vanilla extract	2 mL
	Vegetable oil	
	Vanilla ice cream (optional)	

1. *Caramel Apples:* In a large skillet, heat butter over medium heat. Add apples and cook, stirring, for 3 minutes. Add caramel sauce and cook, stirring, for 2 to 4 minutes or until apples are softened. Remove from heat and let cool completely.

2. *Ebelskivers:* In a large bowl, whisk together flour, baking powder and salt.

3. In a medium bowl, whisk together sugar, egg yolks, milk, butter and vanilla until well blended.

4. Add the egg yolk mixture to the flour mixture and stir until just blended (the batter will appear slightly lumpy).

5. In a medium bowl, using an electric mixer on medium-high speed, beat egg whites until frothy. Increase speed to high and beat until stiff, but not dry, peaks form. Using a rubber spatula, gently mix one-third of the egg whites into the batter. Gently fold in the remaining whites.

Tip

An equal amount of diced peeled firm-ripe pears may be used in place of the apples.

6. Brush wells of pan lightly with oil. Set pan over medium heat. When oil begins to sizzle, add 1 tbsp (15 mL) batter to each well. Place $1\frac{1}{2}$ tsp (7 mL) of the caramel apples in the center of each well and top with 1 tbsp (15 mL) batter. Cook for 2 to 4 minutes or until bottoms are golden brown. Using two skewers, flip the puffs over. Cook for 2 to 3 minutes or until bottoms are golden brown and a toothpick inserted in the center comes out with a bit of filling and a few moist crumbs attached. Remove pan from heat and transfer puffs to a plate. Let pan cool slightly.

7. Repeat with the remaining batter, brushing wells with oil and reheating pan before each batch.

8. Serve the ebelskivers warm, with the remaining caramel apples. Serve with ice cream, if desired.

Peach Melba Ebelskivers

Midsummer marks high season at the farmers' market, so why not celebrate with these peach and raspberry ebelskivers? Based on the classic dessert invented by Auguste Escoffier to honor the Australian soprano Dame Nellie Melba, these puffs make the most of summer's bounty.

● **7-well ebelskiver pan**

Raspberry Sauce

2 cups	raspberries	500 mL
2 tbsp	granulated sugar	30 mL

Ebelskivers

1¼ cups	all-purpose flour	300 mL
½ tsp	baking powder	2 mL
½ tsp	baking soda	2 mL
¼ tsp	salt	1 mL
1 tbsp	granulated sugar	15 mL
2	large eggs, separated	2
¾ cup	sour cream	175 mL
⅓ cup	milk	75 mL
2 tbsp	unsalted butter, melted	30 mL
1 tsp	vanilla extract	5 mL
	Vegetable oil	
½ cup	peach preserves	125 mL
	Vanilla ice cream or lightly sweetened whipped cream	

1. *Sauce:* In a medium bowl, coarsely crush raspberries with the tines of a fork. Stir in sugar. Let stand at room temperature while preparing the ebelskivers.

2. *Ebelskivers:* In a large bowl, whisk together flour, baking powder, baking soda and salt.

3. In a medium bowl, whisk together sugar, egg yolks, sour cream, milk, butter and vanilla until well blended.

4. Add the egg yolk mixture to the flour mixture and stir until just blended (the batter will appear slightly lumpy).

5. In a medium bowl, using an electric mixer on medium-high speed, beat egg whites until frothy. Increase speed to high and beat until stiff, but not dry, peaks form. Using a rubber spatula, gently mix one-third of the egg whites into the batter. Gently fold in the remaining whites.

Tips

An equal amount of thawed frozen raspberries (undrained) may be used in place of fresh.

Apricot jam may be used in place of the peach jam.

6. Brush wells of pan lightly with oil. Set pan over medium heat. When oil begins to sizzle, add 1 tbsp (15 mL) batter to each well. Place 1 tsp (5 mL) preserves in the center of each well and top with 1 tbsp (15 mL) batter. Cook for 2 to 4 minutes or until bottoms are golden brown. Using two skewers, flip the puffs over. Cook for 2 to 3 minutes or until bottoms are golden brown and a toothpick inserted in the center comes out with a bit of filling and a few moist crumbs attached. Remove pan from heat and transfer puffs to a plate. Let pan cool slightly.

7. Repeat with the remaining batter and preserves, brushing wells with oil and reheating pan before each batch.

8. Serve the ebelskivers warm, with the raspberry sauce and ice cream or whipped cream.

Strawberries and Cream Ebelskivers

Although I appreciate traditional shortcakes, I am always up for innovation. This ebelskiver rendering of the summertime classic, in which ebelskivers take the place of shortcake biscuits, is the perfect case in point.

Variation

Other fresh berries, such as blueberries, raspberries or blackberries, or other diced summer fruits, such as peaches or apricots, may be used in place of the strawberries.

● **7-well ebelskiver pan**

8 oz	strawberries, hulled and diced	250 g
2 tbsp	granulated sugar, divided	30 mL
1¼ cups	all-purpose flour	300 mL
¾ tsp	baking powder	3 mL
¼ tsp	salt	1 mL
2	large eggs, separated	2
1 cup	milk	250 mL
2 tbsp	unsalted butter, melted	30 mL
1 tsp	vanilla extract	5 mL
	Vegetable oil	
	Lightly sweetened whipped cream	

1. In a medium bowl, combine strawberries and 1 tbsp (15 mL) of the sugar. Let stand while preparing the ebelskivers.

2. In a large bowl, whisk together flour, baking powder and salt.

3. In a medium bowl, whisk together the remaining sugar, egg yolks, milk, butter and vanilla until well blended.

4. Add the egg yolk mixture to the flour mixture and stir until just blended (the batter will appear slightly lumpy).

5. In a medium bowl, using an electric mixer on medium-high speed, beat egg whites until frothy. Increase speed to high and beat until stiff, but not dry, peaks form. Using a rubber spatula, gently mix one-third of the egg whites into the batter. Gently fold in the remaining whites.

6. Brush wells of pan lightly with oil. Set pan over medium heat. When oil begins to sizzle, add 2 tbsp (30 mL) batter to each well. Cook for 2 to 4 minutes or until bottoms are golden brown. Using two skewers, flip the puffs over. Cook for 2 to 3 minutes or until bottoms are golden brown and a toothpick inserted in the center comes out with a few moist crumbs attached. Remove pan from heat and transfer puffs to a plate. Let pan cool slightly.

7. Repeat with the remaining batter, brushing wells with oil and reheating pan before each batch.

8. Serve the ebelskivers warm, with the strawberries and whipped cream.

Neapolitan Ebelskivers

In this interpretation of the beloved trio of vanilla, strawberry and chocolate, I've flecked vanilla ebelskivers with dark chocolate, then filled them with sweet strawberry centers. I predict many new memories in the making.

Tips

Raspberry jam or preserves may be used in place of the strawberry preserves.

An equal amount of regular semisweet chocolate chips may be used in place of the miniature chocolate chips. Coarsely chop the chips for more even distribution of the chocolate throughout the ebelskivers.

● **7-well ebelskiver pan**

1¼ cups	all-purpose flour	300 mL
½ tsp	baking powder	2 mL
½ tsp	baking soda	2 mL
¼ tsp	salt	1 mL
2 tbsp	granulated sugar	30 mL
2	large eggs, separated	2
¾ cup	sour cream	175 mL
⅓ cup	milk	75 mL
2 tbsp	unsalted butter, melted	30 mL
1 tsp	vanilla extract	5 mL
⅔ cup	miniature semisweet chocolate chips	150 mL
	Vegetable oil	
½ cup	strawberry preserves or jam	125 mL
	Confectioners' (icing) sugar	

1. In a large bowl, whisk together flour, baking powder, baking soda and salt.

2. In a medium bowl, whisk together sugar, egg yolks, sour cream, milk, butter and vanilla until well blended.

3. Add the egg yolk mixture to the flour mixture and stir until just blended (the batter will appear slightly lumpy). Gently stir in chocolate chips.

4. In a medium bowl, using an electric mixer on medium-high speed, beat egg whites until frothy. Increase speed to high and beat until stiff, but not dry, peaks form. Using a rubber spatula, gently mix one-third of the egg whites into the batter. Gently fold in the remaining whites.

5. Brush wells of pan lightly with oil. Set pan over medium heat. When oil begins to sizzle, add 1 tbsp (15 mL) batter to each well. Place 1 tsp (5 mL) preserves in the center of each well and top with 1 tbsp (15 mL) batter. Cook for 2 to 4 minutes or until bottoms are golden brown. Using two skewers, flip the puffs over. Cook for 2 to 3 minutes or until bottoms are golden brown and a toothpick inserted in the center comes out with a bit of filling and a few moist crumbs attached. Remove pan from heat and transfer puffs to a plate. Let pan cool slightly.

6. Repeat with the remaining batter and preserves, brushing wells with oil and reheating pan before each batch.

7. Dust the ebelskivers with confectioners' sugar. Serve warm or at room temperature.

Browned Butter Raspberry Ebelskivers

Thanks to a few French-inspired additions — browned butter (*beurre noisette*), raspberries and plenty of cream and eggs — these pretty puffs have both charm and exquisite flavor to spare.

● **7-well ebelskiver pan**

¼ cup	unsalted butter	60 mL
1¼ cups	all-purpose flour	300 mL
½ tsp	baking soda	2 mL
¼ tsp	baking powder	1 mL
¼ tsp	salt	1 mL
2 tbsp	packed light brown sugar	30 mL
2	large eggs, separated	2
½ cup	sour cream	125 mL
⅓ cup	milk	75 mL
1 tsp	vanilla extract	5 mL
	Vegetable oil	
21	fresh raspberries	21
	Confectioners' (icing) sugar	

1. In a medium, heavy skillet, heat butter over medium heat until foam subsides and butter is beginning to brown. Continue to cook, stirring, for 1 to 2 minutes or until butter is golden brown. Immediately transfer to a medium bowl and let cool to room temperature.

2. In a large bowl, whisk together flour, baking soda, baking powder and salt.

3. Add brown sugar, egg yolks, sour cream, milk and vanilla to the browned butter and whisk until well blended.

4. Add the egg yolk mixture to the flour mixture and stir until just blended (the batter will appear slightly lumpy).

5. In a medium bowl, using an electric mixer on medium-high speed, beat egg whites until frothy. Increase speed to high and beat until stiff, but not dry, peaks form. Using a rubber spatula, gently mix one-third of the egg whites into the batter. Gently fold in the remaining whites.

Tips

For best results, do not use frozen raspberries for this recipe.

An equal amount of blackberries may be used in place of the raspberries.

6. Brush wells of pan lightly with oil. Set pan over medium heat. When oil begins to sizzle, add 1 tbsp (15 mL) batter to each well. Place 1 raspberry in the center of each well and top with 1 tbsp (15 mL) batter. Cook for 2 to 4 minutes or until bottoms are golden brown. Using two skewers, flip the puffs over. Cook for 2 to 3 minutes or until bottoms are golden brown and a toothpick inserted in the center comes out with a few moist crumbs attached. Remove pan from heat and transfer puffs to a plate. Let pan cool slightly.

7. Repeat with the remaining batter and raspberries, brushing wells with oil and reheating pan before each batch.

8. Dust the ebelskivers with confectioner's sugar. Serve warm.

Toasted Almond and Cherry Ebelskivers

These ebelskivers showcase the exquisite, complementary flavors of cherries and almonds through and through.

Variation

An equal amount of dried cranberries can be used in place of the dried cherries.

● **7-well ebelskiver pan**

1¼ cups	all-purpose flour	300 mL
¾ tsp	baking powder	3 mL
¼ tsp	salt	1 mL
¼ tsp	ground nutmeg	1 mL
1 tbsp	packed light brown sugar	15 mL
2	large eggs, separated	2
1 cup	milk	250 mL
2 tbsp	unsalted butter, melted	30 mL
1 tsp	almond extract	5 mL
½ cup	toasted sliced almonds, chopped	125 mL
½ cup	dried cherries, finely chopped	125 mL
	Vegetable oil	
	Confectioners' (icing) sugar	

1. In a large bowl, whisk together flour, baking powder, salt and nutmeg.

2. In a medium bowl, whisk together brown sugar, egg yolks, milk, butter and almond extract until well blended.

3. Add the egg yolk mixture to the flour mixture and stir until just blended (the batter will appear slightly lumpy). Gently stir in almonds and cherries.

4. In a medium bowl, using an electric mixer on medium-high speed, beat egg whites until frothy. Increase speed to high and beat until stiff, but not dry, peaks form. Using a rubber spatula, gently mix one-third of the egg whites into the batter. Gently fold in the remaining whites.

5. Brush wells of pan lightly with oil. Set pan over medium heat. When oil begins to sizzle, add 2 tbsp (30 mL) batter to each well. Cook for 2 to 4 minutes or until bottoms are golden brown. Using two skewers, flip the puffs over. Cook for 2 to 3 minutes or until bottoms are golden brown and a toothpick inserted in the center comes out with a few moist crumbs attached. Remove pan from heat and transfer puffs to a plate. Let pan cool slightly.

6. Repeat with the remaining batter, brushing wells with oil and reheating pan before each batch.

7. Dust the ebelskivers with confectioners' sugar. Serve warm or at room temperature.

Lemon Lavender Ebelskivers

If you're new to using lavender in cooking or baking, these ebelskivers are the perfect place to begin, as it adds subtle yet bewitching floral notes to the finished puffs. With olive oil and lemon zest in the batter, plus tart lemon curd centers, they will transport you to northern California wine country, or perhaps sunny Provence.

Tips

Look for dried lavender at health food, specialty food and cooking stores, and from online herb and spice companies. It is crucial to make sure you buy culinary-grade lavender, not the kind made for potpourri or other crafts. This means the plant has been raised and harvested in a manner that makes it safe for human consumption. Buying certified organic lavender is a good way to make sure it has not been treated with pesticides or other unwanted chemicals.

If you can't find culinary lavender, 1 tsp (5 mL) minced fresh rosemary may be used in its place.

● **Food processor or clean coffee grinder**
● **7-well ebelskiver pan**

1¼ cups	all-purpose flour	300 mL
¾ tsp	baking powder	3 mL
¼ tsp	salt	1 mL
3 tbsp	granulated sugar	45 mL
2 tsp	finely grated lemon zest	10 mL
1¼ tsp	dried lavender flowers	6 mL
2	large eggs, separated	2
1 cup	milk	250 mL
2 tbsp	extra virgin olive oil	30 mL
	Vegetable oil	
½ cup	lemon curd	125 mL
	Confectioners' (icing) sugar	

1. In a large bowl, whisk together flour, baking powder and salt.

2. In food processor, combine sugar, lemon zest and lavender; process until lavender is finely chopped. Transfer to a medium bowl.

3. Whisk egg yolks, milk and olive oil into lavender mixture until well blended.

4. Add the egg yolk mixture to the flour mixture and stir until just blended (the batter will appear slightly lumpy).

5. In a medium bowl, using an electric mixer on medium-high speed, beat egg whites until frothy. Increase speed to high and beat until stiff, but not dry, peaks form. Using a rubber spatula, gently mix one-third of the egg whites into the batter. Gently fold in the remaining whites.

6. Brush wells of pan lightly with oil. Set pan over medium heat. When oil begins to sizzle, add 1 tbsp (15 mL) batter to each well. Place 1 tsp (5 mL) lemon curd in the center of each well and top with 1 tbsp (15 mL) batter. Cook for 2 to 4 minutes or until bottoms are golden brown. Using two skewers, flip the puffs over. Cook for 2 to 3 minutes or until bottoms are golden brown and a toothpick inserted in the center comes out with a bit of filling and a few moist crumbs attached. Remove pan from heat and transfer puffs to a plate. Let pan cool slightly.

7. Repeat with the remaining batter and lemon curd, brushing wells with oil and reheating pan before each batch.

8. Dust the ebelskivers with confectioners' sugar. Serve warm or at room temperature.

Lemon Poppy Seed Ebelskivers with Lemon Cream

Polka-dotted and perfectly delicious, these puffs boast creamy citrus centers as well as a lemony batter.

Tips

Poppy seeds have a high oil content, which means they can become rancid quickly. For optimal freshness, store them in an airtight container in the refrigerator or freezer for up to 6 months.

The poppy seeds may be omitted, if desired.

● **7-well ebelskiver pan**

Lemon Cream Filling

3 tbsp	granulated sugar	45 mL
8 oz	cream cheese, softened	250 g
1 tsp	finely grated lemon zest	5 mL
2 tbsp	freshly squeezed lemon juice	30 mL

Ebelskivers

1¾ cups	all-purpose flour	425 mL
1 tsp	baking powder	5 mL
¼ tsp	salt	1 mL
2 tbsp	granulated sugar	30 mL
3	large eggs, separated	3
2 tbsp	unsalted butter, melted	30 mL
1 tsp	finely grated lemon zest	5 mL
1⅓ cups	milk	325 mL
3 tbsp	poppy seeds	45 mL
	Vegetable oil	
	Confectioners' (icing) sugar	

1. *Filling:* In a medium bowl, using an electric mixer on medium-high speed, beat sugar, cream cheese lemon zest and lemon juice until smooth and creamy. Cover and refrigerate while preparing the batter. Clean the beaters.

2. *Ebelskivers:* In a large bowl, whisk together flour, baking powder and salt.

3. In a medium bowl, whisk together sugar, egg yolks, butter and lemon zest. Whisk in milk until well blended.

4. Add the egg yolk mixture to the flour mixture and stir until just blended (the batter will appear slightly lumpy). Gently stir in poppy seeds.

Variation

Replace the cream cheese filling with 1 cup (250 mL) prepared lemon curd.

5. In a medium bowl, using an electric mixer on medium-high speed, beat egg whites until frothy. Increase speed to high and beat until stiff, but not dry, peaks form. Using a rubber spatula, gently mix one-third of the egg whites into the batter. Gently fold in the remaining whites.

6. Brush wells of pan lightly with oil. Set pan over medium heat. When oil begins to sizzle, add 1 tbsp (15 mL) batter to each well. Place 1 tsp (5 mL) filling in the center of each well and top with 1 tbsp (15 mL) batter. Cook for 2 to 4 minutes or until bottoms are golden brown. Using two skewers, flip the puffs over. Cook for 2 to 3 minutes or until bottoms are golden brown and a toothpick inserted in the center comes out with a bit of filling and a few moist crumbs attached. Remove pan from heat and transfer puffs to a plate. Let pan cool slightly.

7. Repeat with the remaining batter and filling, brushing wells with oil and reheating pan before each batch.

8. Dust the ebelskivers with confectioners' sugar. Serve warm or at room temperature.

Lime Ebelskivers with Mango Sauce

Indian ingredients —
mango, cardamom and
yogurt — make these
otherwise humble
ebelskivers something
special.

Tip

To choose a good mango,
smell it. It should have
a faintly sweet aroma,
especially around the
stem; if the mango has no
perfume at all, do not buy
it. Additionally, if the fruit
smells sour or like alcohol,
it's past its prime. Choose
firm fruit that just beginning
to show some yellow or
red in the skin. The skin
should be tight around the
flesh; loose skin means the
mango is old.

- **Blender or food processor**
- **7-well ebelskiver pan**

Mango Sauce

2 cups	diced fresh or thawed frozen mango	500 mL
3 tbsp	granulated sugar	45 mL
2 tbsp	freshly squeezed lime juice	30 mL

Ebelskivers

1¼ cups	all-purpose flour	300 mL
1 tsp	ground cardamom or ginger	5 mL
½ tsp	baking powder	2 mL
½ tsp	baking soda	2 mL
¼ tsp	salt	1 mL
2 tbsp	granulated sugar	30 mL
2	large eggs, separated	2
⅔ cup	plain whole-milk yogurt	150 mL
⅔ cup	milk	150 mL
2 tbsp	unsalted butter, melted	30 mL
1 tbsp	finely grated lime zest	15 mL
	Vegetable oil	

1. *Sauce:* In blender, combine mango, sugar and lime juice; purée until smooth. Transfer to a small bowl or pitcher and set aside.

2. *Ebelskivers:* In a large bowl, whisk together flour, cardamom, baking powder, baking soda and salt.

3. In a medium bowl, whisk together sugar, egg yolks, yogurt, milk, butter and lime zest until well blended.

4. Add the egg yolk mixture to the flour mixture and stir until just blended (the batter will appear slightly lumpy).

5. In a medium bowl, using an electric mixer on medium-high speed, beat egg whites until frothy. Increase speed to high and beat until stiff, but not dry, peaks form. Using a rubber spatula, gently mix one-third of the egg whites into the batter. Gently fold in the remaining whites.

Tips

You can use 1¼ tsp (6 mL) pure lime oil in place of the lime zest.

These lime-scented ebelskivers are also wonderful with Salted Caramel Sauce (page 108), Chocolate Coconut Sauce (page 132) or straight up with a simple sprinkle of confectioners' (icing) sugar.

6. Brush wells of pan lightly with oil. Set pan over medium heat. When oil begins to sizzle, add 2 tbsp (30 mL) batter to each well. Cook for 2 to 4 minutes or until bottoms are golden brown. Using two skewers, flip the puffs over. Cook for 2 to 3 minutes or until bottoms are golden brown and a toothpick inserted in the center comes out with a few moist crumbs attached. Remove pan from heat and transfer puffs to a plate. Let pan cool slightly.

7. Repeat with the remaining batter, brushing wells with oil and reheating pan before each batch.

8. Serve the ebelskivers warm, with the mango sauce.

Orange Dreamsicle Puffs

It's no mystery why orange sherbet–vanilla ice cream bars — sweet, citrusy and mellow — are nostalgic childhood favorites. Reinterpreted as ebelskivers filled with white chocolate and marmalade, the vanilla-orange duet evokes the spirit of summer, even in the depths of winter.

Tips

An equal amount of orange curd may be used in place of the marmalade.

You can use ⅔ cup (150 mL) white chocolate chips, finely chopped, in place of the white chocolate.

● **7-well ebelskiver pan**

1¼ cups	all-purpose flour	300 mL
¾ tsp	baking powder	3 mL
¼ tsp	salt	1 mL
1 tbsp	granulated sugar	15 mL
2	large eggs, separated	2
1 cup	milk	250 mL
2 tbsp	unsalted butter, melted	30 mL
2 tsp	finely grated orange zest	10 mL
1 tsp	vanilla extract	5 mL
4 oz	white chocolate, finely chopped	125 g
	Vegetable oil	
½ cup	orange marmalade	125 mL
	Confectioners' (icing) sugar	

1. In a large bowl, whisk together flour, baking powder and salt.

2. In a medium bowl, whisk together sugar, egg yolks, milk, butter, orange zest and vanilla until well blended.

3. Add the egg yolk mixture to the flour mixture and stir until just blended (the batter will appear slightly lumpy). Gently stir in white chocolate.

4. In a medium bowl, using an electric mixer on medium-high speed, beat egg whites until frothy. Increase speed to high and beat until stiff, but not dry, peaks form. Using a rubber spatula, gently mix one-third of the egg whites into the batter. Gently fold in the remaining whites.

6. Brush wells of pan lightly with oil. Set pan over medium heat. When oil begins to sizzle, add 1 tbsp (15 mL) batter to each well. Place 1 tsp (5 mL) marmalade in the center of each well and top with 1 tbsp (15 mL) batter. Cook for 2 to 4 minutes or until bottoms are golden brown. Using two skewers, flip the puffs over. Cook for 2 to 3 minutes or until bottoms are golden brown and a toothpick inserted in the center comes out with a bit of filling and a few moist crumbs attached. Remove pan from heat and transfer puffs to a plate. Let pan cool slightly.

7. Repeat with the remaining batter and marmalade, brushing wells with oil and reheating pan before each batch.

8. Dust the puffs with confectioners' sugar. Serve warm or at room temperature.

Citrus Ricotta Puffs

Extra virgin olive oil adds a sophisticated, fruity nuance to these tender, citrus-scented puffs. The accompanying citrusy syrup delivers sweet-tart sophistication that belies its simplicity.

Tips

You'll need about 2 large lemons to yield the zest and juice needed for these ebelskivers.

For best results, do not use nonfat ricotta cheese in this recipe.

● **7-well ebelskiver pan**

1¼ cups	all-purpose flour	300 mL
½ tsp	baking powder	2 mL
½ tsp	ground coriander or ginger	2 mL
¼ tsp	salt	1 mL
¼ tsp	baking soda	1 mL
2 tsp	granulated sugar	10 mL
2	large eggs, separated	2
⅔ cup	buttermilk	150 mL
⅔ cup	ricotta cheese	150 mL
2 tbsp	extra virgin olive oil	30 mL
2 tsp	finely grated lemon zest	10 mL
	Vegetable oil	
⅔ cup	orange marmalade	150 mL
3 tbsp	freshly squeezed lemon juice	45 mL
	Confectioners' (icing) sugar	

1. In a large bowl, whisk together flour, baking powder, coriander, salt and baking soda.

2. In a medium bowl, whisk together sugar, egg yolks, buttermilk, ricotta, olive oil and lemon zest until well blended.

3. Add the egg yolk mixture to the flour mixture and stir until just blended (the batter will appear slightly lumpy).

4. In a medium bowl, using an electric mixer on medium-high speed, beat egg whites until frothy. Increase speed to high and beat until stiff, but not dry, peaks form. Using a rubber spatula, gently mix one-third of the egg whites into the batter. Gently fold in the remaining whites.

5. Brush wells of pan lightly with vegetable oil. Set pan over medium heat. When oil begins to sizzle, add 2 tbsp (30 mL) batter to each well. Cook for 2 to 4 minutes or until bottoms are golden brown. Using two skewers, flip the puffs over. Cook for 2 to 3 minutes or until bottoms are golden brown and a toothpick inserted in the center comes out with a few moist crumbs attached. Remove pan from heat and transfer puffs to a plate. Let pan cool slightly.

6. Repeat with the remaining batter, brushing wells with oil and reheating pan before each batch.

7. In a small saucepan, combine marmalade and lemon juice. Heat over medium-low heat, whisking, until melted and warmed through.

8. Dust the puffs with confectioners' sugar and drizzle with marmalade syrup. Serve warm or at room temperature.

Banana Split Puffs

Bananas, chocolate, cherries and toasted nuts have a natural affinity for each other, so it's no surprise that they are so popular in ice cream sundae form. The same flavors are equally enchanting in decadent puffs.

Tip

There are two good reasons to use very ripe bananas: first, very ripe bananas will mash to near liquid consistency, yielding tender ebelskivers; second, the riper the bananas, the greater the banana flavor.

Variation

Chocolate Chip Banana Puffs: Omit the chocolate sauce and the cherry jam filling (the pecans remain optional). Add ⅔ cup miniature semisweet chocolate chips to the batter in step 3.

• 7-well ebelskiver pan

1½ cups	all-purpose flour	375 mL
¾ tsp	baking powder	3 mL
½ tsp	baking soda	2 mL
¼ tsp	salt	1 mL
3 tbsp	packed light brown sugar	45 mL
2	large eggs, separated	2
1 cup	milk	250 mL
1 cup	mashed very ripe bananas	250 mL
2 tbsp	unsalted butter, melted	30 mL
½ cup	chopped toasted pecans or walnuts (optional)	125 mL
	Vegetable oil	
⅔ cup	cherry or strawberry jam or preserves	150 mL
	Chocolate Sauce (page 90)	

1. In a large bowl, whisk together flour, baking powder, baking soda and salt.

2. In a medium bowl, whisk together brown sugar, egg yolks, milk, bananas and butter until well blended.

3. Add the egg yolk mixture to the flour mixture and stir until just blended (the batter will appear slightly lumpy). Gently stir in pecans (if using).

4. In a medium bowl, using an electric mixer on medium-high speed, beat egg whites until frothy. Increase speed to high and beat until stiff, but not dry, peaks form. Using a rubber spatula, gently mix one-third of the egg whites into the batter. Gently fold in the remaining whites.

5. Brush wells of pan lightly with oil. Set pan over medium heat. When oil begins to sizzle, add 1 tbsp (15 mL) batter to each well. Place 1 tsp (5 mL) jam in the center of each well and top with 1 tbsp (15 mL) batter. Cook for 2 to 4 minutes or until bottoms are golden brown. Using two skewers, flip the puffs over. Cook for 2 to 3 minutes or until bottoms are golden brown and a toothpick inserted in the center comes out with a bit of filling and a few moist crumbs attached. Remove pan from heat and transfer puffs to a plate. Let pan cool slightly.

6. Repeat with the remaining batter and jam, brushing wells with oil and reheating pan before each batch.

7. Drizzle the ebelskivers with chocolate sauce. Serve warm or at room temperature.

Turkish Coffee Ebelskivers

**Makes about
21 puffs**

The primary ingredients in Turkish coffee — dark coffee and cardamom — make these otherwise humble ebelskivers something extraordinary.

Variation

Cappuccino Ebelskivers:
Omit the cardamom and add ½ tsp (2 mL) ground cinnamon. Sprinkle the ebelskivers with cocoa powder and serve warm, with lightly sweetened whipped cream.

● **7-well ebelskiver pan**

1¼ cups	all-purpose flour	300 mL
1 tsp	ground cardamom	5 mL
¾ tsp	baking powder	3 mL
¼ tsp	salt	1 mL
2 tbsp	packed light brown sugar	30 mL
1 tbsp	instant espresso powder	15 mL
2	large eggs, separated	2
1 cup	milk	250 mL
2 tbsp	unsalted butter, melted	30 mL
1 tsp	vanilla extract	5 mL
	Vegetable oil	
	Confectioners' (icing) sugar	

1. In a large bowl, whisk together flour, cardamom, baking powder and salt.

2. In a medium bowl, whisk together brown sugar, espresso powder, egg yolks, milk, butter and vanilla until well blended.

3. Add the egg yolk mixture to the flour mixture and stir until just blended (the batter will appear slightly lumpy).

4. In a medium bowl, using an electric mixer on medium-high speed, beat egg whites until frothy. Increase speed to high and beat until stiff, but not dry, peaks form. Using a rubber spatula, gently mix one-third of the egg whites into the batter. Gently fold in the remaining whites.

5. Brush wells of pan lightly with oil. Set pan over medium heat. When oil begins to sizzle, add 2 tbsp (30 mL) batter to each well. Cook for 2 to 4 minutes or until bottoms are golden brown. Using two skewers, flip the puffs over. Cook for 2 to 3 minutes or until bottoms are golden brown and a toothpick inserted in the center comes out with a few moist crumbs attached. Remove pan from heat and transfer puffs to a plate. Let pan cool slightly.

6. Repeat with the remaining batter, brushing wells with oil and reheating pan before each batch.

7. Dust the ebelskivers with confectioners' sugar. Serve warm.

Coconut Ebelskivers with Coconut Chocolate Sauce

Here, a coconut-rich batter is imbued with fragrant vanilla, and the finished ebelskivers are drizzled with a ribbon of coconut chocolate sauce. It's a recipe that's sure to make you go weak in the knees.

● **7-well ebelskiver pan**

Coconut Chocolate Sauce

1 cup	semisweet chocolate chips	250 mL
2/3 cup	well-stirred canned coconut milk	150 mL
1 tbsp	dark rum	15 mL

Ebelskivers

1¼ cups	all-purpose flour	300 mL
¾ tsp	baking powder	3 mL
¼ tsp	salt	1 mL
2 tbsp	granulated sugar	30 mL
3	large eggs, separated	3
1 cup	milk	250 mL
2 tbsp	unsalted butter, melted	30 mL
1 tsp	vanilla extract	5 mL
1 cup	sweetened flaked coconut, divided	250 mL
	Vegetable oil	

1. *Sauce:* In a small saucepan, combine chocolate chips and coconut milk. Heat over low heat, whisking until melted and smooth. Remove from heat, whisk in rum and let cool while preparing the ebelskivers.

2. *Ebelskivers:* In a large bowl, whisk together flour, baking powder and salt.

3. In a medium bowl, whisk together sugar, egg yolks, milk, butter and vanilla until well blended.

4. Add the egg yolk mixture to the flour mixture and stir until just blended (the batter will appear slightly lumpy). Gently stir in ¾ cup (175 mL) of the coconut.

5. In a medium bowl, using an electric mixer on medium-high speed, beat egg whites until frothy. Increase speed to high and beat until stiff, but not dry, peaks form. Using a rubber spatula, gently mix one-third of the egg whites into the batter. Gently fold in the remaining whites.

Tips

For best results, do not use light coconut milk in the chocolate sauce recipe.

You can use 1 tsp (5 mL) rum extract in place of the rum, or omit it altogether.

6. Brush wells of pan lightly with oil. Set pan over medium heat. When oil begins to sizzle, add $1/2$ tsp (2 mL) coconut to each well. Immediately add 2 tbsp (30 mL) batter to each well. Cook for 2 to 4 minutes or until bottoms are golden brown. Using two skewers, flip the puffs over. Cook for 2 to 3 minutes or until bottoms are golden brown and a toothpick inserted in the center comes out with a few moist crumbs attached. Remove pan from heat and transfer puffs to a plate. Let pan cool slightly.

7. Repeat with the remaining coconut and batter, brushing wells with oil and reheating pan before each batch.

8. Drizzle the ebelskivers with the coconut chocolate sauce. Serve warm or at room temperature.

Piña Colada Puffs

**Makes about
35 puffs**

A double dose of coconut
delivers extra tropical
richness to a newfangled
take on a favorite flavor
combination. A dash of
ground ginger adds a
spicy-sweet note to these
rum-rich puffs.

Tips

For best results, do not use
light coconut milk.

● **7-well ebelskiver pan**

1⅔ cups	all-purpose flour	400 mL
1 tsp	baking powder	5 mL
1 tsp	ground ginger	5 mL
¾ tsp	salt	3 mL
3 tbsp	granulated sugar	45 mL
3	large eggs, separated	3
1	can (8 oz/227 mL) crushed pineapple, drained	1
¾ cup	coconut milk	175 mL
¼ cup	dark rum	60 mL
2 tbsp	unsalted butter, melted	30 mL
1 cup	sweetened flaked or shredded coconut	250 mL
	Vegetable oil	
	Confectioners' (icing) sugar	

1. In a large bowl, whisk together flour, baking powder, ginger and salt.

2. In a medium bowl, whisk together sugar, egg yolks, pineapple, coconut milk, rum and butter until well blended.

3. Add the egg yolk mixture to the flour mixture and stir until just blended (the batter will appear slightly lumpy). Gently stir in coconut.

4. In a medium bowl, using an electric mixer on medium-high speed, beat egg whites until frothy. Increase speed to high and beat until stiff, but not dry, peaks form. Using a rubber spatula, gently mix one-third of the egg whites into the batter. Gently fold in the remaining whites.

5. Brush wells of pan lightly with oil. Set pan over medium heat. When oil begins to sizzle, add 2 tbsp (30 mL) batter to each well. Cook for 2 to 4 minutes or until bottoms are golden brown. Using two skewers, flip the puffs over. Cook for 2 to 3 minutes or until bottoms are golden brown and a toothpick inserted in the center comes out with a few moist crumbs attached. Remove pan from heat and transfer puffs to a plate. Let pan cool slightly.

6. Repeat with the remaining batter, brushing wells with oil and reheating pan before each batch.

7. Dust the puffs with confectioners' sugar. Serve warm or at room temperature.

Pineapple Inside-Out Ebelskivers

Although this whimsical dessert bears little resemblance to the pineapple upside-down cake my mother would whip up at a moment's notice, it captures all of the essential elements: juicy pineapple, cherries and a gooey, brown sugar–based sauce.

Tips

You can use 1 cup (250 mL) purchased caramel sauce, warmed slightly, in place of the Salted Caramel Sauce.

An equal amount of dried cranberries may be used in place of the cherries.

● **7-well ebelskiver pan**

1¼ cups	all-purpose flour	300 mL
½ tsp	baking soda	2 mL
½ tsp	baking powder	2 mL
¼ tsp	salt	1 mL
2 tbsp	granulated sugar	30 mL
2	large eggs, separated	2
¾ cup	drained canned crushed pineapple	175 mL
¼ cup	sour cream or plain yogurt	60 mL
2 tbsp	unsalted butter, melted	30 mL
1 tsp	vanilla extract	5 mL
½ cup	dried cherries, chopped	125 mL
	Vegetable oil	
	Salted Caramel Sauce (page 108)	

1. In a large bowl, whisk together flour, baking soda, baking powder and salt.

2. In a medium bowl, whisk together sugar, egg yolks, pineapple, sour cream, butter and vanilla until well blended.

3. Add the egg yolk mixture to the flour mixture and stir until just blended (the batter will appear slightly lumpy). Gently stir in cherries.

4. In a medium bowl, using an electric mixer on medium-high speed, beat egg whites until frothy. Increase speed to high and beat until stiff, but not dry, peaks form. Using a rubber spatula, gently mix one-third of the egg whites into the batter. Gently fold in the remaining whites.

5. Brush wells of pan lightly with oil. Set pan over medium heat. When oil begins to sizzle, add 2 tbsp (30 mL) batter to each well. Cook for 2 to 4 minutes or until bottoms are golden brown. Using two skewers, flip the puffs over. Cook for 2 to 3 minutes or until bottoms are golden brown and a toothpick inserted in the center comes out with a few moist crumbs attached. Remove pan from heat and transfer puffs to a plate. Let pan cool slightly.

6. Repeat with the remaining batter, brushing wells with oil and reheating pan before each batch.

7. Serve the ebelskivers warm, with caramel sauce.

Tennessee Jam Cake Puffs

These puffs are based on Tennessee jam cake, a beloved dessert in the American South invented by some innovative home baker years ago. And oh, what an invention: blackberry jam, warm spices, buttery brown sugar cake and a creamy butterscotch frosting make it nothing short of magnificent. I've made the delectable experience available in minutes thanks to the ebelskiver pan.

● **7-well ebelskiver pan**

Butterscotch Icing

¼ cup	unsalted butter	60 mL
½ cup	packed dark brown sugar	125 mL
2 tbsp	milk	30 mL
1 cup	confectioners' (icing) sugar, sifted	250 mL

Puffs

1¼ cups	all-purpose flour	300 mL
1¼ tsp	ground cinnamon	6 mL
¾ tsp	baking powder	3 mL
½ tsp	ground allspice	2 mL
¼ tsp	salt	1 mL
¼ tsp	ground cloves	1 mL
3 tbsp	packed light brown sugar	15 mL
2	large eggs, separated	2
1 cup	milk	250 mL
3 tbsp	unsalted butter, melted	45 mL
1 tsp	vanilla extract	5 mL
½ cup	dried currants	125 mL
½ cup	chopped toasted pecans	125 mL
	Vegetable oil	
⅔ cup	blackberry jam	150 mL

1. *Icing:* In a small, heavy saucepan, melt butter over medium heat. Add brown sugar and bring to a gentle boil, whisking. Whisk in milk and return to a boil. Boil, whisking, for 2 minutes. Remove from heat and let cool. Whisk in confectioners' sugar.

2. *Puffs:* In a large bowl, whisk together flour, cinnamon, baking powder, allspice, salt and cloves.

3. In a medium bowl, whisk together brown sugar, egg yolks, milk, butter and vanilla until well blended.

4. Add the egg yolk mixture to the flour mixture and stir until just blended (the batter will appear slightly lumpy). Gently stir in currants and pecans.

5. In a medium bowl, using an electric mixer on medium-high speed, beat egg whites until frothy. Increase speed to high and beat until stiff, but not dry, peaks form. Using a rubber spatula, gently mix one-third of the egg whites into the batter. Gently fold in the remaining whites.

6. Brush wells of pan lightly with oil. Set pan over medium heat. When oil begins to sizzle, add 1 tbsp (15 mL) batter to each well. Place 1 tsp (5 mL) jam in the center of each well and top with 1 tbsp (15 mL) batter. Cook for 2 to 4 minutes or until bottoms are golden brown. Using two skewers, flip the puffs over. Cook for 2 to 3 minutes or until bottoms are golden brown and a toothpick inserted in the center comes out with a bit of filling and a few moist crumbs attached. Remove pan from heat and transfer puffs to a plate. Let pan cool slightly.

7. Repeat with the remaining batter and jam, brushing wells with oil and reheating pan before each batch.

8. Drizzle the ebelskivers with the butterscotch icing. Serve warm.

Fruitcake Puffs with Brandy Icing

There's no chance of these light, buttery fruitcake puffs hanging around unnoticed; they will disappear as fast as you make them.

• **7-well ebelskiver pan**

Puffs

1¼ cups	all-purpose flour	300 mL
¾ tsp	ground allspice	3 mL
½ tsp	baking powder	2 mL
¼ tsp	salt	1 mL
¼ tsp	baking soda	1 mL
3 tbsp	granulated sugar	45 mL
2	large eggs, separated	2
1 cup	milk	250 mL
2 tbsp	unsalted butter, melted	30 mL
⅔ cup	chopped assorted dried fruit	150 mL
½ cup	chopped toasted pecans or walnuts	125 mL
	Vegetable oil	

Brandy Icing

2 cups	confectioners' (icing) sugar	500 mL
1½ tbsp	brandy or dark rum	22 mL

1. *Puffs:* In a large bowl, whisk together flour, allspice, baking powder, salt and baking soda.

2. In a medium bowl, whisk together sugar, egg yolks, milk and butter until well blended.

3. Add the egg yolk mixture to the flour mixture and stir until just blended (the batter will appear slightly lumpy). Gently stir in dried fruit and pecans.

4. In a medium bowl, using an electric mixer on medium-high speed, beat egg whites until frothy. Increase speed to high and beat until stiff, but not dry, peaks form. Using a rubber spatula, gently mix one-third of the egg whites into the batter. Gently fold in the remaining whites.

Tips

For the dried fruit, try an assortment of apricots, cherries, cranberries, blueberries and/or dates.

An equal amount of milk may be used in place of the brandy in the icing.

5. Brush wells of pan lightly with oil. Set pan over medium heat. When oil begins to sizzle, add 2 tbsp (30 mL) batter to each well. Cook for 2 to 4 minutes or until bottoms are golden brown. Using two skewers, flip the puffs over. Cook for 2 to 3 minutes or until bottoms are golden brown and a toothpick inserted in the center comes out with a few moist crumbs attached. Remove pan from heat and transfer puffs to a plate. Let pan cool slightly.

6. Repeat with the remaining batter, brushing wells with oil and reheating pan before each batch.

7. *Icing:* In a small bowl, stir together confectioners' sugar and brandy until smooth.

8. Drizzle the puffs with the brandy icing. Serve warm or at room temperature.

Rum Raisin Ebelskivers

No need to wait for rum raisin ice cream to come back in vogue. This ebelskiver expression of the favorite flavor duo — further accentuated by a touch of nutmeg in the batter and a wickedly decadent rum sauce drizzled on top — amps things up like never before.

● **7-well ebelskiver pan**

Rum Sauce

½ cup	packed dark brown sugar	125 mL
½ cup	heavy or whipping (35%) cream	125 mL
¼ cup	unsalted butter	60 mL
¼ tsp	salt	1 mL
2 tbsp	dark rum	30 mL

Ebelskivers

1¼ cups	all-purpose flour	300 mL
¾ tsp	baking powder	3 mL
½ tsp	ground nutmeg	2 mL
¼ tsp	salt	1 mL
2 tbsp	granulated sugar	30 mL
2	large eggs, separated	2
1 cup	milk	250 mL
2 tbsp	unsalted butter, melted	30 mL
1 tsp	vanilla extract	5 mL
⅔ cup	raisins	150 mL
	Vegetable oil	

1. *Sauce:* In a medium, heavy saucepan, combine brown sugar, cream, butter and salt. Bring to a very gentle boil over medium heat, whisking often. Boil, whisking occasionally, for 5 to 6 minutes or until sugar is dissolved and sauce is slightly thickened. Remove from heat and whisk in rum. Let cool while preparing the ebelskivers.

2. *Ebelskivers:* In a large bowl, whisk together flour, baking powder, nutmeg and salt.

3. In a medium bowl, whisk together sugar, egg yolks, milk, butter and vanilla until well blended.

4. Add the egg yolk mixture to the flour mixture and stir until just blended (the batter will appear slightly lumpy). Gently stir in raisins.

Tips

You can use 2 tsp (10 mL) rum extract in place of the rum.

If the raisins are particularly large, coarsely chop them before adding them to the batter.

5. In a medium bowl, using an electric mixer on medium-high speed, beat egg whites until frothy. Increase speed to high and beat until stiff, but not dry, peaks form. Using a rubber spatula, gently mix one-third of the egg whites into the batter. Gently fold in the remaining whites.

6. Brush wells of pan lightly with oil. Set pan over medium heat. When oil begins to sizzle, add 2 tbsp (30 mL) batter to each well. Cook for 2 to 4 minutes or until bottoms are golden brown. Using two skewers, flip the puffs over. Cook for 2 to 3 minutes or until bottoms are golden brown and a toothpick inserted in the center comes out with a few moist crumbs attached. Remove pan from heat and transfer puffs to a plate. Let pan cool slightly.

7. Repeat with the remaining batter, brushing wells with oil and reheating pan before each batch.

8. Serve the ebelskivers warm, with the rum sauce.

Gingerbread Ebelskivers with Lemon Icing

Makes about 21 puffs

Too many ginger cakes, cookies and muffins lean toward the soothingly subtle. These are the opposite — they're spicy, with an ample amount of ginger, as well as cinnamon, cloves and dark molasses. A drizzle of lemon icing pushes the flavor to the max.

- **7-well ebelskiver pan**

Ebelskivers

1¼ cups	all-purpose flour	300 mL
2 tsp	ground ginger	10 mL
1 tsp	ground cinnamon	5 mL
½ tsp	baking powder	2 mL
¼ tsp	salt	1 mL
¼ tsp	baking soda	1 mL
¼ tsp	ground cloves	1 mL
2	large eggs, separated	2
1 cup	milk	250 mL
½ cup	dark (cooking) molasses	125 mL
2 tbsp	unsalted butter, melted	30 mL

Lemon Icing

2 cups	confectioners' (icing) sugar	500 mL
1 tsp	finely grated lemon zest	5 mL
1½ tbsp	freshly squeezed lemon juice	22 mL

1. *Ebelskivers:* In a large bowl, whisk together flour, ginger, cinnamon, baking powder, salt, baking powder and cloves.

2. In a medium bowl, whisk together egg yolks, milk, molasses and butter until well blended.

3. Add the egg yolk mixture to the flour mixture and stir until just blended (the batter will appear slightly lumpy).

4. In a medium bowl, using an electric mixer on medium-high speed, beat egg whites until frothy. Increase speed to high and beat until stiff, but not dry, peaks form. Using a rubber spatula, gently mix one-third of the egg whites into the batter. Gently fold in the remaining whites.

Tip

For a milder flavor, use an equal amount of liquid honey or pure maple syrup in place of the molasses.

5. Brush wells of pan lightly with oil. Set pan over medium heat. When oil begins to sizzle, add 2 tbsp (30 mL) batter to each well. Cook for 2 to 4 minutes or until bottoms are firm to the touch. Using two skewers, flip the puffs over. Cook for 2 to 3 minutes or until bottoms are firm to the touch and a toothpick inserted in the center comes out with a few moist crumbs attached. Remove pan from heat and transfer puffs to a plate. Let pan cool slightly.

6. Repeat with the remaining batter, brushing wells with oil and reheating pan before each batch.

7. *Icing:* In a small bowl, stir together confectioners' sugar, lemon zest and lemon juice until smooth.

8. Drizzle the ebelskivers with the lemon icing. Serve warm or at room temperature.

Vanilla Malt Ebelskivers

One word expresses the typical reaction to a candy-inspired dessert: "Yippee!" The toasty malt flavor of these puffs is amped up with a chocolate-covered malt ball at the center of each, making this dessert terrifically adult- and child-friendly.

Tip

Look for malted milk powder in the coffee aisle of the supermarket, where chocolate milk mixes are shelved, or in the baking aisle, where dried powdered milk is shelved.

- **7-well ebelskiver pan**

Ebelskivers

1¼ cups	all-purpose flour	300 mL
¾ tsp	baking powder	3 mL
¼ tsp	salt	1 mL
3 tbsp	granulated sugar	45 mL
2	large eggs, separated	2
1 cup	milk	250 mL
½ cup	malted milk powder	125 mL
3 tbsp	unsalted butter, melted	45 mL
1½ tsp	vanilla extract	7 mL
	Vegetable oil	
21	chocolate-covered malt ball candies	21

Vanilla Icing

2 cups	confectioners' (icing) sugar	500 mL
1½ tbsp	milk	22 mL
½ tsp	vanilla extract	2 mL

1. *Ebelskivers:* In a large bowl, whisk together flour, baking powder and salt.

2. In a medium bowl, whisk together sugar, egg yolks, milk, malted milk powder, butter and vanilla until well blended.

3. Add the egg yolk mixture to the flour mixture and stir until just blended (the batter will appear slightly lumpy).

4. In a medium bowl, using an electric mixer on medium-high speed, beat egg whites until frothy. Increase speed to high and beat until stiff, but not dry, peaks form. Using a rubber spatula, gently mix one-third of the egg whites into the batter. Gently fold in the remaining whites.

Variation

Chocolate-Covered Malt Puffs: Omit the vanilla icing. Serve the finished ebelskivers warm, drizzled with Chocolate Sauce (page 90).

5. Brush wells of pan lightly with oil. Set pan over medium heat. When oil begins to sizzle, add 1 tbsp (15 mL) batter to each well. Place 1 malt ball in the center of each well and top with 1 tbsp (15 mL) batter. Cook for 2 to 4 minutes or until bottoms are golden brown. Using two skewers, flip the pancakes over. Cook for 2 to 3 minutes or until bottoms are golden brown and a toothpick inserted in the center comes out with a bit of filling and a few moist crumbs attached. Remove pan from heat and transfer puffs to a plate. Let pan cool slightly.

6. Repeat with the remaining batter and malt balls, brushing wells with oil and reheating pan before each batch.

7. *Icing:* In a small bowl, stir together confectioners' sugar, milk and vanilla until smooth.

8. Drizzle the ebelskivers with the vanilla icing. Serve warm or at room temperature.

Mint Julep Ebelskivers

**Makes about
21 puffs**

Just the dessert for Derby
Day, or any Southern-
style celebration, these
puffs play on mint
julep flavors — notably
bourbon and fresh mint.

Tip

The Bourbon Mint Sauce
can be prepared up to
1 day in advance. Let cool
completely, then store in
an airtight container in the
refrigerator. Let come to
room temperature before
use.

● **7-well ebelskiver pan**

Bourbon Mint Sauce

½ cup	granulated sugar	125 mL
Pinch	salt	Pinch
¼ cup	unsalted butter, cut into small pieces	60 mL
3 tbsp	bourbon or whisky	45 mL
2 tbsp	chopped fresh mint	30 mL

Ebelskivers

1¼ cups	all-purpose flour	300 mL
½ tsp	baking powder	2 mL
¼ tsp	salt	1 mL
¼ tsp	baking soda	1 mL
2 tbsp	granulated sugar	30 mL
2	large eggs, separated	2
⅔ cup	sour cream	150 mL
½ cup	milk	125 mL
2 tbsp	unsalted butter, melted	30 mL
1 tsp	vanilla extract	5 mL
	Vegetable oil	
	Confectioners' (icing) sugar	
	Vanilla ice cream or lightly sweetened whipped cream	
	Fresh mint sprigs	

1. *Sauce:* In a small saucepan, combine sugar, salt, butter, bourbon and mint. Bring to a boil over medium-high heat, stirring. Boil, stirring, for 2 minutes or until sugar is dissolved. Remove from heat and let cool while preparing the ebelskivers.

2. *Ebelskivers:* In a large bowl, whisk together flour, baking powder, salt and baking soda.

3. In a medium bowl, whisk together sugar, egg yolks, sour cream, milk, butter and vanilla until well blended.

4. Add the egg yolk mixture to the flour mixture and stir until just blended (the batter will appear slightly lumpy).

Variation

Basil Julep Ebelskivers:
Substitute an equal amount of chopped fresh basil for the mint.

5. In a medium bowl, using an electric mixer on medium-high speed, beat egg whites until frothy. Increase speed to high and beat until stiff, but not dry, peaks form. Using a rubber spatula, gently mix one-third of the egg whites into the batter. Gently fold in the remaining whites.

6. Brush wells of pan lightly with oil. Set pan over medium heat. When oil begins to sizzle, add 2 tbsp (30 mL) batter to each well. Cook for 2 to 4 minutes or until bottoms are golden brown. Using two skewers, flip the puffs over. Cook for 2 to 3 minutes or until bottoms are golden brown and a toothpick inserted in the center comes out with a few moist crumbs attached. Remove pan from heat and transfer puffs to a plate. Let pan cool slightly.

7. Repeat with the remaining batter, brushing wells with oil and reheating pan before each batch.

8. Dust the ebelskivers with confectioners' sugar and drizzle with the bourbon mint sauce. Serve warm, with ice cream and mint sprigs.

Eggnog Ebelskivers

Regardless of your feelings for eggnog as a beverage, you will love it as ebelskivers. Ample amounts of cinnamon and nutmeg, as well as the rounded complexity of dark rum, lend the ebelskivers deep, delicious richness, plus an inviting fragrance that will put you in the holiday spirit as they sizzle on the stove.

Tip

The rum may be replaced with an equal amount of milk and 1 tsp (5 mL) rum, brandy or whiskey extract.

● **7-well ebelskiver pan**

1½ cups	all-purpose flour	375 mL
1 tsp	baking powder	5 mL
1 tsp	ground nutmeg	5 mL
¾ tsp	ground cinnamon	3 mL
¼ tsp	salt	1 mL
3 tbsp	granulated sugar	45 mL
3	large eggs, separated	3
1 cup	milk	250 mL
3 tbsp	unsalted butter, melted	45 mL
3 tbsp	dark rum, brandy or whiskey	45 mL
	Vegetable oil	
	Confectioners' (icing) sugar	

1. In a large bowl, whisk together flour, baking powder, nutmeg, cinnamon and salt.

2. In a medium bowl, whisk together sugar, egg yolks, milk, butter and rum until well blended.

3. Add the egg yolk mixture to the flour mixture and stir until just blended (the batter will appear slightly lumpy).

4. In a medium bowl, using an electric mixer on medium-high speed, beat egg whites until frothy. Increase speed to high and beat until stiff, but not dry, peaks form. Using a rubber spatula, gently mix one-third of the egg whites into the batter. Gently fold in the remaining whites.

5. Brush wells of pan lightly with oil. Set pan over medium heat. When oil begins to sizzle, add 2 tbsp (30 mL) batter to each well. Cook for 2 to 4 minutes or until bottoms are golden brown. Using two skewers, flip the puffs over. Cook for 2 to 3 minutes or until bottoms are golden brown and a toothpick inserted in the center comes out with a few moist crumbs attached. Remove pan from heat and transfer puffs to a plate. Let pan cool slightly.

6. Repeat with the remaining batter, brushing wells with oil and reheating pan before each batch.

7. Dust the ebelskivers with confectioners' sugar. Serve warm or at room temperature.

Savory Puffs for Appetizers, Snacks, Breakfast and Lunch

continued...

Popover Puffs

The egg-rich batter for these puffs produces a crisp-light appetizer akin to a popover, without ever turning on the oven.

● **7-well ebelskiver pan**

1¼ cups	all-purpose flour	300 mL
¾ tsp	baking powder	3 mL
½ tsp	salt	2 mL
4	large eggs, separated	4
¾ cup	milk	175 mL
2 tbsp	unsalted butter, melted	30 mL
	Vegetable oil	

1. In a large bowl, whisk together flour, baking powder and salt.

2. In a medium bowl, whisk together egg yolks, milk and butter until well blended.

3. Add the egg yolk mixture to the flour mixture and stir until just blended (the batter will appear slightly lumpy).

4. In a medium bowl, using an electric mixer on medium-high speed, beat egg whites until frothy. Increase speed to high and beat until stiff, but not dry, peaks form. Using a rubber spatula, gently mix one-third of the egg whites into the batter. Gently fold in the remaining whites.

5. Brush wells of pan lightly with oil. Set pan over medium heat. When oil begins to sizzle, add 2 tbsp (30 mL) batter to each well. Cook for 2 to 4 minutes or until bottoms are golden brown. Using two skewers, flip the puffs over. Cook for 2 to 3 minutes or until bottoms are golden brown and the puffs feel firm to the touch. Remove pan from heat and transfer puffs to a plate. Let pan cool slightly.

6. Repeat with the remaining batter, brushing wells with oil and reheating pan before each batch. Serve warm.

Stone-Ground Cornmeal Ebelskivers

Turns out the lightest, finest-textured cornbread in the world isn't baked at all! In fact, once you try these cornmeal puffs — as cute and fun to eat as they are lickety-split simple to prepare — you may never make cornbread any other way.

Tips

Although these ebelskivers are terrific with any variety of yellow cornmeal, they have the best texture and flavor when made with stone-ground cornmeal.

If you don't have any buttermilk on hand, stir 2 tsp (10 mL) lemon juice or white vinegar into 1 cup (250 mL) milk. Let stand for 5 to 10 minutes or until thickened. Use in place of the buttermilk.

Variation

Smoky Cornmeal Ebelskivers: Add 1 tsp (5 mL) chipotle chile powder and ½ tsp (2 mL) ground cumin in step 1, and gently stir in 1 cup (175 mL) shredded smoked Gouda cheese at the end of step 3.

● **7-well ebelskiver pan**

¾ cup	all-purpose flour	175 mL
½ cup	stone-ground yellow cornmeal	125 mL
½ tsp	baking soda	2 mL
¼ tsp	baking powder	1 mL
¼ tsp	salt	1 mL
1 tsp	granulated sugar	5 mL
2	large eggs, separated	2
1 cup	buttermilk	250 mL
2 tbsp	unsalted butter, melted	30 mL
	Vegetable oil	

1. In a large bowl, whisk together flour, cornmeal, baking soda, baking powder and salt.

2. In a medium bowl, whisk together sugar, egg yolks, buttermilk and butter until well blended.

3. Add the egg yolk mixture to the flour mixture and stir until just blended (the batter will appear slightly lumpy).

4. In a medium bowl, using an electric mixer on medium-high speed, beat egg whites until frothy. Increase speed to high and beat until stiff, but not dry, peaks form. Using a rubber spatula, gently mix one-third of the egg whites into the batter. Gently fold in the remaining whites.

5. Brush wells of pan lightly with oil. Set pan over medium heat. When oil begins to sizzle, add 2 tbsp (30 mL) batter to each well. Cook for 2 to 4 minutes or until bottoms are golden brown. Using two skewers, flip the puffs over. Cook for 2 to 3 minutes or until bottoms are golden brown and a toothpick inserted in the center comes out with a few moist crumbs attached. Remove pan from heat and transfer puffs to a plate. Let pan cool slightly.

6. Repeat with the remaining batter, brushing wells with oil and reheating pan before each batch. Serve warm or at room temperature.

Fresh Corn Spoon Bread Puffs

Spoon bread is to Southerners what soufflés are to the French: cloudlike and classic. Here, I've made double-corn puffs that taste just like time-intensive spoon bread (perhaps even better).

Variation

Basil-Corn Spoon Bread Puffs: Omit the Monterey Jack cheese and green onions. Gently stir in ⅓ cup (75 mL) freshly grated Parmesan cheese and ¼ cup (60 mL) chopped fresh basil leaves at the end of step 3.

- Blender or food processor
- 7-well ebelskiver pan

1 cup	fresh or thawed frozen corn kernels	250 mL
½ cup	milk	125 mL
¾ cup	all-purpose flour	175 mL
½ cup	yellow cornmeal	125 mL
¾ tsp	baking powder	3 mL
½ tsp	salt	2 mL
1 tbsp	seeded minced jalapeño pepper	15 mL
1 tsp	granulated sugar	5 mL
3	large eggs, separated	3
2 tbsp	unsalted butter, melted	30 mL
1 cup	shredded Monterey Jack cheese	250 mL
⅓ cup	finely chopped green onions	75 mL
	Vegetable oil	

1. In blender, combine corn and milk; process until smooth.

2. In a large bowl, whisk together flour, cornmeal, baking powder and salt.

3. In a medium bowl, whisk together corn mixture, jalapeño, sugar, egg yolks and butter until well blended.

4. Add the egg yolk mixture to the flour mixture and stir until just blended (the batter will appear slightly lumpy). Gently stir in cheese and green onions.

5. In a medium bowl, using an electric mixer on medium-high speed, beat egg whites until frothy. Increase speed to high and beat until stiff, but not dry, peaks form. Using a rubber spatula, gently mix one-third of the egg whites into the batter. Gently fold in the remaining whites.

6. Brush wells of pan lightly with oil. Set pan over medium heat. When oil begins to sizzle, add 2 tbsp (30 mL) batter to each well. Cook for 2 to 4 minutes or until bottoms are golden brown. Using two skewers, flip the puffs over. Cook for 2 to 3 minutes or until bottoms are golden brown and a toothpick inserted in the center comes out with a few moist crumbs attached. Remove pan from heat and transfer puffs to a plate. Let pan cool slightly.

7. Repeat with the remaining batter, brushing wells with oil and reheating pan before each batch. Serve warm or at room temperature.

Rosemary Parmesan Puffs

The sweet-salty umami flavor of Parmesan is a perfect match for the aromatic intensity of rosemary in these easy-peasy puffs.

Tips

For a milder flavor, use regular olive oil in place of the extra virgin olive oil.

An equal amount of another hard Italian cheese, such as Romano or Asiago, may be used in place of the Parmesan.

● **7-well ebelskiver pan**

1¼ cups	all-purpose flour	300 mL
¾ tsp	baking powder	3 mL
¼ tsp	salt	1 mL
¼ tsp	freshly cracked black pepper	1 mL
1 tsp	granulated sugar	5 mL
2	large eggs, separated	2
2	cloves garlic, minced	2
1 cup	milk	250 mL
2 tbsp	extra virgin olive oil	30 mL
2 tsp	finely chopped fresh rosemary	10 mL
¾ cup	freshly grated Parmesan cheese	175 mL
	Olive oil or vegetable oil	

1. In a large bowl, whisk together flour, baking powder, salt and pepper.

2. In a medium bowl, whisk together sugar, egg yolks, garlic, milk, oil and rosemary until well blended.

3. Add the egg yolk mixture to the flour mixture and stir until just blended (the batter will appear slightly lumpy). Gently stir in cheese.

4. In a medium bowl, using an electric mixer on medium-high speed, beat egg whites until frothy. Increase speed to high and beat until stiff, but not dry, peaks form. Using a rubber spatula, gently mix one-third of the egg whites into the batter. Gently fold in the remaining whites.

5. Brush wells of pan lightly with oil. Set pan over medium heat. When oil begins to sizzle, add 2 tbsp (30 mL) batter to each well. Cook for 2 to 4 minutes or until bottoms are golden brown. Using two skewers, flip the puffs over. Cook for 2 to 3 minutes or until bottoms are golden brown and a toothpick inserted in the center comes out with a few moist crumbs attached. Remove pan from heat and transfer puffs to a plate. Let pan cool slightly.

6. Repeat with the remaining batter, brushing wells with oil and reheating pan before each batch. Serve warm or at room temperature.

Olivada Ebelskivers

Olivada, an olive spread made of olives, olive oil and herbs and spices, is the sophisticated surprise nestled in these rosemary-scented ebelskivers. In answer to your question, yes, they make sublime appetizers.

Tip

Look for jars of prepared olivada in the section of the supermarket where olives are shelved or in the international foods section. Olivada and tapenade are virtually identical products and can be used interchangeably in this recipe. *Olivada* is the Italian name for the olive spread; *tapenade* is the French name.

● **7-well ebelskiver pan**

1¼ cups	all-purpose flour	300 mL
¾ tsp	baking powder	3 mL
¼ tsp	salt	1 mL
1 tsp	granulated sugar	5 mL
2	large eggs, separated	2
1 cup	milk	250 mL
2 tbsp	extra virgin olive oil	30 mL
2 tsp	minced fresh rosemary	10 mL
	Olive oil or vegetable oil	
⅔ cup	prepared olivada (black olive tapenade)	150 mL

1. In a large bowl, whisk together flour, baking powder and salt.

2. In a medium bowl, whisk together sugar, egg yolks, milk, oil and rosemary until well blended.

3. Add the egg yolk mixture to the flour mixture and stir until just blended (the batter will appear slightly lumpy).

4. In a medium bowl, using an electric mixer on medium-high speed, beat egg whites until frothy. Increase speed to high and beat until stiff, but not dry, peaks form. Using a rubber spatula, gently mix one-third of the egg whites into the batter. Gently fold in the remaining whites.

5. Brush wells of pan lightly with oil. Set pan over medium heat. When oil begins to sizzle, add 1 tbsp (15 mL) batter to each well. Place 1 tsp (5 mL) olivada in the center of each pancake and top with 1 tbsp (15 mL) batter. Cook for 2 to 4 minutes or until bottoms are golden brown. Using two skewers, flip the puffs over. Cook for 2 to 3 minutes or until bottoms are golden brown and a toothpick inserted in the center comes out with a bit of filling and a few moist crumbs attached. Remove pan from heat and transfer puffs to a plate. Let pan cool slightly.

6. Repeat with the remaining batter and olivada, brushing wells with oil and reheating pan before each batch. Serve warm or at room temperature.

Smoked Paprika Ebelskivers with Chimichurri

Chimichurri, a quick blended sauce of olive oil, fresh herbs, acid (such as lemon juice or vinegar) and a touch of heat, is the national condiment of both Uruguay and Argentina. Although it is renowned for pairing up with grilled steak, it also plays well with these smoky, cheese-filled puffs.

- Blender
- 7-well ebelskiver pan

Chimichurri

2	cloves garlic	2
1 cup	packed fresh cilantro or flat-leaf (Italian) parsley leaves	250 mL
1/4 tsp	hot pepper flakes	1 mL
1/4 cup	extra virgin olive oil	60 mL
2 tbsp	red wine vinegar	30 mL
	Salt	

Ebelskivers

1 1/4 cups	all-purpose flour	300 mL
1 1/2 tsp	hot or sweet smoked paprika	7 mL
3/4 tsp	baking powder	3 mL
1/4 tsp	salt	1 mL
1 tsp	granulated sugar	5 mL
2	large eggs, separated	2
1 cup	milk	250 mL
2 tbsp	unsalted butter, melted	30 mL
	Olive oil or vegetable oil	
3 oz	queso fresco or cotija cheese, cut into 1/2-inch (1 cm) cubes	90 g

1. *Chimichurri:* In blender, combine garlic, cilantro, hot pepper flakes, oil and vinegar; purée until smooth. Season to taste with salt. Set aside.

2. *Ebelskivers:* In a large bowl, whisk together flour, paprika, baking powder and salt.

3. In a medium bowl, whisk together sugar, egg yolks, milk and butter until well blended.

4. Add the egg yolk mixture to the flour mixture and stir until just blended (the batter will appear slightly lumpy).

Tips

An equal amount of chipotle chile powder may be used in place of the smoked paprika.

Mild feta cheese may be used in place of the queso fresco.

5. In a medium bowl, using an electric mixer on medium-high speed, beat egg whites until frothy. Increase speed to high and beat until stiff, but not dry, peaks form. Using a rubber spatula, gently mix one-third of the egg whites into the batter. Gently fold in the remaining whites.

6. Brush wells of pan lightly with oil. Set pan over medium heat. When oil begins to sizzle, add 1 tbsp (15 mL) batter to each well. Place 1 cheese cube in the center of each well and top with 1 tbsp (15 mL) batter. Cook for 2 to 4 minutes or until bottoms are golden brown. Using two skewers, flip the puffs over. Cook for 2 to 3 minutes or until bottoms are golden brown and a toothpick inserted in the center comes out with a bit of cheese and a few moist crumbs attached. Remove pan from heat and transfer puffs to a plate. Let pan cool slightly.

7. Repeat with the remaining batter and cheese cubes, brushing wells with oil and reheating pan before each batch.

8. Serve the ebelskivers warm, with the chimichurri.

Stuffed Tamale Puffs

Makes about 28 puffs

Thanks to a few Southwestern additions — yellow cornmeal, cumin, corn and cilantro — these puffs have real pizzazz. Best of all, they require little more than a quick whisk, stir and sizzle to prepare.

Tip

If you don't have any buttermilk on hand, stir 2 tsp (10 mL) lemon juice or white vinegar into 1 cup (250 mL) milk. Let stand for 5 to 10 minutes or until thickened. Use in place of the buttermilk.

- **7-well ebelskiver pan**

¾ cup	stone-ground yellow cornmeal	175 mL
⅓ cup	all-purpose flour	75 mL
2 tsp	ground cumin	10 mL
½ tsp	baking soda	2 mL
¼ tsp	baking powder	1 mL
¼ tsp	salt	1 mL
¼ tsp	cayenne pepper	1 mL
2	large eggs, separated	2
1 cup	buttermilk	250 mL
2 tbsp	unsalted butter, melted	30 mL
1 cup	fresh or thawed frozen corn kernels	250 mL
¼ cup	chopped fresh cilantro	60 mL
	Vegetable oil	
4 oz	pepper Jack cheese, cut into ½-inch (1 cm) cubes	125 g
	Tomato salsa	

1. In a large bowl, whisk together cornmeal, flour, cumin, baking soda, baking powder, salt and cayenne.

2. In a medium bowl, whisk together egg yolks, buttermilk and butter until well blended.

3. Add the egg yolk mixture to the flour mixture and stir until just blended (the batter will appear slightly lumpy). Gently stir in corn and cilantro.

4. In a medium bowl, using an electric mixer on medium-high speed, beat egg whites until frothy. Increase speed to high and beat until stiff, but not dry, peaks form. Using a rubber spatula, gently mix one-third of the egg whites into the batter. Gently fold in the remaining whites.

Tips

If you are not a cilantro fan, replace it with an equal amount of chopped green onions.

An equal amount of Monterey Jack or sharp (old) Cheddar cheese may be used in place of the pepper Jack cheese.

5. Brush wells of pan lightly with oil. Set pan over medium heat. When oil begins to sizzle, add 1 tbsp (15 mL) batter to each well. Place 1 cheese cube in the center of each well and top with 1 tbsp (15 mL) batter. Cook for 2 to 4 minutes or until bottoms are golden brown. Using two skewers, flip the puffs over. Cook for 2 to 3 minutes or until bottoms are golden brown and a toothpick inserted in the center comes out with a bit of cheese and a few moist crumbs attached. Remove pan from heat and transfer puffs to a plate. Let pan cool slightly.

6. Repeat with the remaining batter and cheese cubes, brushing wells with oil and reheating pan before each batch.

7. Serve the puffs warm, with the salsa.

Roasted Pepper Feta Puffs

Cheesy, herbed, roasted pepper–flecked puffs are sure to please a crowd, not to mention you. The batter can be stirred up and the puffs ready to serve in less than 20 minutes.

Tip

An equal amount of water-packed mozzarella or fontina may be used in place of the feta cheese. Goat cheese can also be used: use 1 tsp (5 mL) mild, creamy goat cheese in place of each cheese cube.

● **7-well ebelskiver pan**

1¼ cups	all-purpose flour	300 mL
1¼ tsp	dried oregano	6 mL
¾ tsp	baking powder	3 mL
¼ tsp	salt	1 mL
¼ tsp	cayenne pepper	1 mL
1 tsp	granulated sugar	5 mL
2	large eggs, separated	2
1 cup	milk	250 mL
2 tbsp	extra virgin olive oil	30 mL
½ cup	finely chopped drained roasted red bell peppers	125 mL
	Olive oil or vegetable oil	
3 oz	feta cheese, cut into ½-inch (1 cm) cubes and patted dry	90 g

1. In a large bowl, whisk together flour, oregano, baking powder, salt and cayenne.

2. In a medium bowl, whisk together sugar, egg yolks, milk and oil until well blended.

3. Add the egg yolk mixture to the flour mixture and stir until just blended (the batter will appear slightly lumpy). Gently stir in roasted peppers.

4. In a medium bowl, using an electric mixer on medium-high speed, beat egg whites until frothy. Increase speed to high and beat until stiff, but not dry, peaks form. Using a rubber spatula, gently mix one-third of the egg whites into the batter. Gently fold in the remaining whites.

5. Brush wells of pan lightly with oil. Set pan over medium heat. When oil begins to sizzle, add 1 tbsp (15 mL) batter to each well. Place 1 cheese cube in the center of each well and top with 1 tbsp (15 mL) batter. Cook for 2 to 4 minutes or until bottoms are golden brown. Using two skewers, flip the puffs over. Cook for 2 to 3 minutes or until bottoms are golden brown and a toothpick inserted in the center comes out with a bit of cheese and a few moist crumbs attached. Remove pan from heat and transfer puffs to a plate. Let pan cool slightly.

6. Repeat with the remaining batter and cheese cubes, brushing wells with oil and reheating pan before each batch. Serve warm or at room temperature.

Scallion Curry Puffs with Chutney (page 162)

Zucchini Dill Ebelskivers (page 170)

Blue Cheese and Pecan Ebelskivers
with Pear Compote (page 174)

Antipasto Puffs (page 186)

Mayan Chocolate Puffs (page 197)

Linzer Puffs *(at top)* (page 214) and Barazek Puffs (page 229)

Buckwheat Blini Puffs (page 209)

Pa Jeon (page 243)

Green Chile and Jalapeño Ebelskivers

Ebelskivers seem like something new — by way of the American Southwest — in these moist, rich puffs dolled up with pepper Jack cheese, green chiles and jalapeño.

Tips

Any variety of yellow cornmeal works well in this recipe, but for the best texture and corn flavor, use stone-ground cornmeal.

An equal amount of Monterey Jack or sharp (old) Cheddar cheese may be used in place of the pepper Jack cheese.

● **7-well ebelskiver pan**

1 cup	all-purpose flour	250 mL
¼ cup	yellow cornmeal	60 mL
1 tsp	ground cumin	5 mL
¾ tsp	baking powder	3 mL
½ tsp	salt	1 mL
1 tsp	granulated sugar	5 mL
2	large eggs, separated	2
1	jalapeño pepper, seeded and chopped	1
1	can (4½ oz/127 mL) green chiles	1
½ cup	milk	125 mL
	Vegetable oil	
3 oz	pepper Jack cheese, cut into ½-inch (1 cm) cubes	90 g

1. In a large bowl, whisk together flour, cornmeal, cumin, baking powder and salt.

2. In a medium bowl, whisk together sugar, egg yolks, jalapeño, green chiles, milk and 2 tbsp (30 mL) oil until well blended.

3. Add the egg yolk mixture to the flour mixture and stir until just blended (the batter will appear slightly lumpy).

4. In a medium bowl, using an electric mixer on medium-high speed, beat egg whites until frothy. Increase speed to high and beat until stiff, but not dry, peaks form. Using a rubber spatula, gently mix one-third of the egg whites into the batter. Gently fold in the remaining whites.

5. Brush wells of pan lightly with oil. Set pan over medium heat. When oil begins to sizzle, add 1 tbsp (15 mL) batter to each well. Place 1 cheese cube in the center of each well and top with 1 tbsp (15 mL) batter. Cook for 2 to 4 minutes or until bottoms are golden brown. Using two skewers, flip the puffs over. Cook for 2 to 3 minutes or until bottoms are golden brown and a toothpick inserted in the center comes out with a bit of cheese and a few moist crumbs attached. Remove pan from heat and transfer puffs to a plate. Let pan cool slightly.

6. Repeat with the remaining batter and cheese cubes, brushing wells with oil and reheating pan before each batch. Serve warm or at room temperature.

Scallion Curry Puffs with Chutney

These puffs feature the flavors of India: aromatic curry powder, yogurt and spicy-sweet chutney. I love to pair them with cold chicken or chicken salad on hot summer nights, or with steaming mugs of soup in mid-winter.

● **7-well ebelskiver pan**

1¼ cups	all-purpose flour	300 mL
2 tsp	curry powder (mild, medium or hot)	10 mL
½ tsp	baking soda	2 mL
½ tsp	salt	2 mL
¼ tsp	baking powder	1 mL
1 tsp	granulated sugar	5 mL
2	large eggs, separated	2
2 cups	plain yogurt, divided	500 mL
2 tbsp	unsalted butter, melted	30 mL
½ cup	chopped green onions (scallions)	125 mL
	Vegetable oil	
½ cup	mango or Major Grey's chutney	125 mL

1. In a large bowl, whisk together flour, curry powder, baking soda, salt and baking powder.

2. In a medium bowl, whisk together sugar, egg yolks, 1 cup (250 mL) of the yogurt and butter until well blended.

3. Add the egg yolk mixture to the flour mixture and stir until just blended (the batter will appear slightly lumpy). Gently stir in green onions.

4. In a medium bowl, using an electric mixer on medium-high speed, beat egg whites until frothy. Increase speed to high and beat until stiff, but not dry, peaks form. Using a rubber spatula, gently mix one-third of the egg whites into the batter. Gently fold in the remaining whites.

Supermarkets use the names "scallions" and "green onions" interchangeably for the same vegetable.

For best results, do not use nonfat yogurt in this recipe.

5. Brush wells of pan lightly with oil. Set pan over medium heat. When oil begins to sizzle, add 1 tbsp (15 mL) batter to each well. Place 1 tsp (5 mL) chutney in the center of each well and top with 1 tbsp (15 mL) batter. Cook for 2 to 4 minutes or until bottoms are golden brown. Using two skewers, flip the puffs over. Cook for 2 to 3 minutes or until bottoms are golden brown and a toothpick inserted in the center comes out with a bit of filling and a few moist crumbs attached. Remove pan from heat and transfer puffs to a plate. Let pan cool slightly.

6. Repeat with the remaining batter and chutney, brushing wells with oil and reheating pan before each batch.

7. Serve the puffs warm, with the remaining yogurt.

Mushroom-Stuffed Puffs

Mushrooms have a rich earthiness that is best accentuated in straight-forward preparations such as these inside-out stuffed mushroom puffs.

● **7-well ebelskiver pan**

Mushroom Filling

1 tbsp	extra virgin olive oil	15 mL
2	cloves garlic, minced	2
1¼ cups	chopped mushrooms	300 mL
	Salt and freshly cracked black pepper	

Puffs

1¼ cups	all-purpose flour	300 mL
¾ tsp	baking powder	3 mL
¼ tsp	salt	1 mL
1 tsp	granulated sugar	5 mL
2	large eggs, separated	2
1 cup	milk	250 mL
2 tbsp	unsalted butter, melted	30 mL
2 tsp	minced fresh thyme	10 mL
	Olive oil or vegetable oil	

1. *Filling:* In a large skillet, heat oil over medium-high heat. Add garlic and cook, stirring, for 30 seconds. Add mushrooms and cook, stirring, for 2 to 4 minutes or until mushrooms have given off their juices and softened. Remove from heat and season to taste with salt and pepper. Let cool completely.

2. *Puffs:* In a large bowl, whisk together flour, baking powder and salt.

3. In a medium bowl, whisk together sugar, egg yolks, milk, butter and thyme until well blended.

4. Add the egg yolk mixture to the flour mixture and stir until just blended (the batter will appear slightly lumpy).

5. In a medium bowl, using an electric mixer on medium-high speed, beat egg whites until frothy. Increase speed to high and beat until stiff, but not dry, peaks form. Using a rubber spatula, gently mix one-third of the egg whites into the batter. Gently fold in the remaining whites.

Use any variety of mushrooms you prefer, including button, cremini or wild mushrooms.

One tsp (5 mL) dried thyme may be used in place of the fresh thyme.

6. Brush wells of pan lightly with oil. Set pan over medium heat. When oil begins to sizzle, add 1 tbsp (15 mL) batter to each well. Place 1 tsp (5 mL) filling in the center of each well and top with 1 tbsp (15 mL) batter. Cook for 2 to 4 minutes or until bottoms are golden brown. Using two skewers, flip the puffs over. Cook for 2 to 3 minutes or until bottoms are golden brown and a toothpick inserted in the center comes out with a bit of filling and a few moist crumbs attached. Remove pan from heat and transfer puffs to a plate. Let pan cool slightly.

7. Repeat with the remaining batter and filling, brushing wells with oil and reheating pan before each batch. Serve warm or at room temperature.

NYC Onion Rye Puffs

I have had my share of
New York City onion rye
bread, and these puffs are
worthy of their eponym.
They are easy to make,
but that's not the point
here — deliciousness is.

● **7-well ebelskiver pan**

Onion Filling

1½ tbsp	unsalted butter	22 mL
1¼ cups	chopped onion	300 mL
	Salt and freshly ground black pepper	

Puffs

¾ cup	all-purpose flour	175 mL
⅓ cup	rye flour	75 mL
1½ tbsp	yellow cornmeal	22 mL
1 tbsp	caraway seeds, crushed	15 mL
¾ tsp	baking powder	3 mL
½ tsp	salt	2 mL
2 tsp	packed light brown sugar	10 mL
2	large eggs, separated	2
1 cup	milk	250 mL
2 tbsp	unsalted butter, melted	30 mL
	Vegetable oil	

1. *Filling:* In a large skillet, melt butter over medium-high heat. Add onion and cook, stirring, for 5 to 8 minutes or until softened and golden. Remove from heat and season to taste with salt and pepper. Let cool completely.

2. *Puffs:* In a large bowl, whisk together all-purpose flour, rye flour, cornmeal, caraway, baking powder and salt.

3. In a medium bowl, whisk together brown sugar, egg yolks, milk and butter until well blended.

4. Add the egg yolk mixture to the flour mixture and stir until just blended (the batter will appear slightly lumpy).

5. In a medium bowl, using an electric mixer on medium-high speed, beat egg whites until frothy. Increase speed to high and beat until stiff, but not dry, peaks form. Using a rubber spatula, gently mix one-third of the egg whites into the batter. Gently fold in the remaining whites.

Tips

One medium onion will yield about 1¼ cups (300 mL) chopped onion.

Either light or dark rye flour may be used in this recipe.

6. Brush wells of pan lightly with oil. Set pan over medium heat. When oil begins to sizzle, add 1 tbsp (15 mL) batter to each well. Place 1 tsp (5 mL) filling in the center of each well and top with 1 tbsp (15 mL) batter. Cook for 2 to 4 minutes or until bottoms are golden brown. Using two skewers, flip the puffs over. Cook for 2 to 3 minutes or until bottoms are golden brown and a toothpick inserted in the center comes out with a bit of filling and a few moist crumbs attached. Remove pan from heat and transfer puffs to a plate. Let pan cool slightly.

7. Repeat with the remaining batter and filling, brushing wells with oil and reheating pan before each batch. Serve warm or at room temperature.

Potato Latke Puffs

This new way with latkes is a delicious main course for brunch as well as a super supper side dish. The batter for these crispy, puffy potato pancakes is enhanced by the simple addition of green onions, which add a hit of freshness and color.

Tips

One lb (500 g) of potatoes is about 3 medium.

An equal amount of thawed frozen shredded potatoes may be used in place of the fresh potatoes.

Variation

Sweet Potato Latke Puffs: Replace the potatoes with shredded peeled sweet potatoes.

● **7-well ebelskiver pan**

3 cups	coarsely shredded peeled russet potatoes (about 1 lb/500 g)	750 mL
2/3 cup	all-purpose flour	150 mL
3/4 tsp	baking powder	3 mL
1/4 tsp	salt	1 mL
1/4 tsp	freshly cracked black pepper	1 mL
2	large eggs, separated	2
1 cup	milk	250 mL
2 tbsp	unsalted butter, melted	30 mL
3/4 cup	chopped green onions	175 mL
	Vegetable oil	

1. Place potatoes between several layers of paper towels, wrap tightly and squeeze out as much water as possible.

2. In a large bowl, whisk together flour, baking powder, salt and pepper.

3. In a medium bowl, whisk together egg yolks, milk and butter until well blended.

4. Add the egg yolk mixture to the flour mixture and stir until just blended (the batter will appear slightly lumpy). Gently stir in potatoes and green onions.

5. In a medium bowl, using an electric mixer on medium-high speed, beat egg whites until frothy. Increase speed to high and beat until stiff, but not dry, peaks form. Using a rubber spatula, gently mix one-third of the egg whites into the batter. Gently fold in the remaining whites.

6. Brush wells of pan lightly with oil. Set pan over medium heat. When oil begins to sizzle, add 2 tbsp (30 mL) batter to each well. Cook for 2 to 4 minutes or until bottoms are golden brown. Using two skewers, flip the puffs over. Cook for 2 to 3 minutes or until bottoms are golden brown and a toothpick inserted in the center comes out with a few moist crumbs attached. Remove pan from heat and transfer puffs to a plate. Let pan cool slightly.

7. Repeat with the remaining batter, brushing wells with oil and reheating pan before each batch. Serve warm.

Butternut Squash Ebelskivers

No doubt about it, anything with butternut squash in it, on it or beside it is just right by me. Here, it is shredded and stirred into the batter for what is sure to be your favorite new appetizer too.

Tip

An equal amount of grated Romano, Manchego or Asiago cheese may be used in place of the Parmesan.

Variation

An equal amount of finely shredded carrots may be used in place of the squash.

● **7-well ebelskiver pan**

1¼ cups	all-purpose flour	300 mL
1 tsp	baking powder	5 mL
½ tsp	salt	2 mL
¼ tsp	freshly ground black pepper	1 mL
1	clove garlic, minced	1
1½ tsp	minced fresh thyme	7 mL
2	large eggs, separated	2
1 cup	milk	250 mL
2 tbsp	unsalted butter, melted	30 mL
1 cup	finely shredded butternut or other winter squash	250 mL
½ cup	freshly grated Parmesan cheese Vegetable oil	125 mL

1. In a large bowl, whisk together flour, baking powder, salt and pepper.

2. In a medium bowl, whisk together garlic, thyme, egg yolks, milk and butter until well blended.

3. Add the egg yolk mixture to the flour mixture and stir until just blended (the batter will appear slightly lumpy). Gently stir in squash and cheese.

4. In a medium bowl, using an electric mixer on medium-high speed, beat egg whites until frothy. Increase speed to high and beat until stiff, but not dry, peaks form. Using a rubber spatula, gently mix one-third of the egg whites into the batter. Gently fold in the remaining whites.

5. Brush wells of pan lightly with oil. Set pan over medium heat. When oil begins to sizzle, add 2 tbsp (30 mL) batter to each well. Cook for 2 to 4 minutes or until bottoms are golden brown. Using two skewers, flip the puffs over. Cook for 2 to 3 minutes or until bottoms are golden brown and a toothpick inserted in the center comes out with a few moist crumbs attached. Remove pan from heat and transfer puffs to a plate. Let pan cool slightly.

6. Repeat with the remaining batter, brushing wells with oil and reheating pan before each batch. Serve warm.

Zucchini Dill Ebelskivers

Zucchini and dill have a real affinity. Here, they come together in tender ebelskivers, which highlight their delicate flavors.

Tip

Other shredded summer squash varieties, such as pattypan or crookneck, may be used in place of the zucchini.

● **7-well ebelskiver pan**

1½ cups	all-purpose flour	375 mL
1½ tsp	baking powder	7 mL
¼ tsp	salt	1 mL
¼ tsp	freshly cracked black pepper	1 mL
3	large eggs, separated	3
1 cup	milk	250 mL
2 tbsp	unsalted butter, melted	30 mL
2 tbsp	chopped fresh dill	30 mL
1 cup	shredded zucchini	250 mL
⅓ cup	freshly grated Romano or Parmesan cheese	75 mL
	Vegetable oil	

1. In a large bowl, whisk together flour, baking powder, salt and pepper.

2. In a medium bowl, whisk together egg yolks, milk, butter and dill until well blended.

3. Add the egg yolk mixture to the flour mixture and stir until just blended (the batter will appear slightly lumpy). Gently stir in zucchini and cheese.

4. In a medium bowl, using an electric mixer on medium-high speed, beat egg whites until frothy. Increase speed to high and beat until stiff, but not dry, peaks form. Using a rubber spatula, gently mix one-third of the egg whites into the batter. Gently fold in the remaining whites.

5. Brush wells of pan lightly with oil. Set pan over medium heat. When oil begins to sizzle, add 2 tbsp (30 mL) batter to each well. Cook for 2 to 4 minutes or until bottoms are golden brown. Using two skewers, flip the puffs over. Cook for 2 to 3 minutes or until bottoms are golden brown and a toothpick inserted in the center comes out with a few moist crumbs attached. Remove pan from heat and transfer puffs to a plate. Let pan cool slightly.

6. Repeat with the remaining batter, brushing wells with oil and reheating pan before each batch. Serve warm.

Double-Cheese Ebelskivers

Makes about 21 puffs

Extra-sharp (extra-old) Cheddar and Parmesan cheese star in these flavorful, easy-to-make ebelskivers.

Tip

An equal amount of grated Romano, Asiago or Manchego cheese may be used in place of the Parmesan.

● **7-well ebelskiver pan**

1¼ cups	all-purpose flour	300 mL
¾ tsp	baking powder	3 mL
¼ tsp	salt	1 mL
1 tsp	granulated sugar	5 mL
2	large eggs, separated	2
1 cup	milk	250 mL
2 tbsp	unsalted butter, melted	30 mL
2 tsp	Dijon mustard	10 mL
½ cup	freshly grated Parmesan cheese	125 mL
	Vegetable oil	
3 oz	extra-sharp (extra-old) Cheddar cheese, cut into ½-inch (1 cm) cubes	90 g

1. In a large bowl, whisk together flour, baking powder and salt.

2. In a medium bowl, whisk together sugar, egg yolks, milk, butter and mustard until well blended.

3. Add the egg yolk mixture to the flour mixture and stir until just blended (the batter will appear slightly lumpy). Gently stir in Parmesan.

4. In a medium bowl, using an electric mixer on medium-high speed, beat egg whites until frothy. Increase speed to high and beat until stiff, but not dry, peaks form. Using a rubber spatula, gently mix one-third of the egg whites into the batter. Gently fold in the remaining whites.

5. Brush wells of pan lightly with oil. Set pan over medium heat. When oil begins to sizzle, add 1 tbsp (15 mL) batter to each well. Place 1 Cheddar cheese cube in the center of each well and top with 1 tbsp (15 mL) batter. Cook for 2 to 4 minutes or until bottoms are golden brown. Using two skewers, flip the puffs over. Cook for 2 to 3 minutes or until bottoms are golden brown and a toothpick inserted in the center comes out with a bit of cheese and a few moist crumbs attached. Remove pan from heat and transfer puffs to a plate. Let pan cool slightly.

6. Repeat with the remaining batter and cheese cubes, brushing wells with oil and reheating pan before each batch. Serve warm or at room temperature.

Parisian Soufflé Puffs

Makes about 21 puffs

Soufflés are terrific but are typically terrifying to home chefs. Fear no more: with the ebelskiver pan, popable cheese soufflés can be made in minutes with minimal fuss and muss but all of the expected style. *Bon appétit!*

Tip

An equal amount of shredded Swiss, Cheddar or Manchego cheese may be used in place of the Gruyère.

● **7-well ebelskiver pan**

1¼ cups	all-purpose flour	300 mL
¾ tsp	baking powder	3 mL
¼ tsp	salt	1 mL
¼ tsp	ground black pepper	1 mL
1 tsp	granulated sugar	5 mL
3	large eggs, separated	3
¾ cup	milk	175 mL
¼ cup	unsalted butter, melted	60 mL
1 cup	shredded Gruyère cheese	250 mL
	Unsalted butter, melted	

1. In a large bowl, whisk together flour, baking powder, salt and pepper.

2. In a medium bowl, whisk together sugar, egg yolks, milk and butter until well blended.

3. Add the egg yolk mixture to the flour mixture and stir until just blended (the batter will appear slightly lumpy). Gently stir in cheese.

4. In a medium bowl, using an electric mixer on medium-high speed, beat egg whites until frothy. Increase speed to high and beat until stiff, but not dry, peaks form. Using a rubber spatula, gently mix one-third of the egg whites into the batter. Gently fold in the remaining whites.

5. Brush wells of pan lightly with melted butter. Set pan over medium heat. When butter begins to sizzle, add 2 tbsp (30 mL) batter to each well. Cook for 2 to 4 minutes or until bottoms are golden brown. Using two skewers, flip the puffs over. Cook for 2 to 3 minutes or until bottoms are golden brown and a toothpick inserted in the center comes out with a few moist crumbs attached. Remove pan from heat and transfer puffs to a plate. Let pan cool slightly.

6. Repeat with the remaining batter, brushing wells with butter before each use. Serve warm or at room temperature.

Caprese Puffs

Savory-sweet sun-dried tomatoes, creamy mozzarella cheese and basil pesto are the stars of these irresistible puffs. Serve them as appetizers, pack them in a lunch bag, or pair them with soup or a green salad for a light supper.

Tip

Other varieties of creamy white cheese, such as Monterey Jack, fontina or Brie, may be used in place of the mozzarella.

- **7-well ebelskiver pan**

1⅓ cups	all-purpose flour	325 mL
¾ tsp	baking powder	3 mL
1 tsp	granulated sugar	5 mL
2	large eggs, separated	2
¾ cup	milk	175 mL
½ cup	prepared basil pesto	125 mL
⅔ cup	packed drained oil-packed sun-dried tomatoes, chopped	150 mL
	Vegetable oil	
3 oz	drained water-packed mozzarella cheese, cut into ½-inch (1 cm) cubes and patted dry	90 g
	Chopped fresh basil and/or additional basil pesto (optional)	

1. In a large bowl, whisk together flour and baking powder.

2. In a medium bowl, whisk together sugar, egg yolks, milk and pesto until well blended.

3. Add the egg yolk mixture to the flour mixture and stir until just blended (the batter will appear slightly lumpy). Gently stir in tomatoes.

4. In a medium bowl, using an electric mixer on medium-high speed, beat egg whites until frothy. Increase speed to high and beat until stiff, but not dry, peaks form. Using a rubber spatula, gently mix one-third of the egg whites into the batter. Gently fold in the remaining whites.

5. Brush wells of pan lightly with oil. Set pan over medium heat. When oil begins to sizzle, add 1 tbsp (15 mL) batter to each well. Place 1 cheese cube in the center of each well and top with 1 tbsp (15 mL) batter. Cook for 2 to 4 minutes or until bottoms are golden brown. Using two skewers, flip the puffs over. Cook for 2 to 3 minutes or until bottoms are golden brown and a toothpick inserted in the center comes out with a bit of cheese and a few moist crumbs attached. Remove pan from heat and transfer puffs to a plate. Let pan cool slightly.

6. Repeat with the remaining batter and cheese cubes, brushing wells with oil and reheating pan before each batch.

7. Serve the puffs warm, with basil and/or pesto, if desired.

Blue Cheese and Pecan Ebelskivers with Pear Compote

The peppery pear compote accompanying and filling these ebelskivers is the catalyst that makes the blue cheese and toasted pecan flavors jump out of the airy centers. Keep a crowd nearby or you may find yourself "sampling" half a batch (or more) as they emerge from the pan.

● **7-well ebelskiver pan**

Pear Compote

2 tbsp	unsalted butter	30 mL
1 tbsp	liquid honey	15 mL
1/4 tsp	freshly cracked black pepper	1 mL
1/8 tsp	salt	0.5 mL
2	medium-large pears, peeled and chopped	2

Ebelskivers

1 1/4 cups	all-purpose flour	300 mL
3/4 tsp	baking powder	3 mL
1/4 tsp	salt	1 mL
1 tsp	granulated sugar	5 mL
2	large eggs, separated	2
1 cup	milk	250 mL
2 tbsp	unsalted butter, melted	30 mL
1/2 cup	chopped toasted pecans or walnuts	125 mL
1/3 cup	crumbled blue cheese	75 mL
	Vegetable oil	

1. *Compote:* In a medium saucepan, melt butter over medium-high heat. Add honey, pepper and salt; cook, stirring, for 30 seconds, until bubbly. Add pears, reduce heat to medium and cook, stirring occasionally, for 3 to 4 minutes or until pears are tender. Remove from heat and let cool completely.

2. *Ebelskivers:* In a large bowl, whisk together flour, baking powder and salt.

3. In a medium bowl, whisk together sugar, egg yolks, milk and butter until well blended.

4. Add the egg yolk mixture to the flour mixture and stir until just blended (the batter will appear slightly lumpy). Gently stir in pecans and blue cheese.

5. In a medium bowl, using an electric mixer on medium-high speed, beat egg whites until frothy. Increase speed to high and beat until stiff, but not dry, peaks form. Using a rubber spatula, gently mix one-third of the egg whites into the batter. Gently fold in the remaining whites.

6. Brush wells of pan lightly with oil. Set pan over medium heat. When oil begins to sizzle, add 1 tbsp (15 mL) batter to each well. Place 1 tsp (5 mL) compote in the center of each well and top with 1 tbsp (15 mL) batter. Cook for 2 to 4 minutes or until bottoms are golden brown. Using two skewers, flip the puffs over. Cook for 2 to 3 minutes or until bottoms are golden brown and a toothpick inserted in the center comes out with a bit of filling and a few moist crumbs attached. Remove pan from heat and transfer puffs to a plate. Let pan cool slightly.

7. Repeat with the remaining batter and compote, brushing wells with oil and reheating pan before each batch.

8. Serve the ebelskivers warm, with the remaining pear compote.

Blue Cheese and Fig Ebelskivers

Blue cheese and figs have a natural affinity for one another. A bit of black pepper and nutmeg in the batter contribute nuanced counterpoints.

Tip

For best results, use dried figs that are very moist (e.g., packed in vacuum-sealed packages). If using chopped dried figs that are particularly hard, soak them in hot (not boiling) water for 2 minutes, then drain and pat dry.

● **7-well ebelskiver pan**

1¼ cups	all-purpose flour	300 mL
¾ tsp	baking powder	3 mL
¼ tsp	salt	1 mL
⅛ tsp	ground nutmeg	0.5 mL
⅛ tsp	freshly cracked black pepper	0.5 mL
2	large eggs, separated	2
1 cup	milk	250 mL
2 tbsp	unsalted butter, melted	30 mL
2 tsp	liquid honey	10 mL
½ cup	chopped dried figs	125 mL
	Vegetable oil	
3 oz	firm blue cheese, cut into ½-inch (1 cm) cubes	90 g

1. In a large bowl, whisk together flour, baking powder, salt, nutmeg and pepper.

2. In a medium bowl, whisk together egg yolks, milk, butter and honey until well blended.

3. Add the egg yolk mixture to the flour mixture and stir until just blended (the batter will appear slightly lumpy). Gently stir in figs.

4. In a medium bowl, using an electric mixer on medium-high speed, beat egg whites until frothy. Increase speed to high and beat until stiff, but not dry, peaks form. Using a rubber spatula, gently mix one-third of the egg whites into the batter. Gently fold in the remaining whites.

Tip

Softer varieties of blue cheese may also be used; simply measure 1 tsp (5 mL) of cheese in place of each cheese cube in step 5.

5. Brush wells of pan lightly with oil. Set pan over medium heat. When oil begins to sizzle, add 1 tbsp (15 mL) batter to each well. Place 1 cheese cube in the center of each pancake and top with 1 tbsp (15 mL) batter. Cook for 2 to 4 minutes or until bottoms are golden brown. Using two skewers, flip the puffs over. Cook for 2 to 3 minutes or until bottoms are golden brown and a toothpick inserted in the center comes out with a bit of cheese and a few crumbs attached. Remove pan from heat and transfer puffs to a plate. Let pan cool slightly.

6. Repeat with the remaining batter and cheese cubes, brushing wells with oil and reheating pan before each batch. Serve warm or at room temperature.

Sage and Brown Butter Puffs with Goat Cheese

Makes about 21 puffs

The simple step of browning the butter adds a subtle nuttiness to these puffs, a flavor that marries harmoniously with the fresh sage. Goat cheese contributes creamy, tangy contrast.

● **7-well ebelskiver pan**

3 tbsp	unsalted butter	45 mL
2 tsp	chopped fresh sage	10 mL
1¼ cups	all-purpose flour	300 mL
¾ tsp	baking powder	3 mL
¼ tsp	salt	1 mL
1 tsp	granulated sugar	5 mL
2	large eggs, separated	2
1 cup	milk	250 mL
	Vegetable oil	
½ cup	creamy goat cheese	125 mL

1. In a small, heavy skillet, heat butter over medium heat until foam subsides and butter is beginning to brown. Stir in sage and cook, stirring, for 1 to 2 minutes or until butter is golden brown. Immediately transfer to a medium bowl and let cool to room temperature.

2. In a large bowl, whisk together flour, baking powder and salt.

3. Add sugar, egg yolks and milk to the browned butter and whisk until well blended.

4. Add the egg yolk mixture to the flour mixture and stir until just blended (the batter will appear slightly lumpy).

5. In a medium bowl, using an electric mixer on medium-high speed, beat egg whites until frothy. Increase speed to high and beat until stiff, but not dry, peaks form. Using a rubber spatula, gently mix one-third of the egg whites into the batter. Gently fold in the remaining whites.

Tip

An equal amount of chopped fresh thyme or 1 tsp (5 mL) dry rubbed sage may be used in place of the fresh sage.

6. Brush wells of pan lightly with oil. Set pan over medium heat. When oil begins to sizzle, add 1 tbsp (15 mL) batter to each well. Place 1 tsp (5 mL) cheese in the center of each well and top with 1 tbsp (15 mL) batter. Cook for 2 to 4 minutes or until bottoms are golden brown. Using two skewers, flip the puffs over. Cook for 2 to 3 minutes or until bottoms are golden brown and a toothpick inserted in the center comes out with a bit of cheese and a few moist crumbs attached. Remove pan from heat and transfer puffs to a plate. Let pan cool slightly.

7. Repeat with the remaining batter and cheese, brushing wells with oil and reheating pan before each batch. Serve warm or at room temperature.

Cheese-Stuffed Macaroni and Cheese Puffs

Makes about 28 puffs

Mini macaroni and cheese puffs stuffed with even more Cheddar cheese? Please and thank you! If you're wondering what's not to love, the answer is nothing. Absolutely nothing.

Tip

The recipe works best if the macaroni and cheese is at room temperature as opposed to cold.

● **7-well ebelskiver pan**

⅔ cup	all-purpose flour	150 mL
¾ tsp	baking powder	3 mL
¼ tsp	salt	1 mL
2	large eggs, separated	2
¾ cup	milk	175 mL
2 tbsp	unsalted butter, melted	30 mL
2½ cups	prepared macaroni and cheese, cooled (see tip, at left)	625 mL
	Vegetable oil	
3 oz	sharp (old) Cheddar cheese, cut into ½-inch (1 cm) cubes	90 g

1. In a large bowl, whisk together flour, baking powder and salt.

2. In a medium bowl, whisk together egg yolks, milk and butter until well blended.

3. Add the egg yolk mixture to the flour mixture and stir until just blended (the batter will appear slightly lumpy). Gently stir in macaroni and cheese.

4. In a medium bowl, using an electric mixer on medium-high speed, beat egg whites until frothy. Increase speed to high and beat until stiff, but not dry, peaks form. Using a rubber spatula, gently mix one-third of the egg whites into the batter. Gently fold in the remaining whites.

5. Brush wells of pan lightly with oil. Set pan over medium heat. When oil begins to sizzle, add 1 tbsp (15 mL) batter to each well. Place 1 cheese cube in the center of each well and top with 1 tbsp (15 mL) batter. Cook for 2 to 4 minutes or until bottoms are golden brown. Using two skewers, flip the puffs over. Cook for 2 to 3 minutes or until bottoms are golden brown and a toothpick inserted in the center comes out with a bit of cheese and a few moist crumbs attached. Remove pan from heat and transfer puffs to a plate. Let pan cool slightly.

6. Repeat with the remaining batter and cheese cubes, brushing wells with oil and reheating pan before each batch. Serve warm or at room temperature.

Spinach Omelet Puffs

Omelets may be familiar breakfast and brunch fare, but they don't have to be boring and predictable. Take eggs, add some spinach, garlic and cheese, cook into puffy minis with the ebelskiver pan, and you have a fresh new crowd-pleaser, whether it's just the family or a last-minute gathering of friends. And thanks to the convenience of frozen chopped spinach, I bet you won't want to wait for the weekend to make them.

Tips

This recipe uses 3 tbsp (45 mL) batter for each omelet, so each well is filled to nearly the top. The reason for the greater volume is that the omelets do not puff as much as ebelskiver recipes.

For the cheese, try Cheddar, Parmesan or Gruyère.

● **7-well ebelskiver pan**

¼ cup	all-purpose flour	60 mL
¼ tsp	baking powder	1 mL
¼ tsp	salt	1 mL
¼ tsp	freshly cracked black pepper	1 mL
4	large eggs	4
2	cloves garlic, mashed	2
¼ cup	milk	60 mL
2 tbsp	unsalted butter, melted	30 mL
1	package (10 oz/300 g) frozen chopped spinach, thawed and squeezed dry	1
½ cup	freshly grated or shredded cheese of choice	125 mL
	Vegetable oil	

1. In a large bowl, whisk together flour, baking powder, salt and pepper.

2. In a medium bowl, whisk together eggs, garlic, milk and butter until well blended.

3. Gradually whisk the egg mixture into the flour mixture until just blended (the batter will appear slightly lumpy). Gently stir in spinach and cheese.

4. Brush wells of pan lightly with oil. Set pan over medium heat. When oil begins to sizzle, add 3 tbsp (45 mL) batter to each well. Cook for 2 to 4 minutes or until bottoms are golden brown. Using two skewers, flip the omelets over. Cook for 2 to 3 minutes or until bottoms are golden brown and puffs feel set when lightly touched with your fingertips. Remove pan from heat and transfer omelets to a plate. Let pan cool slightly.

5. Repeat with the remaining batter, brushing wells with oil and reheating pan before each batch. Serve warm or at room temperature.

Quiche Lorraine Puffs

These French finger foods are at once sophisticated and adorable, with all the favorite flavors of quiche Lorraine: bacon, onions, Gruyère and a pinch of nutmeg.

● **7-well ebelskiver pan**

1 tbsp	extra virgin olive oil	15 mL
1 cup	chopped onion	250 mL
	Salt and freshly ground black pepper	
1¼ cups	all-purpose flour	300 mL
¾ tsp	baking powder	3 mL
⅛ tsp	ground nutmeg	0.5 mL
1 tsp	granulated sugar	5 mL
3	large eggs, separated	3
¾ cup	milk	175 mL
2 tbsp	unsalted butter, melted	30 mL
½ cup	crumbled cooked bacon	125 mL
	Olive oil or vegetable oil	
3 oz	Gruyère cheese, cut into ½-inch (1 cm) cubes	90 g

1. In a large skillet, heat oil over medium-high heat. Add onion and cook, stirring, for 5 to 8 minutes or until softened and golden. Remove from heat and season to taste with salt and pepper. Let cool completely.

2. In a large bowl, whisk together flour, baking powder, ¼ tsp (1 mL) salt and nutmeg.

3. In a medium bowl, whisk together sugar, egg yolks, milk and butter until well blended.

4. Add the egg yolk mixture to the flour mixture and stir until just blended (the batter will appear slightly lumpy). Gently stir in onion mixture and bacon.

5. In a medium bowl, using an electric mixer on medium-high speed, beat egg whites until frothy. Increase speed to high and beat until stiff, but not dry, peaks form. Using a rubber spatula, gently mix one-third of the egg whites into the batter. Gently fold in the remaining whites.

Tip

An equal amount of Swiss cheese may be used in place of the Gruyère.

6. Brush wells of pan lightly with oil. Set pan over medium heat. When oil begins to sizzle, add 1 tbsp (15 mL) batter to each well. Place 1 cheese cube in the center of each well and top with 1 tbsp (15 mL) batter. Cook for 2 to 4 minutes or until bottoms are golden brown. Using two skewers, flip the puffs over. Cook for 2 to 3 minutes or until bottoms are golden brown and a toothpick inserted in the center comes out with a bit of cheese and a few moist crumbs attached. Remove pan from heat and transfer puffs to a plate. Let pan cool slightly.

7. Repeat with the remaining batter and cheese cubes, brushing wells with oil and reheating pan before each batch. Serve warm or at room temperature.

Pepperoni Pizza Puffs

A riff on an American classic, these puffs have the toppings (pepperoni, parsley and mozzarella) stirred and stuffed right into the batter. The sauce comes alongside, ready for delicious dipping.

Tip

For a vegetarian take on these puffs, simply omit the pepperoni.

Variation

Sausage Pizza Puffs: Replace the pepperoni with 6 oz (175 g) Italian sausage, cooked, crumbled, drained of fat and cooled.

● **7-well ebelskiver pan**

1¼ cups	all-purpose flour	300 mL
¾ tsp	baking powder	3 mL
¼ tsp	salt	1 mL
1 tsp	granulated sugar	5 mL
2	large eggs, separated	2
1 cup	milk	250 mL
2 tbsp	extra virgin olive oil	30 mL
½ cup	chopped pepperoni	125 mL
3 tbsp	chopped fresh flat-leaf (Italian) parsley	45 mL
	Olive oil or vegetable oil	
3 oz	drained water-packed mozzarella, cut into ½-inch (1 cm) cubes, patted dry	90 g
1 cup	marinara sauce, warmed	250 mL

1. In a large bowl, whisk together flour, baking powder and salt.

2. In a medium bowl, whisk together sugar, egg yolks, milk and oil until well blended.

3. Add the egg yolk mixture to the flour mixture and stir until just blended (the batter will appear slightly lumpy). Gently stir in pepperoni and parsley.

4. In a medium bowl, using an electric mixer on medium-high speed, beat egg whites until frothy. Increase speed to high and beat until stiff, but not dry, peaks form. Using a rubber spatula, gently mix one-third of the egg whites into the batter. Gently fold in the remaining whites.

5. Brush wells of pan lightly with oil. Set pan over medium heat. When oil begins to sizzle, add 1 tbsp (15 mL) batter to each well. Place 1 cheese cube in the center of each well and top with 1 tbsp (15 mL) batter. Cook for 2 to 4 minutes or until bottoms are golden brown. Using two skewers, flip the puffs over. Cook for 2 to 3 minutes or until bottoms are golden brown and a toothpick inserted in the center comes out with a bit of cheese and a few moist crumbs attached. Remove pan from heat and transfer puffs to a plate. Let pan cool slightly.

6. Repeat with the remaining batter and cheese cubes, brushing wells with oil and reheating pan before each batch.

7. Serve the puffs warm, with marinara sauce.

Italian Sausage Puffs

Makes about 28 puffs

Resistance is futile: no one can possibly eat just one of these sausage- and cheese-stuffed puffs.

Variation

Cheeseburger Puffs: Replace the sausage with lean ground beef, and the provolone with sharp (old) Cheddar cheese.

● **7-well ebelskiver pan**

8 oz	sweet Italian sausage (bulk or removed from casings)	250 g
1¼ cups	all-purpose flour	300 mL
¾ tsp	dried oregano	3 mL
¾ tsp	baking powder	3 mL
¼ tsp	salt	1 mL
1 tsp	granulated sugar	5 mL
2	large eggs, separated	2
1 cup	milk	250 mL
2 tbsp	extra virgin olive oil	30 mL
1 cup	shredded smoked provolone cheese	250 mL
	Olive oil or vegetable oil	

1. In a large nonstick skillet, cook sausage over medium heat, breaking it up with a spoon, for 5 to 6 minutes or until no longer pink. Transfer to a plate lined with paper towels to drain. Let cool completely.

2. In a large bowl, whisk together flour, oregano, baking powder and salt.

3. In a medium bowl, whisk together sugar, egg yolks, milk and oil until well blended.

4. Add the egg yolk mixture to the flour mixture and stir until just blended (the batter will appear slightly lumpy). Gently stir in sausage and cheese.

5. In a medium bowl, using an electric mixer on medium-high speed, beat egg whites until frothy. Increase speed to high and beat until stiff, but not dry, peaks form. Using a rubber spatula, gently mix one-third of the egg whites into the batter. Gently fold in the remaining whites.

6. Brush wells of pan lightly with oil. Set pan over medium heat. When oil begins to sizzle, add 2 tbsp (30 mL) batter to each well. Cook for 2 to 4 minutes or until bottoms are golden brown. Using two skewers, flip the puffs over. Cook for 2 to 3 minutes or until bottoms are golden brown and a toothpick inserted in the center comes out with a few moist crumbs attached. Remove pan from heat and transfer puffs to a plate. Let pan cool slightly.

7. Repeat with the remaining batter, brushing wells with oil and reheating pan before each batch. Serve warm or at room temperature.

Antipasto Puffs

Salami, artichoke hearts, sun-dried tomatoes and cheese go well together on more than a platter. These puffs are staggeringly simple to make, belying their complex taste.

● **7-well ebelskiver pan**

1¼ cups	all-purpose flour	300 mL
¾ tsp	baking powder	3 mL
¼ tsp	salt	1 mL
⅛ tsp	freshly cracked black pepper	0.5 mL
2	large eggs, separated	2
1 cup	milk	250 mL
2 tbsp	extra virgin olive oil	30 mL
¾ cup	chopped drained marinated artichoke hearts	175 mL
⅓ cup	packed fresh basil leaves, chopped	75 mL
¼ cup	chopped drained oil-packed sun-dried tomatoes	60 mL
¼ cup	chopped salami	60 mL
	Olive oil or vegetable oil	
3 oz	fontina or Brie cheese, cut into ½-inch (1 cm) cubes	90 g

1. In a large bowl, whisk together flour, baking powder, salt and pepper.

2. In a medium bowl, whisk together egg yolks, milk and oil until well blended.

3. Add the egg yolk mixture to the flour mixture and stir until just blended (the batter will appear slightly lumpy). Gently stir in artichoke hearts, basil, tomatoes and salami.

4. In a medium bowl, using an electric mixer on medium-high speed, beat egg whites until frothy. Increase speed to high and beat until stiff, but not dry, peaks form. Using a rubber spatula, gently mix one-third of the egg whites into the batter. Gently fold in the remaining whites.

5. Brush wells of pan lightly with oil. Set pan over medium heat. When oil begins to sizzle, add 1 tbsp (15 mL) batter to each well. Place 1 cheese cube in the center of each well and top with 1 tbsp (15 mL) batter. Cook for 2 to 4 minutes or until bottoms are golden brown. Using two skewers, flip the puffs over. Cook for 2 to 3 minutes or until bottoms are golden brown and a toothpick inserted in the center comes out with a bit of cheese and a few moist crumbs attached. Remove pan from heat and transfer puffs to a plate. Let pan cool slightly.

6. Repeat with the remaining batter and cheese cubes, brushing wells with oil and reheating pan before each batch. Serve warm or at room temperature.

Ham and Swiss in Rye Puffs

This play on the deli classic ham on rye forgoes sliced bread for a dark rye, caraway and ham-flecked batter with Swiss cheese filling. The airy puffs offset the richness of the meat and cheese.

Tips

To crush the caraway seeds with ease, grind them with a mortar and pestle or in a spice grinder. Alternatively, place the seeds in a small sealable plastic bag and crush them with a mallet or rolling pin.

An equal amount of crushed fennel seeds may be used in place of the caraway seeds.

● **7-well ebelskiver pan**

¾ cup	dark rye flour	175 mL
½ cup	all-purpose flour	125 mL
1 tsp	caraway seeds, crushed	5 mL
¾ tsp	baking powder	3 mL
¼ tsp	salt	1 mL
1 tsp	granulated sugar	5 mL
2	large eggs, separated	2
1 cup	milk	250 mL
2 tbsp	unsalted butter, melted	30 mL
2 tsp	Dijon mustard	10 mL
½ cup	chopped smoked ham	125 mL
	Vegetable oil	
3 oz	Swiss or Gruyère cheese, cut into ½-inch (1 cm) cubes	90 g

1. In a large bowl, whisk together rye flour, all-purpose flour, caraway seeds, baking powder and salt.

2. In a medium bowl, whisk together sugar, egg yolks, milk, butter and mustard until well blended.

3. Add the egg yolk mixture to the flour mixture and stir until just blended (the batter will appear slightly lumpy). Gently stir in ham.

4. In a medium bowl, using an electric mixer on medium-high speed, beat egg whites until frothy. Increase speed to high and beat until stiff, but not dry, peaks form. Using a rubber spatula, gently mix one-third of the egg whites into the batter. Gently fold in the remaining whites.

5. Brush wells of pan lightly with oil. Set pan over medium heat. When oil begins to sizzle, add 1 tbsp (15 mL) batter to each well. Place 1 cheese cube in the center of each pancake and top with 1 tbsp (15 mL) batter. Cook for 2 to 4 minutes or until bottoms are golden brown. Using two skewers, flip the puffs over. Cook for 2 to 3 minutes or until bottoms are golden brown and a toothpick inserted in the center comes out with a bit of cheese and a few moist crumbs attached. Remove pan from heat and transfer puffs to a plate. Let pan cool slightly.

6. Repeat with the remaining batter and cheese cubes, brushing wells with oil and reheating pan before each batch. Serve warm or at room temperature.

Buttermilk Puffs with Greens and Ham

The combination of buttermilk, greens and ham has true Southern synergy. The greens cut the smokiness of the ham, turning these humble puffs into something extra-special — just what's needed to accompany a simple repast of soup or salad.

● **7-well ebelskiver pan**

	Vegetable oil	
1 cup	chopped kale (stems removed)	250 mL
½ cup	chopped smoked ham	125 mL
½ tsp	hot pepper sauce (such as Tabasco)	2 mL
1 cup	all-purpose flour	250 mL
¼ cup	yellow cornmeal	60 mL
½ tsp	baking soda	2 mL
¼ tsp	baking powder	1 mL
¼ tsp	salt	1 mL
¼ tsp	freshly cracked black pepper	1 mL
1 tsp	granulated sugar	5 mL
2	large eggs, separated	2
1 cup	buttermilk	250 mL

1. In a large skillet, heat 1 tbsp (15 mL) oil over medium-high heat. Add kale and cook for 4 to 5 minutes or until wilted. Add ham and hot pepper sauce; cook, stirring, for 1 minute. Remove from heat and let cool completely.

2. In a large bowl, whisk together flour, cornmeal, baking soda, baking powder, salt and pepper.

3. In a medium bowl, whisk together sugar, egg yolks, buttermilk and 2 tbsp (30 mL) oil until well blended.

4. Add the egg yolk mixture to the flour mixture and stir until just blended (the batter will appear slightly lumpy). Gently stir in kale mixture.

5. In a medium bowl, using an electric mixer on medium-high speed, beat egg whites until frothy. Increase speed to high and beat until stiff, but not dry, peaks form. Using a rubber spatula, gently mix one-third of the egg whites into the batter. Gently fold in the remaining whites.

Tips

Other greens, such as spinach or turnip greens, may be used in place of the kale.

If you don't have any buttermilk on hand, stir 2 tsp (10 mL) lemon juice or white vinegar into 1 cup (250 mL) milk. Let stand for 5 to 10 minutes or until thickened. Use in place of the buttermilk.

6. Brush wells of pan lightly with oil. Set pan over medium heat. When oil begins to sizzle, add 2 tbsp (30 mL) batter to each well. Cook for 2 to 4 minutes or until bottoms are golden brown. Using two skewers, flip the puffs over. Cook for 2 to 3 minutes or until bottoms are golden brown and a toothpick inserted in the center comes out with a few moist crumbs attached. Remove pan from heat and transfer puffs to a plate. Let pan cool slightly.

7. Repeat with the remaining batter, brushing wells with oil and reheating pan before each batch. Serve warm or at room temperature.

Lox and Cream Cheese Ebelskivers

These petite puffs embrace the flavors of a classic bagel loaded with the very best toppings.

Tips

An equal amount of minced green onions may be used in place of the chives.

Other smoked fish, such as trout or herring, may be used in place of the lox.

● **7-well ebelskiver pan**

1¼ cups	all-purpose flour	300 mL
¾ tsp	baking powder	3 mL
¼ tsp	salt	1 mL
⅛ tsp	freshly ground black pepper	0.5 mL
1 tsp	granulated sugar	5 mL
2	large eggs, separated	2
1 cup	milk	250 mL
2 tbsp	unsalted butter, melted	30 mL
2 tsp	finely grated lemon zest	10 mL
¼ cup	minced fresh chives	60 mL
	Vegetable oil	
½ cup	whipped cream cheese	125 mL
¼ cup	finely chopped lox or other smoked or cured salmon	60 mL

1. In a large bowl, whisk together flour, baking powder, salt and pepper.

2. In a medium bowl, whisk together sugar, egg yolks, milk, butter and lemon zest until well blended.

3. Add the egg yolk mixture to the flour mixture and stir until just blended (the batter will appear slightly lumpy). Gently stir in chives.

4. In a medium bowl, using an electric mixer on medium-high speed, beat egg whites until frothy. Increase speed to high and beat until stiff, but not dry, peaks form. Using a rubber spatula, gently mix one-third of the egg whites into the batter. Gently fold in the remaining whites.

Variation

Lemon-Dill Lox Ebelskivers: Use an equal amount of chopped fresh dill in place of the chives. Omit the cream cheese and increase the lox to ¾ cup (175 mL). Use 1½ tsp (7 mL) lox to fill each ebelskiver.

5. Brush wells of pan lightly with oil. Set pan over medium heat. When oil begins to sizzle, add 1 tbsp (15 mL) batter to each well. Place 1 tsp (5 mL) cream cheese and ½ tsp (2 mL) lox in the center of each well and top with 1 tbsp (15 mL) batter. Cook for 2 to 4 minutes or until bottoms are golden brown. Using two skewers, flip the puffs over. Cook for 2 to 3 minutes or until bottoms are golden brown and a toothpick inserted in the center comes out with a bit of cheese and a few moist crumbs attached. Remove pan from heat and transfer puffs to a plate. Let pan cool slightly.

6. Repeat with the remaining batter, cream cheese and lox, brushing wells with oil and reheating pan before each batch. Serve warm or at room temperature.

Crab Cake Puffs with Lemon Aïoli

Use good mayonnaise, fresh crabmeat and sunny lemons, and these crab cake puffs will really sing.

Tip

If you don't have any buttermilk on hand, stir 2 tsp (10 mL) lemon juice or white vinegar into 1 cup (250 mL) milk. Let stand for 5 to 10 minutes or until thickened. Use in place of the buttermilk.

● **7-well ebelskiver pan**

Lemon Aïoli

1	clove garlic, mashed to a paste	1
¾ cup	mayonnaise (preferably olive oil mayonnaise)	175 mL
1 tsp	finely grated lemon zest	5 mL
2 tbsp	freshly squeezed lemon juice	30 mL
1 tsp	Dijon mustard	5 mL

Puffs

1 cup	all-purpose flour	300 mL
2 tsp	Old Bay seasoning	10 mL
½ tsp	baking soda	2 mL
¼ tsp	baking powder	1 mL
¼ tsp	salt	1 mL
2	large eggs, separated	2
1 cup	buttermilk	250 mL
2 tbsp	unsalted butter, melted	30 mL
8 oz	cooked fresh lump crabmeat, picked over for shell and cartilage pieces	250 g
¼ cup	minced fresh chives	60 mL
	Vegetable oil	

1. *Aïoli:* In a small bowl, whisk together garlic, mayonnaise, lemon zest, lemon juice and mustard until smooth. Cover and refrigerate while preparing the puffs.

2. *Puffs:* In a large bowl, whisk together flour, Old Bay seasoning, baking soda, baking powder and salt.

3. In a medium bowl, whisk together egg yolks, buttermilk and butter until well blended.

4. Add the egg yolk mixture to the flour mixture and stir until just blended (the batter will appear slightly lumpy). Gently stir in crab and chives.

Tips

An equal amount of drained canned or thawed frozen lump crabmeat may be used in place of the fresh crabmeat.

An equal amount of minced green onions may be used in place of the chives.

5. In a medium bowl, using an electric mixer on medium-high speed, beat egg whites until frothy. Increase speed to high and beat until stiff, but not dry, peaks form. Using a rubber spatula, gently mix one-third of the egg whites into the batter. Gently fold in the remaining whites.

6. Brush wells of pan lightly with oil. Set pan over medium heat. When oil begins to sizzle, add 2 tbsp (30 mL) batter to each well. Cook for 2 to 4 minutes or until bottoms are golden brown. Using two skewers, flip the puffs over. Cook for 2 to 3 minutes or until bottoms are golden brown and a toothpick inserted in the center comes out with a few moist crumbs attached. Remove pan from heat and transfer puffs to a plate. Let pan cool slightly.

7. Repeat with the remaining batter, brushing wells with oil and reheating pan before each batch.

8. Serve the puffs warm, with the lemon aïoli.

Thanksgiving Day Puffs

Turkey day just got a whole lot easier: these puffs taste like Thanksgiving dinner in one easy morsel — and you never have to turn on the oven. Use turkey leftovers or buy sliced turkey breast from the deli to make these puffs any time of the year.

Tips

If you don't have any buttermilk on hand, stir 2 tsp (10 mL) lemon juice or white vinegar into 1 cup (250 mL) milk. Let stand for 5 to 10 minutes or until thickened. Use in place of the buttermilk.

You can purchase roasted turkey from the deli counter at the supermarket. Ask for the turkey to be cut into one or two thick pieces, then chop it at home. It will take about 4 oz (125 g) turkey to yield ⅔ cup (150 mL) chopped.

● **7-well ebelskiver pan**

1 cup	all-purpose flour	250 mL
¼ cup	yellow cornmeal	60 mL
1½ tsp	dried rubbed sage	7 mL
½ tsp	dried thyme	2 mL
½ tsp	baking soda	2 mL
¼ tsp	baking powder	1 mL
¼ tsp	salt	1 mL
2 tsp	granulated sugar	10 mL
2	large eggs, separated	2
1 cup	buttermilk	250 mL
2 tbsp	unsalted butter, melted	30 mL
⅔ cup	chopped roasted turkey	150 mL
¼ cup	minced fresh chives or green onions	60 mL
	Vegetable oil	
⅔ cup	cranberry sauce	150 mL

1. In a large bowl, whisk together flour, cornmeal, sage, thyme, baking soda, baking powder and salt.

2. In a medium bowl, whisk together sugar, egg yolks, buttermilk and butter until well blended.

3. Add the egg yolk mixture to the flour mixture and stir until just blended (the batter will appear slightly lumpy). Gently stir in turkey and chives.

4. In a medium bowl, using an electric mixer on medium-high speed, beat egg whites until frothy. Increase speed to high and beat until stiff, but not dry, peaks form. Using a rubber spatula, gently mix one-third of the egg whites into the batter. Gently fold in the remaining whites.

5. Brush wells of pan lightly with oil. Set pan over medium heat. When oil begins to sizzle, add 1 tbsp (15 mL) batter to each well. Place 1 tsp (5 mL) cranberry sauce in the center of each well and top with 1 tbsp (15 mL) batter. Cook for 2 to 4 minutes or until bottoms are golden brown. Using two skewers, flip the puffs over. Cook for 2 to 3 minutes or until bottoms are golden brown and a toothpick inserted in the center comes out with a bit of filling and a few moist crumbs attached. Remove pan from heat and transfer puffs to a plate. Let pan cool slightly.

6. Repeat with the remaining batter and cranberry sauce, brushing wells with oil and reheating pan before each batch. Serve warm or at room temperature.

Global Puffs

continued...

Mayan Chocolate Puffs
(Latin America)

Ready for a showstopper dessert? Look no further than these stylish puffs. Chocolate and spice may be a fashionable combination, but it is a trend backed up with centuries of Central American history.

Tip

An equal amount of regular semisweet chocolate chips may be used in place of the miniature chocolate chips. Coarsely chop the chips for more even distribution of the chocolate throughout the ebelskivers.

● **7-well ebelskiver pan**

1 cup	all-purpose flour	250 mL
1/4 cup	unsweetened cocoa powder (not Dutch process)	60 mL
1 tsp	ground cinnamon	5 mL
1/2 tsp	baking powder	2 mL
1/4 tsp	baking soda	1 mL
1/4 tsp	salt	1 mL
1/8 tsp	cayenne pepper	0.5 mL
2 tbsp	packed light brown sugar	30 mL
2	large eggs, separated	2
1 cup	milk	250 mL
2 tbsp	unsalted butter, melted	30 mL
1/2 tsp	almond extract	2 mL
3/4 cup	miniature semisweet chocolate chips	175 mL
	Vegetable oil	

1. In a large bowl, whisk together flour, cocoa powder, cinnamon, baking powder, baking soda, salt and cayenne.

2. In a medium bowl, whisk together brown sugar, egg yolks, milk, butter and almond extract until well blended.

3. Add the egg yolk mixture to the flour mixture and stir until just blended (the batter will appear slightly lumpy). Gently stir in chocolate chips.

4. In a medium bowl, using an electric mixer on medium-high speed, beat egg whites until frothy. Increase speed to high and beat until stiff, but not dry, peaks form. Using a rubber spatula, gently mix one-third of the egg whites into the batter. Gently fold in the remaining whites.

5. Brush wells of pan lightly with oil. Set pan over medium heat. When oil begins to sizzle, add 2 tbsp (30 mL) batter to each well. Cook for 2 to 4 minutes or until bottoms are crisp-firm to the touch. Using two skewers, flip the puffs over. Cook for 2 to 3 minutes or until crisp-firm to the touch and a toothpick inserted in the center comes out with a few moist crumbs attached. Remove pan from heat and transfer puffs to a plate. Let pan cool slightly.

6. Repeat with the remaining batter, brushing wells with oil and reheating pan before each batch. Serve warm or at room temperature.

Tres Leches Puffs (Ecuador, Mexico)

The origins of *tres leches* — a rich and creamy confection served with *cafecito* throughout Latin America — are disputed, but most culinary historians agree that its roots lie in Ecuador and Mexico. It makes a seamless transition from cake to ebelskiver puff: tender, not too sweet and utterly irresistible.

● **7-well ebelskiver pan**

Filling

6 oz	cream cheese, softened	175 g
3 tbsp	sweetened condensed milk	45 mL

Puffs

1¾ cups	all-purpose flour	425 mL
1½ tsp	baking powder	7 mL
¼ tsp	salt	1 mL
3	large eggs, separated	3
¾ cup	milk	175 mL
½ cup	sweetened condensed milk	125 mL
3 tbsp	unsalted butter, melted	45 mL
1½ tsp	vanilla extract	7 mL
	Vegetable oil	
	Confectioners' (icing) sugar	
	Lightly sweetened whipped cream	

1. *Filling:* In a medium bowl, using an electric mixer on medium-high speed, beat cream cheese and condensed milk until smooth and creamy. Cover and refrigerate while preparing the batter. Clean the beaters.

2. *Puffs:* In a large bowl, whisk together flour, baking powder and salt.

3. In a medium bowl, whisk together egg yolks, milk, condensed milk, butter and vanilla until well blended.

4. Add the egg yolk mixture to the flour mixture and stir until just blended (the batter will appear slightly lumpy).

5. In a medium bowl, using an electric mixer on medium-high speed, beat egg whites until frothy. Increase speed to high and beat until stiff, but not dry, peaks form. Using a rubber spatula, gently mix one-third of the egg whites into the batter. Gently fold in the remaining whites.

6. Brush wells of pan lightly with oil. Set pan over medium heat. When oil begins to sizzle, add 1 tbsp (15 mL) batter to each well. Place 1 tsp (5 mL) filling in the center of each well and top with 1 tbsp (15 mL) batter. Cook for 2 to 4 minutes or until bottoms are golden brown. Using two skewers, flip the puffs over. Cook for 2 to 3 minutes or until bottoms are golden brown and a toothpick inserted in the center comes out with a bit of filling and a few moist crumbs attached. Remove pan from heat and transfer puffs to a plate. Let pan cool slightly.

7. Repeat with the remaining batter and filling, brushing wells with oil and reheating pan before each batch.

8. Dust the puffs with confectioners' sugar. Serve warm, with whipped cream.

Butter Tart Puffs (Canada)

Makes about 28 puffs

Canucks — my mother included — take their butter tarts seriously, and with good reason: the iconic brown sugar and butter confections are quintessential Canadian fare. Here, I've traded the traditional tartlet shells for a buttery ebelskiver batter and stuffed the centers with a butter-tart-like filling. O Canada!

- Food processor
- 7-well ebelskiver pan

Filling

½ cup	toasted walnuts	125 mL
2 tbsp	packed light brown sugar	30 mL
Pinch	salt	Pinch
1 tbsp	unsalted butter, melted	15 mL

Puffs

1¼ cups	all-purpose flour	300 mL
¾ tsp	baking powder	3 mL
¼ tsp	salt	1 mL
2 tbsp	packed light brown sugar	30 mL
3	large eggs, separated	3
¾ cup	milk	175 mL
¼ cup	unsalted butter, melted	60 mL
1 tsp	vanilla extract	5 mL
½ cup	dried currants	125 mL
	Vegetable oil	
	Confectioners' (icing) sugar	

1. *Filling:* In food processor, combine walnuts, brown sugar, salt and butter; process until a paste forms. Set aside.

2. *Puffs:* In a large bowl, whisk together flour, baking powder and salt.

3. In a medium bowl, whisk together brown sugar, egg yolks, milk, butter and vanilla until well blended.

4. Add the egg yolk mixture to the flour mixture and stir until just blended (the batter will appear slightly lumpy). Gently stir in currants.

5. In a medium bowl, using an electric mixer on medium-high speed, beat egg whites until frothy. Increase speed to high and beat until stiff, but not dry, peaks form. Using a rubber spatula, gently mix one-third of the egg whites into the batter. Gently fold in the remaining whites.

6. Brush wells of pan lightly with oil. Set pan over medium heat. When oil begins to sizzle, add 1 tbsp (15 mL) batter to each well. Place 1 tsp (5 mL) filling in the center of each well and top with 1 tbsp (15 mL) batter. Cook for 2 to 4 minutes or until bottoms are golden brown. Using two skewers, flip the puffs over. Cook for 2 to 3 minutes or until bottoms are golden brown and a toothpick inserted in the center comes out with a bit of filling and a few moist crumbs attached. Remove pan from heat and transfer puffs to a plate. Let pan cool slightly.

7. Repeat with the remaining batter and filling, brushing wells with oil and reheating pan before each batch.

8. Dust the puffs with confectioners' sugar. Serve warm or at room temperature.

Banoffee Puffs (Great Britain)

Banoffee pie, from which
these puffs take their
cue, is an indulgent take
on toffee with bananas
(hence the name). It
made its debut at the
Hungry Monk, a pub
in England, in 1972
and has been a hit ever
since. Traditional recipes
involve boiling unopened
cans of condensed milk,
but since that sometimes
results in explosions, I
suggest using ready-made
dulce de leche or a quick
batch of Salted Caramel
Sauce instead.

● **7-well ebelskiver pan**

Filling

2 tbsp	unsalted butter, cut into pieces	30 mL
1 cup	diced firm-ripe bananas	250 mL
3 tbsp	packed light brown sugar	45 mL
Pinch	salt	Pinch

Puffs

1¼ cups	all-purpose flour	300 mL
¾ tsp	baking powder	3 mL
¼ tsp	salt	1 mL
1 tbsp	packed light brown sugar	15 mL
2	large eggs, separated	2
1 cup	milk	250 mL
2 tbsp	unsalted butter, melted	30 mL
1 tsp	vanilla extract	5 mL
	Vegetable oil	
1 cup	dulce de leche (or 1 recipe Salted Caramel Sauce, page 108), warmed	250 mL

1. *Filling:* In a medium skillet, melt butter over medium heat. Add bananas, brown sugar and salt. Cook, stirring, for 5 to 6 minutes or until sugar is melted and bananas are softened. Let cool completely.

2. *Puffs:* In a large bowl, whisk together flour, baking powder and salt.

3. In a medium bowl, whisk together brown sugar, egg yolks, milk, butter and vanilla until well blended.

4. Add the egg yolk mixture to the flour mixture and stir until just blended (the batter will appear slightly lumpy).

5. In a medium bowl, using an electric mixer on medium-high speed, beat egg whites until frothy. Increase speed to high and beat until stiff, but not dry, peaks form. Using a rubber spatula, gently mix one-third of the egg whites into the batter. Gently fold in the remaining whites.

Look for cans or jars of dulce de leche where Latin American foods are shelved in the international foods section of the supermarket.

6. Brush wells of pan lightly with oil. Set pan over medium heat. When oil begins to sizzle, add 1 tbsp (15 mL) batter to each well. Place 1 tsp (5 mL) filling in the center of each well and top with 1 tbsp (15 mL) batter. Cook for 2 to 4 minutes or until bottoms are golden brown. Using two skewers, flip the puffs over. Cook for 2 to 3 minutes or until bottoms are golden brown and a toothpick inserted in the center comes out with a bit of filling and a few moist crumbs attached. Remove pan from heat and transfer puffs to a plate. Let pan cool slightly.

7. Repeat with the remaining batter and filling, brushing wells with oil and reheating pan before each batch.

8. Serve the puffs warm, with dulce de leche.

Cranachan Puffs (Scotland)

Cranachan is Scotland's answer to trifle, a glorious combination of honey-sweetened whipped cream, toasted oats, whisky and raspberries. I've certainly taken liberties with this transformation from pudding to puff, but I'm confident that with one taste any Scot would be *hert gled* (delighted).

Tips

An equal amount of pure maple syrup or agave nectar may be used in place of the honey.

The whisky may be replaced with 2½ tbsp (37 mL) additional milk and 1½ tsp (7 mL) whisky extract.

● **7-well ebelskiver pan**

¾ cup	all-purpose flour	175 mL
½ cup	quick-cooking rolled oats	125 mL
¾ tsp	baking powder	3 mL
¼ tsp	salt	1 mL
¼ tsp	baking soda	1 mL
2	large eggs, separated	2
1 cup	milk	250 mL
3 tbsp	whisky	45 mL
3 tbsp	unsalted butter, melted	45 mL
3 tbsp	liquid honey	45 mL
½ cup	raspberry jam or preserves	125 mL
	Confectioners' (icing) sugar	
	Lightly sweetened whipped cream	
	Raspberries	

1. In a large bowl, whisk together flour, oats, baking powder, salt and baking soda.

2. In a medium bowl, whisk together egg yolks, milk, whisky, butter and honey until well blended.

3. Add the egg yolk mixture to the flour mixture and stir until just blended (the batter will appear slightly lumpy).

4. In a medium bowl, using an electric mixer on medium-high speed, beat egg whites until frothy. Increase speed to high and beat until stiff, but not dry, peaks form. Using a rubber spatula, gently mix one-third of the egg whites into the batter. Gently fold in the remaining whites.

5. Brush wells of pan lightly with oil. Set pan over medium heat. When oil begins to sizzle, add 1 tbsp (15 mL) batter to each well. Place 1 tsp (5 mL) jam in the center of each well and top with 1 tbsp (15 mL) batter. Cook for 2 to 4 minutes or until bottoms are golden brown. Using two skewers, flip the puffs over. Cook for 2 to 3 minutes or until bottoms are golden brown and a toothpick inserted in the center comes out with a bit of filling and a few moist crumbs attached. Remove pan from heat and transfer puffs to a plate. Let pan cool slightly.

6. Repeat with the remaining batter and jam, brushing wells with oil and reheating pan before each batch.

7. Dust the puffs with confectioners' sugar. Serve warm or at room temperature, with whipped cream and raspberries.

Santa Lucia Ebelskivers (Sweden)

Swedish lore has it that
on December 13, 1764, a
gentleman was awakened
in the middle of the night
by the singing of a young,
winged woman in white.
It was Saint Lucia, and
she arrived bearing light,
food and wine as comfort
on what was, in the
Gregorian calendar, the
longest night of the year.
Saint Lucia continues
to be celebrated on
December 13 in Sweden,
marked by children
walking with lit candles,
singing the beautiful
Lucia carol and bringing
the Lucia bread. This
yeast-free, ebelskiver
interpretation of Santa
Lucia buns will give you
a taste of the beauty and
magic of the day.

Tip

An equal amount of raisins,
chopped, may be used in
place of the currants.

● **7-well ebelskiver pan**

¼ tsp	saffron threads	1 mL
1 tbsp	hot water	15 mL
1¼ cups	all-purpose flour	300 mL
¾ tsp	baking powder	3 mL
¼ tsp	salt	1 mL
2 tbsp	granulated sugar	30 mL
2	large eggs, separated	2
1 cup	milk	250 mL
3 tbsp	unsalted butter, melted	45 mL
⅔ cup	currants	150 mL
	Vegetable oil	
	Confectioners' (icing) sugar	

1. In a small bowl, combine saffron and hot water. Let stand
   for 5 minutes.

2. In a large bowl, whisk together flour, baking powder and
   salt.

3. In a medium bowl, whisk together sugar, egg yolks, milk,
   butter and the saffron mixture until well blended.

4. Add the egg yolk mixture to the flour mixture and stir
   until just blended (the batter will appear slightly lumpy).
   Gently stir in currants.

5. In a medium bowl, using an electric mixer on medium-
   high speed, beat egg whites until frothy. Increase speed to
   high and beat until stiff, but not dry, peaks form. Using
   a rubber spatula, gently mix one-third of the egg whites
   into the batter. Gently fold in the remaining whites.

6. Brush wells of pan lightly with oil. Set pan over medium
   heat. When oil begins to sizzle, add 2 tbsp (30 mL) batter
   to each well. Cook for 2 to 4 minutes or until bottoms
   are golden brown. Using two skewers, flip the puffs over.
   Cook for 2 to 3 minutes or until bottoms are golden
   brown and a toothpick inserted in the center comes out
   with a few moist crumbs attached. Remove pan from heat
   and transfer puffs to a plate. Let pan cool slightly.

7. Repeat with the remaining batter, brushing wells with oil
   and reheating pan before each batch.

8. Dust the ebelskivers with confectioners' sugar. Serve
   warm or at room temperature.

Cardamom Semlor Puffs
(Sweden)

Semlor — small yeast buns flavored with cardamom and filled with almond paste and cream — have become an iconic Swedish treat. The traditions of *semla* (the singular of *semlor*) are rooted in *fettisdag* (Shrove Tuesday), when the buns were eaten at a last celebratory feast before Lenten fasting. Refashioned with the use of an ebelskiver pan, they are a breeze to make, and are a heavenly accompaniment to coffee.

● **7-well ebelskiver pan**

Filling		
6 oz	cream cheese, softened	175 g
1/3 cup	almond paste or filling	75 mL
1/4 tsp	ground cardamom	1 mL
Puffs		
1¾ cups	all-purpose flour	425 mL
1½ tsp	baking powder	7 mL
1 tsp	ground cardamom	5 mL
1/4 tsp	salt	1 mL
2 tbsp	granulated sugar	30 mL
3	large eggs, separated	3
3 tbsp	unsalted butter, melted	45 mL
1½ tsp	vanilla extract	7 mL
1¼ cups	milk	300 mL
	Vegetable oil	
	Confectioners' (icing) sugar	

1. *Filling:* In a medium bowl, using an electric mixer on medium-high speed, beat cream cheese, almond paste and cardamom until smooth and creamy. Cover and refrigerate while preparing the batter. Clean the beaters.

2. *Puffs:* In a large bowl, whisk together flour, baking powder, cardamom and salt.

3. In a medium bowl, whisk together sugar, egg yolks, butter and vanilla. Whisk in milk until well blended.

4. Add the egg yolk mixture to the flour mixture and stir until just blended (the batter will appear slightly lumpy).

5. In a medium bowl, using an electric mixer on medium-high speed, beat egg whites until frothy. Increase speed to high and beat until stiff, but not dry, peaks form. Using a rubber spatula, gently mix one-third of the egg whites into the batter. Gently fold in the remaining whites.

6. Brush wells of pan lightly with oil. Set pan over medium heat. When oil begins to sizzle, add 1 tbsp (15 mL) batter to each well. Place 1 tsp (5 mL) filling in the center of each well and top with 1 tbsp (15 mL) batter. Cook for 2 to 4 minutes or until bottoms are golden brown. Using two skewers, flip the puffs over. Cook for 2 to 3 minutes or until bottoms are golden brown and a toothpick inserted in the center comes out with a bit of filling and a few moist crumbs attached. Remove pan from heat and transfer puffs to a plate. Let pan cool slightly.

7. Repeat with the remaining batter and filling, brushing wells with oil and reheating pan before each batch.

8. Dust the puffs with confectioners' sugar. Serve warm or at room temperature.

Babka Puffs (Poland, Russia)

Laden with chocolate, butter and Old World charm, these babka-inspired puffs are spectacular served with coffee or espresso drinks.

Variation

Dried Fruit and Almond Babka Puffs: Omit the cinnamon and chocolate, and replace the vanilla with ¾ tsp (3 mL) almond extract. Stir in ½ cup (125 mL) toasted sliced almonds and ½ cup (125 mL) assorted chopped dried fruit (such as cherries, apricots or golden raisins) at the end of step 3.

● **7-well ebelskiver pan**

1¼ cups	all-purpose flour	300 mL
1 tsp	ground cinnamon	5 mL
½ tsp	baking powder	2 mL
¼ tsp	salt	1 mL
¼ tsp	baking soda	1 mL
2 tbsp	granulated sugar	30 mL
2	large eggs, separated	2
⅔ cup	sour cream	150 mL
¼ cup	milk	60 mL
3 tbsp	unsalted butter, melted	45 mL
1 tsp	vanilla extract	5 mL
4 oz	bittersweet chocolate, chopped	125 g
	Vegetable oil	

1. In a large bowl, whisk together flour, cinnamon, baking powder, salt and baking soda.

2. In a medium bowl, whisk together sugar, egg yolks, sour cream, milk, butter and vanilla until well blended.

3. Add the egg yolk mixture to the flour mixture and stir until just blended (the batter will appear slightly lumpy). Gently stir in chocolate.

4. In a medium bowl, using an electric mixer on medium-high speed, beat egg whites until frothy. Increase speed to high and beat until stiff, but not dry, peaks form. Using a rubber spatula, gently mix one-third of the egg whites into the batter. Gently fold in the remaining whites.

5. Brush wells of pan lightly with oil. Set pan over medium heat. When oil begins to sizzle, add 2 tbsp (30 mL) batter to each well. Cook for 2 to 4 minutes or until bottoms are golden brown. Using two skewers, flip the puffs over. Cook for 2 to 3 minutes or until bottoms are golden brown and a toothpick inserted in the center comes out with a few moist crumbs attached. Remove pan from heat and transfer puffs to a plate. Let pan cool slightly.

6. Repeat with the remaining batter, brushing wells with oil and reheating pan before each batch. Serve warm or at room temperature.

Buckwheat Blini Puffs (Russia)

Makes about 21 puffs

This version of blini is innovative in both form and prep: puffed instead of flat for the former, and super-quick instead of time-consuming for the latter (because baking powder and eggs, not yeast, do the leavening).

Tips

If buckwheat flour is unavailable, whole wheat flour makes a good substitute.

Plain Greek yogurt may be used in place of the sour cream.

- 7-well ebelskiver pan

1¼ cups	buckwheat flour	300 mL
¾ tsp	baking powder	3 mL
¼ tsp	salt	1 mL
1 tbsp	packed dark brown sugar	15 mL
2	large eggs, separated	2
1 cup	milk	250 mL
2 tbsp	unsalted butter, melted	30 mL
	Vegetable oil	
¾ cup	sour cream	175 mL
3 tbsp	minced fresh chives	45 mL
2 oz	caviar (optional)	60 g

1. In a large bowl, whisk together flour, baking powder and salt.

2. In a medium bowl, whisk together brown sugar, egg yolks, milk and butter until well blended.

3. Add the egg yolk mixture to the flour mixture and stir until just blended (the batter will appear slightly lumpy).

4. In a medium bowl, using an electric mixer on medium-high speed, beat egg whites until frothy. Increase speed to high and beat until stiff, but not dry, peaks form. Using a rubber spatula, gently mix one-third of the egg whites into the batter. Gently fold in the remaining whites.

5. Brush wells of pan lightly with oil. Set pan over medium heat. When oil begins to sizzle, add 2 tbsp (30 mL) batter to each well. Cook for 2 to 4 minutes or until bottoms are golden brown. Using two skewers, flip the puffs over. Cook for 2 to 3 minutes or until bottoms are golden brown and a toothpick inserted in the center comes out with a few moist crumbs attached. Remove pan from heat and transfer puffs to a plate. Let pan cool slightly.

6. Repeat with the remaining batter, brushing wells with oil and reheating pan before each batch.

7. To serve, make a slit in the top of each puff. Spoon in a dollop of sour cream and top with chives and caviar (if using).

Poffertjes (Holland)

Given its close geographical proximity to Denmark, it is not surprising that Holland has its own version of ebelskivers: *poffertjes*. The pan and the cooking method are identical, but the batter differs: where ebelskivers use baking powder and baking soda, *poffertjes* use yeast. Additionally, the eggs are not separated in *poffertje* batters. The texture and the traditional flavorings of citrus zest and almond extract are reminiscent of Italian panettone.

Tip

This *poffertje* batter is every bit as versatile as the Classic Ebelskiver batter (page 20). Have fun experimenting with myriad sweet and savory filling ideas and mix-ins.

- 7-well ebelskiver pan

2 tsp	granulated sugar	10 mL
1¼ cups	milk	300 mL
2¼ tsp	quick-rising (instant) yeast	11 mL
2 cups	all-purpose flour	500 mL
¼ tsp	salt	1 mL
2	large eggs	2
2 tbsp	unsalted butter, melted	30 mL
2 tsp	finely grated lemon zest	10 mL
½ tsp	almond extract	2 mL
	Vegetable oil	
¾ cup	berry jam or preserves	175 mL
	Confectioners' (icing) sugar	

1. In a small saucepan, combine sugar and milk. Heat over medium-low heat for 1 to 2 minutes or until just barely warm. Remove from heat and sprinkle with yeast. Let stand for 3 minutes.

2. Meanwhile, in a large bowl, whisk together flour and salt.

3. In a medium bowl, whisk together eggs, butter, lemon zest and almond extract until well blended. Gradually whisk in milk mixture.

4. Add the egg mixture to the flour mixture and stir until just blended (the batter will appear slightly lumpy). Loosely cover with a clean tea towel and let stand in a warm, draft-free place for 45 minutes, until the batter appears puffy and has nearly doubled in volume.

5. Brush wells of pan lightly with oil. Set pan over medium heat. When oil begins to sizzle, add 1 tbsp (15 mL) batter to each well. Place 1 tsp (5 mL) jam in the center of each well and top with 1 tbsp (15 mL) batter. Cook for 2 to 4 minutes or until bottoms are golden brown. Using two skewers, flip the puffs over. Cook for 2 to 3 minutes or until bottoms are golden brown and a toothpick inserted in the center comes out with a bit of filling and a few moist crumbs attached. Remove pan from heat and transfer puffs to a plate. Let pan cool slightly.

6. Repeat with the remaining batter and jam, brushing wells with oil and reheating pan before each batch.

7. Dust the puffs with confectioners' sugar. Serve warm or at room temperature.

Golden Sherry and Orange Ebelskivers (Spain)

The mellow almond flavor of amontillado sherry works especially well in these refined ebelskivers, but truth be told, almost any type of sweet sherry will yield stellar results.

Tip

An equal amount of Marsala may be used in place of the sherry.

- **7-well ebelskiver pan**

1¼ cups	all-purpose flour	300 mL
¾ tsp	baking powder	3 mL
¼ tsp	salt	1 mL
¼ tsp	ground nutmeg	1 mL
2 tbsp	granulated sugar	30 mL
2	large eggs, separated	2
⅔ cup	milk	150 mL
⅓ cup	sherry	75 mL
2 tbsp	unsalted butter, melted	30 mL
	Vegetable oil	
½ cup	orange marmalade	125 mL
	Confectioners' (icing) sugar	

1. In a large bowl, whisk together flour, baking powder, salt and nutmeg.

2. In a medium bowl, whisk together sugar, egg yolks, milk, sherry and butter until well blended.

3. Add the egg yolk mixture to the flour mixture and stir until just blended (the batter will appear slightly lumpy).

4. In a medium bowl, using an electric mixer on medium-high speed, beat egg whites until frothy. Increase speed to high and beat until stiff, but not dry, peaks form. Using a rubber spatula, gently mix one-third of the egg whites into the batter. Gently fold in the remaining whites.

5. Brush wells of pan lightly with oil. Set pan over medium heat. When oil begins to sizzle, add 1 tbsp (15 mL) batter to each well. Place 1 tsp (5 mL) marmalade in the center of each well and top with 1 tbsp (15 mL) batter. Cook for 2 to 4 minutes or until bottoms are golden brown. Using two skewers, flip the puffs over. Cook for 2 to 3 minutes or until bottoms are golden brown and a toothpick inserted in the center comes out with a bit of filling and a few moist crumbs attached. Remove pan from heat and transfer puffs to a plate. Let pan cool slightly.

6. Repeat with the remaining batter and marmalade, brushing wells with oil and reheating pan before each batch.

7. Dust the ebelskivers with confectioners' sugar. Serve warm or at room temperature.

Pain d'Épices Puffs (France)

Pain d'épices is a dark, aromatic French loaf, part cake, part bread, with a mélange of spices and a generous dose of honey. These delicate puffs taste just like the real thing, with a fraction of the time and effort.

● **7-well ebelskiver pan**

1 cup	all-purpose flour	250 mL
1/4 cup	dark rye flour	60 mL
1 tsp	ground cinnamon	5 mL
1 tsp	ground ginger	5 mL
3/4 tsp	baking powder	3 mL
1/4 tsp	salt	1 mL
1/4 tsp	ground nutmeg	1 mL
1/4 tsp	anise seeds, crushed	1 mL
1/8 tsp	freshly ground black pepper	0.5 mL
2	large eggs, separated	2
1 cup	milk	250 mL
1/4 cup	liquid honey	60 mL
2 tbsp	unsalted butter, melted	30 mL
1 1/2 tsp	finely grated orange zest	7 mL
	Vegetable oil	
	Confectioners' (icing) sugar	

1. In a large bowl, whisk together all-purpose flour, rye flour, cinnamon, ginger, baking powder, salt, nutmeg, anise seeds and pepper.

2. In a medium bowl, whisk together egg yolks, milk, honey, butter and orange zest until well blended.

3. Add the egg yolk mixture to the flour mixture and stir until just blended (the batter will appear slightly lumpy).

4. In a medium bowl, using an electric mixer on medium-high speed, beat egg whites until frothy. Increase speed to high and beat until stiff, but not dry, peaks form. Using a rubber spatula, gently mix one-third of the egg whites into the batter. Gently fold in the remaining whites.

5. Brush wells of pan lightly with oil. Set pan over medium heat. When oil begins to sizzle, add 2 tbsp (30 mL) batter to each well. Cook for 2 to 4 minutes or until bottoms are golden brown. Using two skewers, flip the puffs over. Cook for 2 to 3 minutes or until bottoms are golden brown and a toothpick inserted in the center comes out with a few moist crumbs attached. Remove pan from heat and transfer puffs to a plate. Let pan cool slightly.

6. Repeat with the remaining batter, brushing wells with oil and reheating pan before each batch.

7. Dust the puffs with confectioners' sugar. Serve warm or at room temperature.

Gougère Puffs (France)

These puffs have the lively crisp exterior and cloudlike interior you expect from a gougère — bite-size, oven-baked cheese puffs — including the sharp bite of Dijon mustard and the melted cheesiness of Gruyère. I'm hard-pressed to ask for anything more.

Tip

An equal amount of grated Swiss or white Cheddar cheese may be used in place of the Gruyère.

- **7-well ebelskiver pan**

1¼ cups	all-purpose flour	300 mL
1 tsp	baking powder	5 mL
½ tsp	salt	2 mL
¼ tsp	freshly ground black pepper	1 mL
4	large eggs	4
¾ cup	milk	175 mL
6 tbsp	unsalted butter, melted	90 mL
2 tsp	Dijon mustard	10 mL
1 cup	shredded Gruyère cheese	250 mL
	Vegetable oil	

1. In a large bowl, whisk together flour, baking powder, salt and pepper.

2. In a medium bowl, whisk together eggs, milk, butter and mustard until well blended.

3. Add the egg mixture to the flour mixture and stir until just blended (the batter will appear slightly lumpy). Stir in cheese.

4. Brush wells of pan lightly with oil. Set pan over medium heat. When oil begins to sizzle, add 2 tbsp (30 mL) batter to each well. Cook for 2 to 4 minutes or until bottoms are golden brown. Using two skewers, flip the puffs over. Cook for 2 to 3 minutes or until bottoms are golden brown and puffs feel firm to the touch. Remove pan from heat and transfer puffs to a plate. Let pan cool slightly.

5. Repeat with the remaining batter, brushing wells with oil and reheating pan before each batch. Serve warm.

Linzer Puffs (Austria)

These puffs find inspiration in Vienna's linzertorte, a traditional dessert made with nuts and raspberry jam.

Variation

Sachertorte Puffs: Omit the cinnamon and replace the raspberry jam with apricot jam or preserves. Serve with Chocolate Sauce (page 90).

● **7-well ebelskiver pan**

1¼ cups	all-purpose flour	300 mL
¾ tsp	baking powder	3 mL
½ tsp	ground cinnamon	2 mL
¼ tsp	salt	1 mL
3 tbsp	granulated sugar	45 mL
2	large eggs, separated	2
1 cup	milk	250 mL
3 tbsp	unsalted butter, melted	45 mL
1 tsp	almond extract	5 mL
⅔ cup	chopped toasted hazelnuts or almonds	150 mL
	Vegetable oil	
⅔ cup	raspberry jam or preserves	150 mL
	Confectioners' (icing) sugar	

1. In a large bowl, whisk together flour, baking powder, cinnamon and salt.

2. In a medium bowl, whisk together sugar, egg yolks, milk, butter and almond extract until well blended.

3. Add the egg yolk mixture to the flour mixture and stir until just blended (the batter will appear slightly lumpy). Gently stir in hazelnuts.

4. In a medium bowl, using an electric mixer on medium-high speed, beat egg whites until frothy. Increase speed to high and beat until stiff, but not dry, peaks form. Using a rubber spatula, gently mix one-third of the egg whites into the batter. Gently fold in the remaining whites.

5. Brush wells of pan lightly with oil. Set pan over medium heat. When oil begins to sizzle, add 1 tbsp (15 mL) batter to each well. Place 1 tsp (5 mL) jam in the center of each well and top with 1 tbsp (15 mL) batter. Cook for 2 to 4 minutes or until bottoms are golden brown. Using two skewers, flip the puffs over. Cook for 2 to 3 minutes or until bottoms are golden brown and a toothpick inserted in the center comes out with a bit of filling and a few moist crumbs attached. Remove pan from heat and transfer puffs to a plate. Let pan cool slightly.

6. Repeat with the remaining batter and jam, brushing wells with oil and reheating pan before each batch.

7. Dust the puffs with confectioners' sugar. Serve warm or at room temperature.

Basel Läckerli Puffs (Switzerland)

If you have never had Basel Läckerli, seek them out: they are traditional hard spice biscuits made of honey, almonds, candied peel and Kirsch, a cherry-flavored spirit. In short, scrumptious. According to Swiss lore, they were originally created by local spice merchants in Basel, Switzerland, over 700 years ago. My ebelskiver version is brand-new, but equally delicious.

Tip

One tsp (5 mL) almond extract may be used in place of the Kirsch.

● **7-well ebelskiver pan**

1¼ cups	all-purpose flour	300 mL
¾ tsp	baking powder	3 mL
¾ tsp	ground cinnamon	3 mL
¼ tsp	salt	1 mL
½ tsp	ground nutmeg	2 mL
¼ tsp	ground cloves	1 mL
2	large eggs, separated	2
¾ cup	milk	175 mL
3 tbsp	liquid honey	45 mL
2 tbsp	unsalted butter, melted	30 mL
2 tbsp	Kirsch (cherry brandy)	30 mL
1 tsp	finely grated lemon zest	5 mL
1 tsp	finely grated orange zest	5 mL
½ cup	sliced almonds, toasted	125 mL
	Vegetable oil	

1. In a large bowl, whisk together flour, baking powder, cinnamon, salt, nutmeg and cloves.

2. In a medium bowl, whisk together egg yolks, milk, honey, butter, Kirsch, lemon zest and orange zest until well blended.

3. Add the egg yolk mixture to the flour mixture and stir until just blended (the batter will appear slightly lumpy). Gently stir in almonds.

4. In a medium bowl, using an electric mixer on medium-high speed, beat egg whites until frothy. Increase speed to high and beat until stiff, but not dry, peaks form. Using a rubber spatula, gently mix one-third of the egg whites into the batter. Gently fold in the remaining whites.

5. Brush wells of pan lightly with oil. Set pan over medium heat. When oil begins to sizzle, add 2 tbsp (30 mL) batter to each well. Cook for 2 to 4 minutes or until bottoms are golden brown. Using two skewers, flip the puffs over. Cook for 2 to 3 minutes or until bottoms are golden brown and a toothpick inserted in the center comes out with a few moist crumbs attached. Remove pan from heat and transfer puffs to a plate. Let pan cool slightly.

6. Repeat with the remaining batter, brushing wells with oil and reheating pan before each batch. Serve warm or at room temperature.

Gianduja Puffs (Switzerland, Italy)

The rich hazelnut-flavored chocolate called *gianduja* (or *gianduia* in Italy) — named for the masked character Gianduia of the centuries-old Italian commedia dell'arte — makes for mini puffed pancakes that are sophisticated and intensely delicious.

• **7-well ebelskiver pan**

1 cup	all-purpose flour	250 mL
1/4 cup	unsweetened cocoa powder (not Dutch process)	60 mL
1/2 tsp	baking powder	2 mL
1/4 tsp	baking soda	1 mL
1/4 tsp	salt	1 mL
2 tbsp	packed light brown sugar	30 mL
2	large eggs, separated	2
1 cup	milk	250 mL
2 tbsp	unsalted butter, melted	30 mL
1 tsp	vanilla extract	5 mL
2/3 cup	chopped toasted hazelnuts	150 mL
	Vegetable oil	
2/3 cup	chocolate hazelnut spread	150 mL
	Confectioners' (icing) sugar	

1. In a large bowl, whisk together flour, cocoa powder, baking powder, baking soda and salt.

2. In a medium bowl, whisk together brown sugar, egg yolks, milk, butter and vanilla until well blended.

3. Add the egg yolk mixture to the flour mixture and stir until just blended (the batter will appear slightly lumpy). Gently stir in hazelnuts.

4. In a medium bowl, using an electric mixer on medium-high speed, beat egg whites until frothy. Increase speed to high and beat until stiff, but not dry, peaks form. Using a rubber spatula, gently mix one-third of the egg whites into the batter. Gently fold in the remaining whites.

Tip

An equal amount of chopped toasted almonds may be used in place of the hazelnuts.

5. Brush wells of pan lightly with oil. Set pan over medium heat. When oil begins to sizzle, add 1 tbsp (15 mL) batter to each well. Place 1 tsp (5 mL) chocolate hazelnut spread in the center of each well and top with 1 tbsp (15 mL) batter. Cook for 2 to 4 minutes or until bottoms are crisp-firm to the touch. Using two skewers, flip the puffs over. Cook for 2 to 3 minutes or until bottoms are crisp-firm and a toothpick inserted in the center comes out with a bit of filling and a few moist crumbs attached. Remove pan from heat and transfer puffs to a plate. Let pan cool slightly.

6. Repeat with the remaining batter and chocolate hazelnut spread, brushing wells with oil and reheating pan before each batch.

7. Dust the puffs with confectioners' sugar. Serve warm or at room temperature.

Tiramisu Puffs (Italy)

Tiramisu was a '90s hit, appearing on just about every dessert menu. But while the fad has faded, the appeal of the luxurious confection has not. Here it finds new life in puff form, with a rich rum and espresso ricotta filling.

- 7-well ebelskiver pan

Filling

2 tsp	instant espresso powder	10 mL
1 tbsp	dark rum	15 mL
3 tbsp	granulated sugar	45 mL
1 cup	ricotta cheese	250 mL

Puffs

1¾ cups	all-purpose flour	425 mL
1½ tsp	baking powder	7 mL
¼ tsp	salt	1 mL
2 tbsp	granulated sugar	30 mL
3	large eggs, separated	3
3 tbsp	unsalted butter, melted	45 mL
1½ tsp	vanilla extract	7 mL
1¼ cups	milk	300 mL
	Vegetable oil	
	Confectioners' (icing) sugar	

1. *Filling:* In a small bowl, combine espresso powder and rum, stirring until powder is dissolved. Stir in sugar and cheese until blended. Cover and refrigerate while preparing the batter.

2. *Puffs:* In a large bowl, whisk together flour, baking powder and salt.

3. In a medium bowl, whisk together sugar, egg yolks, butter and vanilla. Whisk in milk until well blended.

4. Add the egg yolk mixture to the flour mixture and stir until just blended (the batter will appear slightly lumpy).

5. In a medium bowl, using an electric mixer on medium-high speed, beat egg whites until frothy. Increase speed to high and beat until stiff, but not dry, peaks form. Using a rubber spatula, gently mix one-third of the egg whites into the batter. Gently fold in the remaining whites.

6. Brush wells of pan lightly with oil. Set pan over medium heat. When oil begins to sizzle, add 1 tbsp (15 mL) batter to each well. Place 1 tsp (5 mL) filling in the center of each well and top with 1 tbsp (15 mL) batter. Cook for 2 to 4 minutes or until bottoms are golden brown. Using two skewers, flip the puffs over. Cook for 2 to 3 minutes or until bottoms are golden brown and a toothpick inserted in the center comes out with a bit of filling and a few moist crumbs attached. Remove pan from heat and transfer puffs to a plate. Let pan cool slightly.

7. Repeat with the remaining batter and filling, brushing wells with oil and reheating pan before each batch.

8. Dust the puffs with confectioners' sugar. Serve warm or at room temperature.

Cannoli Puffs (Italy)

An almond-flavored batter with chocolate chips and flecks of pistachio speckled throughout, plus a sweet ricotta filling, makes for a perfect marriage of Italian and American.

• **7-well ebelskiver pan**

Filling

2 tbsp	granulated sugar	30 mL
1 cup	ricotta cheese	250 mL

Puffs

1¾ cups	all-purpose flour	425 mL
1½ tsp	baking powder	7 mL
¼ tsp	salt	1 mL
2 tbsp	granulated sugar	30 mL
3	large eggs, separated	3
3 tbsp	unsalted butter, melted	45 mL
1¼ tsp	almond extract	6 mL
1¼ cups	milk	300 mL
½ cup	miniature semisweet chocolate chips	125 mL
½ cup	lightly salted roasted pistachios, chopped	125 mL
	Vegetable oil	
	Confectioners' (icing) sugar	

1. *Filling:* In a small bowl, stir together sugar and cheese until blended. Cover and refrigerate while preparing the batter.

2. *Puffs:* In a large bowl, whisk together flour, baking powder and salt.

3. In a medium bowl, whisk together sugar, egg yolks, butter and almond extract. Whisk in milk until well blended.

4. Add the egg yolk mixture to the flour mixture and stir until just blended (the batter will appear slightly lumpy). Gently stir in chocolate chips and pistachios.

5. In a medium bowl, using an electric mixer on medium-high speed, beat egg whites until frothy. Increase speed to high and beat until stiff, but not dry, peaks form. Using a rubber spatula, gently mix one-third of the egg whites into the batter. Gently fold in the remaining whites.

An equal amount of chopped toasted almonds may be used in place of the pistachios.

6. Brush wells of pan lightly with oil. Set pan over medium heat. When oil begins to sizzle, add 1 tbsp (15 mL) batter to each well. Place 1 tsp (5 mL) filling in the center of each well and top with 1 tbsp (15 mL) batter. Cook for 2 to 4 minutes or until bottoms are golden brown. Using two skewers, flip the puffs over. Cook for 2 to 3 minutes or until bottoms are golden brown and a toothpick inserted in the center comes out with a bit of filling and a few moist crumbs attached. Remove pan from heat and transfer puffs to a plate. Let pan cool slightly.

7. Repeat with the remaining batter and filling, brushing wells with oil and reheating pan before each batch.

8. Dust the puffs with confectioners' sugar. Serve warm or at room temperature.

Poppy Seed–Filled Kalács
(Hungary)

Kalács is a traditional
Hungarian egg bread —
similar in taste and
texture to challah — that
is typically scented with
cinnamon and citrus and
filled with a sweet poppy
seed or walnut filling.
The flavors and textures
are equally enchanting
when made in the
ebelskiver pan.

Tip

Poppy seed filling can be
found in cans in the bakery
section of the supermarket,
where almond paste and
pie fillings are shelved.
Leftovers can be frozen in
an airtight container for up
to 3 months.

● **7-well ebelskiver pan**

1¼ cups	all-purpose flour	300 mL
¾ tsp	baking powder	3 mL
¾ tsp	ground cinnamon	3 mL
¼ tsp	salt	1 mL
1 tbsp	granulated sugar	15 mL
3	large eggs, separated	3
¾ cup	milk	175 mL
3 tbsp	unsalted butter, melted	45 mL
1 tsp	finely grated lemon zest	5 mL
½ cup	canned poppy seed filling	125 mL
	Confectioners' (icing) sugar	

1. In a large bowl, whisk together flour, baking powder, cinnamon and salt.

2. In a medium bowl, whisk together sugar, egg yolks, milk, butter and lemon zest until well blended.

3. Add the egg yolk mixture to the flour mixture and stir until just blended (the batter will appear slightly lumpy).

4. In a medium bowl, using an electric mixer on medium-high speed, beat egg whites until frothy. Increase speed to high and beat until stiff, but not dry, peaks form. Using a rubber spatula, gently mix one-third of the egg whites into the batter. Gently fold in the remaining whites.

5. Brush wells of pan lightly with oil. Set pan over medium heat. When oil begins to sizzle, add 1 tbsp (15 mL) batter to each well. Place 1 tsp (5 mL) poppy seed filling in the center of each well and top with 1 tbsp (15 mL) batter. Cook for 2 to 4 minutes or until bottoms are golden brown. Using two skewers, flip the puffs over. Cook for 2 to 3 minutes or until bottoms are golden brown and a toothpick inserted in the center comes out with a bit of filling and a few moist crumbs attached. Remove pan from heat and transfer puffs to a plate. Let pan cool slightly.

6. Repeat with the remaining batter and filling, brushing wells with oil and reheating pan before each batch.

7. Dust the puffs with confectioners' sugar. Serve warm or at room temperature.

Spanakopita Puffs (Greece)

Spanakopita is a Greek spinach pie that is one of the most beloved dishes on the menus of Greek restaurants around the world. Here, I've abandoned the fussy phyllo dough but kept all of the sensational flavors.

● **7-well ebelskiver pan**

1¼ cups	all-purpose flour	300 mL
1½ tsp	dried dillweed	7 mL
¾ tsp	baking powder	3 mL
¼ tsp	salt	1 mL
2	large eggs, separated	2
1 cup	milk	250 mL
2 tbsp	unsalted butter, melted	30 mL
1	package (10 oz/300 g) frozen chopped spinach, thawed and squeezed dry	1
1 cup	crumbled feta cheese	250 mL
	Vegetable oil	

1. In a large bowl, whisk together flour, dill, baking powder and salt.

2. In a medium bowl, whisk together egg yolks, milk and butter until well blended.

3. Add the egg yolk mixture to the flour mixture and stir until just blended (the batter will appear slightly lumpy). Gently stir in spinach and cheese.

4. In a medium bowl, using an electric mixer on medium-high speed, beat egg whites until frothy. Increase speed to high and beat until stiff, but not dry, peaks form. Using a rubber spatula, gently mix one-third of the egg whites into the batter. Gently fold in the remaining whites.

5. Brush wells of pan lightly with oil. Set pan over medium heat. When oil begins to sizzle, add 2 tbsp (30 mL) batter to each well. Cook for 2 to 4 minutes or until bottoms are golden brown. Using two skewers, flip the puffs over. Cook for 2 to 3 minutes or until bottoms are golden brown and a toothpick inserted in the center comes out with a few moist crumbs attached. Remove pan from heat and transfer puffs to a plate. Let pan cool slightly.

6. Repeat with the remaining batter, brushing wells with oil and reheating pan before each batch. Serve warm or at room temperature.

Harcha with Za'atar Olives and Cheese (Morocco)

Harcha is a Moroccan
pan-fried bread that
is served sweet or
savory, plain or stuffed.
Recasting it in puff
form, I've taken it in a
savory, stuffed direction,
featuring spices typical of
za'atar (oregano, thyme
and sesame) and a spicy
olive-cheese filling.

● **7-well ebelskiver pan**

Filling		
½ cup	crumbled feta cheese	125 mL
3 tbsp	chopped black or green brine-cured olives	45 mL
½ tsp	hot smoked paprika	2 mL
Puffs		
1¼ cups	all-purpose flour	300 mL
2 tbsp	sesame seeds, toasted (see tip, at right)	30 mL
1 tsp	dried thyme	5 mL
1 tsp	dried oregano	5 mL
¾ tsp	baking powder	3 mL
¼ tsp	salt	1 mL
2	large eggs, separated	2
1 cup	milk	250 mL
2 tbsp	extra virgin olive oil	30 mL
	Olive oil	

1. *Filling:* In a small bowl, combine cheese, olives and paprika. Set aside.

2. *Puffs:* In a large bowl, whisk together flour, sesame seeds, thyme, oregano, baking powder and salt.

3. In a medium bowl, whisk together egg yolks, milk and oil until well blended.

4. Add the egg yolk mixture to the flour mixture and stir until just blended (the batter will appear slightly lumpy).

5. In a medium bowl, using an electric mixer on medium-high speed, beat egg whites until frothy. Increase speed to high and beat until stiff, but not dry, peaks form. Using a rubber spatula, gently mix one-third of the egg whites into the batter. Gently fold in the remaining whites.

To toast the sesame seeds, place them in a dry skillet set over medium heat. Cook, shaking the pan every few seconds, for 30 to 90 seconds, until the seeds are golden and aromatic and begin to make a popping sound. Immediately transfer to a bowl and let cool.

6. Brush wells of pan lightly with oil. Set pan over medium heat. When oil begins to sizzle, add 1 tbsp (15 mL) batter to each well. Place 1 tsp (5 mL) filling in the center of each well and top with 1 tbsp (15 mL) batter. Cook for 2 to 4 minutes or until bottoms are golden brown. Using two skewers, flip the puffs over. Cook for 2 to 3 minutes or until bottoms are golden brown and a toothpick inserted in the center comes out with a bit of filling and a few moist crumbs attached. Remove pan from heat and transfer puffs to a plate. Let pan cool slightly.

7. Repeat with the remaining batter and filling, brushing wells with oil and reheating pan before each batch. Serve warm or at room temperature.

Sesame Halvah Puffs (Israel)

Tahini is just as delicious — I would argue even more so — in sweets as it is in hummus and baba ghanouj. Halvah, a delicious, fudge-like candy made from tahini, is one such beloved sweet. These halvah-inspired treats may soon become another.

● **7-well ebelskiver pan**

Filling

1 cup	confectioners' (icing) sugar	250 mL
½ cup	well-stirred tahini	125 mL
½ tsp	vanilla extract	2 mL

Puffs

1¼ cups	all-purpose flour	300 mL
¾ tsp	baking powder	3 mL
¼ tsp	salt	1 mL
2 tbsp	packed dark brown sugar	30 mL
2	large eggs, separated	2
1 cup	milk	250 mL
2 tbsp	unsalted butter, melted	30 mL
1 tsp	vanilla extract	5 mL
⅓ cup	sesame seeds, toasted (see tip, at right)	75 mL
	Vegetable oil	
	Confectioners' (icing) sugar	

1. *Filling:* In a small bowl, stir together confectioners' sugar, tahini and vanilla until blended (mixture will be stiff). Set aside.

2. *Puffs:* In a large bowl, whisk together flour, baking powder and salt.

3. In a medium bowl, whisk together brown sugar, egg yolks, milk, butter and vanilla until well blended.

4. Add the egg yolk mixture to the flour mixture and stir until just blended (the batter will appear slightly lumpy). Gently stir in sesame seeds.

5. In a medium bowl, using an electric mixer on medium-high speed, beat egg whites until frothy. Increase speed to high and beat until stiff, but not dry, peaks form. Using a rubber spatula, gently mix one-third of the egg whites into the batter. Gently fold in the remaining whites.

Tip

To toast the sesame seeds, place them in a dry skillet set over medium heat. Cook, shaking the pan every few seconds, for 30 to 90 seconds, until the seeds are golden and aromatic and begin to make a popping sound. Immediately transfer to a bowl and let cool.

6. Brush wells of pan lightly with oil. Set pan over medium heat. When oil begins to sizzle, add 1 tbsp (15 mL) batter to each well. Place 1 tsp (5 mL) filling in the center of each well and top with 1 tbsp (15 mL) batter. Cook for 2 to 4 minutes or until bottoms are golden brown. Using two skewers, flip the puffs over. Cook for 2 to 3 minutes or until bottoms are golden brown and a toothpick inserted in the center comes out with a bit of filling and a few moist crumbs attached. Remove pan from heat and transfer puffs to a plate. Let pan cool slightly.

7. Repeat with the remaining batter and filling, brushing wells with oil and reheating pan before each batch.

8. Dust the puffs with confectioners' sugar. Serve warm or at room temperature.

Orange and Currant Matzo Puffs (Israel)

Unique, easy and light as air, these matzo confections are an ideal addition to the Passover table — or any dessert buffet throughout the year.

Tips

You can make your own matzo cake meal by finely grinding regular matzo meal in a food processor or a clean coffee or spice grinder.

Potato starch is available at most supermarkets, in the health food or baking section, or at health food stores.

● **7-well ebelskiver pan**

1 cup	matzo cake meal	250 mL
1/4 cup	potato starch	60 mL
1/4 tsp	salt	1 mL
2 tbsp	granulated sugar	30 mL
4	large eggs, separated	4
3/4 cup	milk	175 mL
2 tbsp	extra virgin olive oil	30 mL
2 tsp	finely grated orange zest	10 mL
1/2 tsp	almond extract	2 mL
2/3 cup	dried currants or raisins	150 mL
	Olive oil or vegetable oil	
2/3 cup	orange marmalade	150 mL

1. In a large bowl, whisk together matzo cake meal, potato starch and salt.

2. In a medium bowl, whisk together sugar, egg yolks, milk, oil, orange zest and almond extract until well blended.

3. Add the egg yolk mixture to the flour mixture and stir until just blended (the batter will appear slightly lumpy). Gently stir in currants.

4. In a medium bowl, using an electric mixer on medium-high speed, beat egg whites until frothy. Increase speed to high and beat until stiff, but not dry, peaks form. Using a rubber spatula, gently mix one-third of the egg whites into the batter. Gently fold in the remaining whites.

5. Brush wells of pan lightly with oil. Set pan over medium heat. When oil begins to sizzle, add 1 tbsp (15 mL) batter to each well. Place 1 tsp (5 mL) marmalade in the center of each well and top with 1 tbsp (15 mL) batter. Cook for 2 to 4 minutes or until bottoms are golden brown. Using two skewers, flip the puffs over. Cook for 2 to 3 minutes or until bottoms are golden brown and a toothpick inserted in the center comes out with a bit of filling and a few moist crumbs attached. Remove pan from heat and transfer puffs to a plate. Let pan cool slightly.

6. Repeat with the remaining batter and marmalade, brushing wells with oil and reheating pan before each batch. Serve warm or at room temperature.

Barazek Puffs (Syria)

Captivating in their simplicity, these puffs are based on the flavors of *barazek* cookies, which have been peddled on the streets of Damascus for centuries.

Tips

For best results, do not use nonfat yogurt in this recipe.

An equal amount of chopped toasted almonds may be used in place of the pistachios.

● **7-well ebelskiver pan**

1¼ cups	all-purpose flour	300 mL
½ tsp	baking soda	2 mL
¼ tsp	salt	1 mL
2	large eggs, separated	2
1 cup	plain whole-milk yogurt	250 mL
3 tbsp	unsalted butter, melted	45 mL
3 tbsp	liquid honey	45 mL
½ cup	lightly salted roasted pistachios, chopped	125 mL
⅓ cup	sesame seeds, toasted (see tip, page 227)	75 mL
	Vegetable oil	
	Additional liquid honey	

1. In a large bowl, whisk together flour, baking powder and salt.

2. In a medium bowl, whisk together egg yolks, yogurt, butter and honey until well blended.

3. Add the egg yolk mixture to the flour mixture and stir until just blended (the batter will appear slightly lumpy). Gently stir in pistachios and sesame seeds.

4. In a medium bowl, using an electric mixer on medium-high speed, beat egg whites until frothy. Increase speed to high and beat until stiff, but not dry, peaks form. Using a rubber spatula, gently mix one-third of the egg whites into the batter. Gently fold in the remaining whites.

5. Brush wells of pan lightly with oil. Set pan over medium heat. When oil begins to sizzle, add 2 tbsp (30 mL) batter to each well. Cook for 2 to 4 minutes or until bottoms are golden brown. Using two skewers, flip the puffs over. Cook for 2 to 3 minutes or until bottoms are golden brown and a toothpick inserted in the center comes out with a few moist crumbs attached. Remove pan from heat and transfer puffs to a plate. Let pan cool slightly.

6. Repeat with the remaining batter, brushing wells with oil and reheating pan before each batch.

7. Drizzle the puffs with honey. Serve warm or at room temperature.

Katayef (the Middle East)

Makes about 21 puffs

Katayef are nut- and spice-stuffed dessert pancakes made and served in countries throughout the Middle East during the holy month of Ramadan. The traditional recipe involves pinching the still-warm pancakes around the filling, a tricky step easily eliminated by preparing the pancakes in an ebelskiver pan.

- Food processor
- 7-well ebelskiver pan

Filling

1 cup	toasted walnuts	250 mL
2 tbsp	granulated sugar	30 mL
1 tbsp	unsalted butter, melted	15 mL
¼ tsp	ground cinnamon	1 mL
⅛ tsp	ground nutmeg	0.5 mL
Pinch	salt	pinch

Puffs

2¼ tsp	active dry yeast	11 mL
2 tsp	granulated sugar	10 mL
¼ cup	warm water	60 mL
¾ cup	farina or cream of wheat	175 mL
½ cup	all-purpose flour	125 mL
¼ tsp	salt	1 mL
⅛ tsp	baking soda	0.5 mL
1	large egg	1
1 cup	milk	250 mL
2 tbsp	unsalted butter, melted	30 mL
	Vegetable oil	
⅓ cup	liquid honey	75 mL

1. *Filling:* In food processor, combine walnuts, sugar, butter, cinnamon, nutmeg and salt; process until a paste forms. Set aside.

2. *Puffs:* In a small cup, combine yeast, sugar and warm water. Let stand for 5 minutes.

3. In a large bowl, whisk together farina, flour, salt and baking soda.

4. In a medium bowl, whisk together egg, milk, butter and yeast mixture until well blended.

5. Add the egg mixture to the farina mixture and stir until just blended (the batter will appear slightly lumpy). Loosely cover with a clean dish towel and let stand in a warm, draft-free place for 45 minutes, until batter is almost doubled in volume and appears puffy.

Tips

Look for boxes of farina or cream of wheat in the cereal section of the supermarket.

Other nuts, such as pistachios, pine nuts or almonds, may be used in place of the walnuts.

6. Brush wells of pan lightly with oil. Set pan over medium heat. When oil begins to sizzle, add 1 tbsp (15 mL) batter to each well. Place 1 tsp (5 mL) filling in the center of each pancake and top with 1 tbsp (15 mL) batter. Cook for 2 to 4 minutes or until bottoms are golden brown. Using two skewers, flip the puffs over. Cook for 2 to 3 minutes or until bottoms are golden brown and a toothpick inserted in the center comes out with a bit of filling and a few moist crumbs attached. Remove pan from heat and transfer puffs to a plate. Let pan cool slightly.

7. Repeat with the remaining batter and filling, brushing wells with oil and reheating pan before each batch.

8. Drizzle the puffs with honey. Serve warm or at room temperature.

Rose-Scented Pistachio Puffs (India, the Middle East)

These delicate puffs, enriched with yogurt and butter and sweetened with honey, are inspired by aromatic Persian, Turkish and Indian confections.

Tip

Look for rose water in Middle Eastern, Indian and health food stores, or in the international foods section or baking section of well-stocked grocery stores.

Variation

Vanilla Pistachio Puffs: Use an equal amount of vanilla extract in place of the rose water.

- 7-well ebelskiver pan

1¾ cups	all-purpose flour	425 mL
1 tsp	baking powder	5 mL
¾ tsp	baking soda	3 mL
½ tsp	ground cardamom or ground ginger	2 mL
¼ tsp	salt	1 mL
3	large eggs, separated	3
¾ cup	plain yogurt	175 mL
⅓ cup	milk	125 mL
3 tbsp	unsalted butter, melted	45 mL
2 tbsp	liquid honey	30 mL
1 tsp	rose water	5 mL
⅔ cup	roasted lightly salted pistachios, chopped	150 mL
	Vegetable oil	
	Confectioners' (icing) sugar	

1. In a large bowl, whisk together flour, baking powder, baking soda, cardamom and salt.

2. In a medium bowl, whisk together egg yolks, yogurt, milk, butter, honey and rose water until well blended.

3. Add the egg yolk mixture to the flour mixture and stir until just blended (the batter will appear slightly lumpy). Gently stir in pistachios.

4. In a medium bowl, using an electric mixer on medium-high speed, beat egg whites until frothy. Increase speed to high and beat until stiff, but not dry, peaks form. Using a rubber spatula, gently mix one-third of the egg whites into the batter. Gently fold in the remaining whites.

5. Brush wells of pan lightly with oil. Set pan over medium heat. When oil begins to sizzle, add 2 tbsp (30 mL) batter to each well. Cook for 2 to 4 minutes or until bottoms are golden brown. Using two skewers, flip the puffs over. Cook for 2 to 3 minutes or until bottoms are golden brown and a toothpick inserted in the center comes out with a few moist crumbs attached. Remove pan from heat and transfer puffs to a plate. Let pan cool slightly.

6. Repeat with the remaining batter, brushing wells with oil and reheating pan before each batch.

7. Dust the ebelskivers with confectioners' sugar. Serve warm or at room temperature.

Kuzhi Paniyaram (India)

Kuzhi paniyaram is a puffed pancake snack from the southern region of India. The snack can be made savory or sweet, and is a breeze to replicate, given that the *paniyaram* pan is virtually identical to an ebelskiver pan. Although delicious eaten right from the pan, packing them to enjoy at room temperature is traditional, too: *kuzhi paniyaram* used to be made for eating on long-distance trips.

Tips

Either white or brown rice flour may be used in this recipe with equal success.

To make this recipe gluten-free, substitute an equal amount of a gluten-free all-purpose baking mix for the all-purpose flour.

● **7-well ebelskiver pan**

⅔ cup	rice flour	150 mL
½ cup	all-purpose flour	125 mL
1 tsp	ground cumin	5 mL
¼ tsp	salt	1 mL
¼ tsp	baking soda	1 mL
⅓ cup	grated onion	75 mL
¼ cup	chopped fresh cilantro	60 mL
1 tbsp	minced seeded jalapeño pepper	15 mL
1 cup	water	250 mL
¼ cup	plain whole-milk yogurt	60 mL
	Vegetable oil	
	Mango chutney	

1. In a large bowl, whisk together rice flour, all-purpose flour, cumin, salt and baking soda.

2. In a medium bowl, whisk together onion, cilantro, jalapeño, water and yogurt until well blended.

3. Add the onion mixture to the flour mixture and stir until just blended (the batter will appear slightly lumpy).

4. Brush wells of pan lightly with oil. Set pan over medium heat. When oil begins to sizzle, add 2 tbsp (30 mL) batter to each well. Cook for 2 to 4 minutes or until bottoms are golden brown. Using two skewers, flip the puffs over. Cook for 2 to 3 minutes or until bottoms are golden brown and a toothpick inserted in the center comes out with a few moist crumbs attached. Remove pan from heat and transfer puffs to a plate. Let pan cool slightly.

5. Repeat with the remaining batter, brushing wells with oil and reheating pan before each batch.

6. Serve the puffs warm or at room temperature, with chutney.

Paneer-Stuffed Puffs (India)

Makes about 35 puffs

Fried bread stuffed with paneer (a soft, fresh white cheese), herbs and spices can be purchased at street stalls across India. Let these puffs transport you — without the fuss and muss of deep frying.

● **7-well ebelskiver pan**

Filling
1 cup	crumbled paneer	250 mL
2 tbsp	minced fresh cilantro	30 mL
1/8 tsp	cayenne pepper	0.5 mL
1 tbsp	ketchup	15 mL

Puffs
1 3/4 cups	all-purpose flour	425 mL
1 tsp	baking powder	5 mL
1 tsp	ground cumin	5 mL
1/4 tsp	salt	1 mL
3	large eggs, separated	3
1 1/4 cups	milk	300 mL
3 tbsp	unsalted butter, melted	45 mL
2/3 cup	chopped green onions	150 mL
2 tbsp	minced gingerroot	30 mL
	Vegetable oil	

1. *Filling:* In a small bowl, combine paneer, cilantro, cayenne and ketchup. Set aside.

2. *Puffs:* In a large bowl, whisk together flour, baking powder, cumin and salt.

3. In a medium bowl, whisk together egg yolks, milk and butter until well blended.

4. Add the egg yolk mixture to the flour mixture and stir until just blended (the batter will appear slightly lumpy). Gently stir in green onions and ginger.

5. In a medium bowl, using an electric mixer on medium-high speed, beat egg whites until frothy. Increase speed to high and beat until stiff, but not dry, peaks form. Using a rubber spatula, gently mix one-third of the egg whites into the batter. Gently fold in the remaining whites.

An equal amount of crumbled queso blanco, cotija or mild feta cheese can be used in place of the paneer.

6. Brush wells of pan lightly with oil. Set pan over medium heat. When oil begins to sizzle, add 1 tbsp (15 mL) batter to each well. Place 1 tsp (5 mL) filling in the center of each well and top with 1 tbsp (15 mL) batter. Cook for 2 to 4 minutes or until bottoms are golden brown. Using two skewers, flip the puffs over. Cook for 2 to 3 minutes or until bottoms are golden brown and a toothpick inserted in the center comes out with a bit of filling and a few moist crumbs attached. Remove pan from heat and transfer puffs to a plate. Let pan cool slightly.

7. Repeat with the remaining batter and filling, brushing wells with oil and reheating pan before each batch. Serve warm or at room temperature.

Chai Spice Puffs (India)

Makes about 21 puffs

Chai tea spices — ginger, cinnamon, cloves and cardamom — scent these exotic puffs.

- 7-well ebelskiver pan

1¼ cups	all-purpose flour	300 mL
1 tsp	ground ginger	5 mL
¾ tsp	baking powder	3 mL
½ tsp	ground cinnamon	2 mL
½ tsp	ground cardamom	2 mL
¼ tsp	salt	1 mL
⅛ tsp	ground cloves	0.5 mL
2	large eggs, separated	2
1 cup	milk	250 mL
3 tbsp	liquid honey	30 mL
2 tbsp	unsalted butter, melted	30 mL
1 tsp	vanilla extract	5 mL
	Vegetable oil	
	Confectioners' (icing) sugar	

1. In a large bowl, whisk together flour, ginger, baking powder, cinnamon, cardamom, salt and cloves.

2. In a medium bowl, whisk together egg yolks, milk, honey, butter and vanilla until well blended.

3. Add the egg yolk mixture to the flour mixture and stir until just blended (the batter will appear slightly lumpy).

4. In a medium bowl, using an electric mixer on medium-high speed, beat egg whites until frothy. Increase speed to high and beat until stiff, but not dry, peaks form. Using a rubber spatula, gently mix one-third of the egg whites into the batter. Gently fold in the remaining whites.

5. Brush wells of pan lightly with oil. Set pan over medium heat. When oil begins to sizzle, add 2 tbsp (30 mL) batter to each well. Cook for 2 to 4 minutes or until bottoms are golden brown. Using two skewers, flip the puffs over. Cook for 2 to 3 minutes or until bottoms are golden brown and a toothpick inserted in the center comes out with a few moist crumbs attached. Remove pan from heat and transfer puffs to a plate. Let pan cool slightly.

6. Repeat with the remaining batter, brushing wells with oil and reheating pan before each batch.

7. Dust the puffs with confectioners' sugar. Serve warm or at room temperature.

Kanom Krok (Thailand)

Kanom krok is an ubiquitous Thai street snack made in the cast-iron *kanom krok* pan — which just happens to look nearly identical to an ebelskiver pan. This version is rich, custardy (with gooey-sweet coconut centers) and very delicious.

Tips

For best results, do not use light coconut milk.

Be sure to stir the coconut milk well before using — it typically separates in the container.

Stir the batter every time you scoop a batch into the pan, as the rice flour settles to the bottom.

Unlike ebelskivers, *kanom krok* do not puff up into a sphere shape (no eggs or leaveners). Rather, they are half-spheres that are pressed together to form a complete sphere. The result is a snack with a browned, crispy outside and a slightly gooey coconut middle.

- 7-well ebelskiver pan
- Large lid (big enough to cover top of ebelskiver pan)

1¼ cups	white rice flour	300 mL
3 tbsp	granulated sugar	45 mL
2 tbsp	cornstarch or arrowroot	30 mL
1 tsp	salt	5 mL
2 cups	coconut milk (see tips, at left)	500 mL
½ cup	packed unsweetened shredded coconut, very finely chopped	125 mL
⅓ cup	chopped fresh chives or thinly sliced green onions	75 mL
	Vegetable oil	

1. In a large bowl, whisk together flour, sugar, cornstarch and salt. Whisk in coconut milk until blended and smooth. Stir in coconut and chives.

2. Brush wells of pan lightly with oil. Set pan over medium-high heat. When oil begins to sizzle, add 3 tbsp (45 mL) batter to each well (wells should be about three-quarters full). Cover pan with lid and cook for 2 to 4 minutes or until bottoms are golden brown and tops are bubbling (the batter will remain slightly soft in the center). Remove pan from heat. Use a metal soup spoon to scoop out each puff and transfer to a plate. Let pan cool slightly.

3. Repeat with the remaining batter, brushing wells with oil and reheating pan before each batch.

4. To serve, gently press the soft sides of two puffs together to form a little globe. Serve immediately, while still warm.

Jasmine Rice Puffs (Vietnam, Thailand)

Fragrant jasmine rice harmonizes with vanilla and lime in these Southeast Asian–inspired puffs. They will surprise and delight you.

Tip

An equal amount of plain cooled cooked white rice may be used in place of the jasmine rice.

● **7-well ebelskiver pan**

Puffs

1 cup	all-purpose flour	250 mL
¾ tsp	baking powder	3 mL
¼ tsp	salt	1 mL
2 tbsp	granulated sugar	30 mL
2	large eggs, separated	2
¾ cup	milk	175 mL
2 tbsp	unsalted butter, melted	30 mL
2 tsp	finely grated lime zest	10 mL
1 tsp	vanilla extract	5 mL
1 cup	cooled cooked jasmine rice	250 mL
	Vegetable oil	

Lime Icing

2 cups	confectioners' (icing) sugar	500 mL
1 tsp	finely grated lime zest	5 mL
1½ tbsp	freshly squeezed lime juice	22 mL

1. *Puffs:* In a large bowl, whisk together flour, baking powder and salt.

2. In a medium bowl, whisk together sugar, egg yolks, milk, butter, lime zest and vanilla until well blended.

3. Add the egg yolk mixture to the flour mixture and stir until just blended (the batter will appear slightly lumpy). Gently stir in rice.

4. In a medium bowl, using an electric mixer on medium-high speed, beat egg whites until frothy. Increase speed to high and beat until stiff, but not dry, peaks form. Using a rubber spatula, gently mix one-third of the egg whites into the batter. Gently fold in the remaining whites.

Variation

Lemon Risotto Rice Puffs (Italy): Use lemon zest and juice in place of the lime zest and juice, and substitute cooled cooked Arborio rice (or another short-grain rice) for the jasmine rice.

5. Brush wells of pan lightly with oil. Set pan over medium heat. When oil begins to sizzle, add 2 tbsp (30 mL) batter to each well. Cook for 2 to 4 minutes or until bottoms are golden brown. Using two skewers, flip the puffs over. Cook for 2 to 3 minutes or until bottoms are golden brown and a toothpick inserted in the center comes out with a few moist crumbs attached. Remove pan from heat and transfer puffs to a plate. Let pan cool slightly.

6. Repeat with the remaining batter, brushing wells with oil and reheating pan before each batch.

7. *Icing:* In a small bowl, stir together confectioners' sugar, lime zest and lime juice until smooth.

8. Drizzle the puffs with the lime icing. Serve warm or at room temperature.

Char-Siu Bao Puffs (China)

Here, I've transformed one of my all-time favorite dim sum dishes — *char siu bao*, steamed buns stuffed with barbecue pork — into a quick and easy ebelskiver supper to be made anytime, in no time.

● **7-well ebelskiver pan**

Filling

2 tsp	vegetable oil	10 mL
6 oz	extra-lean ground pork	175 g
1½ tbsp	hoisin sauce	22 mL
½ cup	finely chopped green onions	125 mL

Puffs

1¼ cups	all-purpose flour	300 mL
¾ tsp	baking powder	3 mL
¼ tsp	salt	1 mL
3	large eggs, separated	3
¾ cup	water	175 mL
	Vegetable oil	
2 tsp	toasted sesame oil	10 mL

1. *Filling:* In a large, deep skillet, heat oil over medium-high heat. Add pork and cook, breaking it up with a spoon, for 5 to 6 minutes or until no pink. Add hoisin sauce and green onions; cook, stirring, for 1 minute.

2. *Puffs:* In a large bowl, whisk together flour, baking powder and salt.

3. In a medium bowl, whisk together egg yolks, water, 1 tbsp (15 mL) vegetable oil and sesame oil until well blended.

4. Add the egg yolk mixture to the flour mixture and stir until just blended (the batter will appear slightly lumpy).

5. In a medium bowl, using an electric mixer on medium-high speed, beat egg whites until frothy. Increase speed to high and beat until stiff, but not dry, peaks form. Using a rubber spatula, gently mix one-third of the egg whites into the batter. Gently fold in the remaining whites.

Variation

You can use ¾ cup (175 mL) cooled shredded cooked pork or chicken in place of the ground pork. Combine with the hoisin sauce and green onions as directed at the end of step 1.

6. Brush wells of pan lightly with vegetable oil. Set pan over medium heat. When oil begins to sizzle, add 1 tbsp (15 mL) batter to each well. Place 1 tsp (5 mL) filling in the center of each well and top with 1 tbsp (15 mL) batter. Cook for 2 to 4 minutes or until bottoms are golden brown. Using two skewers, flip the puffs over. Cook for 2 to 3 minutes or until bottoms are golden brown and a toothpick inserted in the center comes out with a bit of filling and a few moist crumbs attached. Remove pan from heat and transfer puffs to a plate. Let pan cool slightly.

7. Repeat with the remaining batter and filling, brushing wells with oil and reheating pan before each batch. Serve warm.

Gai Daan Jai (China)

Gai daan jai, also known as Hong Kong eggettes or egg puffs, are a popular street food in Hong Kong and in Chinatowns throughout North America. The pan used to make eggettes has much smaller wells than an ebelskiver pan (it looks like a cross between a waffle iron and an ebelskiver pan), but these are so simple and delicious, you'll be happy to have bigger puffs. Eggettes tend to be much sweeter than traditional ebelskivers, but you can always cut back on the amount of sugar to suit your taste.

Tip

For best results, do not use nonfat evaporated milk.

● **7-well ebelskiver pan**

1 cup	all-purpose flour	250 mL
2 tbsp	cornstarch	30 mL
1 tsp	baking powder	5 mL
¼ tsp	salt	1 mL
⅓ cup	granulated sugar	75 mL
2	large eggs	2
¾ cup	evaporated milk	175 mL
2 tbsp	water	30 mL
	Vegetable oil	
1 tsp	vanilla extract	5 mL

1. In a large bowl, whisk together flour, cornstarch, baking powder and salt.

2. In a medium bowl, whisk together sugar, eggs, evaporated milk, water, 1 tbsp (15 mL) oil and vanilla until well blended.

3. Add the egg mixture to the flour mixture and stir until just blended (the batter will appear slightly lumpy).

4. Brush wells of pan lightly with oil. Set pan over medium heat. When oil begins to sizzle, add 2 tbsp (30 mL) batter to each well. Cook for 2 to 4 minutes or until bottoms are golden brown. Using two skewers, flip the puffs over. Cook for 2 to 3 minutes or until bottoms are golden brown and a toothpick inserted in the center comes out with a few moist crumbs attached. Remove pan from heat and transfer puffs to a plate. Let pan cool slightly.

5. Repeat with the remaining batter, brushing wells with oil and reheating pan before each batch. Serve warm.

Pa Jeon (Korea)

Literally translated as
"green onion pancakes,"
pa jeon are a beloved
Korean dish that is eaten
as a snack or a full meal.
Making them in an
ebelskiver pan is a snap
and results in a greater
puff than when they're
made on a griddle or in
a skillet, and plenty of
crispy edges. Consider
the vegetables in this dish
(other than the green
onions) entirely variable:
the beauty of *pa jeon*
is that it is perfect for
using up bits and pieces
of vegetables you already
have on hand.

● **7-well ebelskiver pan**

Dipping Sauce

1 tbsp	minced gingerroot	15 mL
1½ tsp	granulated sugar	7 mL
1 tsp	sesame seeds, toasted (optional)	5 mL
⅓ cup	soy sauce	75 mL
3 tbsp	unseasoned rice vinegar	45 mL
1 tsp	toasted sesame oil	5 mL

Pancakes

1 cup	all-purpose flour	250 mL
1 cup	rice flour	250 mL
¼ tsp	salt	1 mL
3	large eggs, lightly beaten	3
1¼ cups	chilled seltzer water	300 mL
	Vegetable oil	
1 cup	sliced green onions	250 mL
⅔ cup	coarsely shredded carrots	150 mL
½ cup	chopped shiitake or cremini mushrooms	125 mL
¼ cup	prepared kimchi, chopped	60 mL

1. *Sauce:* In a small bowl, combine ginger, sugar, sesame seeds (if using), soy sauce, vinegar and sesame oil. Set aside.

2. *Pancakes:* In a large bowl, whisk together all-purpose flour, rice flour and salt. Add the eggs, seltzer water and 1 tbsp (15 mL) oil, whisking until blended. Let batter stand for 5 minutes, then gently stir in green onions, carrots, mushrooms and kimchi.

3. Brush wells of pan lightly with oil. Set pan over medium heat. When oil begins to sizzle, add 2 tbsp (30 mL) batter to each well. Cook for 2 to 4 minutes or until bottoms are golden brown. Using two skewers, flip the pancakes over. Cook for 2 to 3 minutes or until bottoms are golden brown and a toothpick inserted in the center comes out with a few moist crumbs attached. Remove pan from heat and transfer pancakes to a plate. Let pan cool slightly.

4. Repeat with the remaining batter, brushing wells with oil and reheating pan before each batch.

5. Serve the pancakes warm, with the dipping sauce.

Takoyaki (Japan)

A traditional Japanese street food, *takoyaki* are savory pancake puffs stuffed with bits of octopus (*tako*). *Takoyaki* pans are virtually identical to ebelskiver pans, although the wells are slightly smaller, so these international snacks are a breeze to make at home.

● **7-well ebelskiver pan**

Takoyaki Sauce

2	cloves garlic, minced	2
2 tsp	minced gingerroot	10 mL
1 tbsp	granulated sugar	15 mL
1/4 cup	ketchup	60 mL
1/4 cup	mirin or cooking sherry	60 mL
2 tbsp	soy sauce	30 mL

Filling

8 oz	cooked octopus, cut into bite-size pieces	250 g
1/3 cup	finely chopped green onions	75 mL
1/4 cup	finely chopped drained pickled ginger	60 mL
1 tbsp	dried shrimp paste	15 mL

Puffs

1 2/3 cups	cake flour	400 mL
1 tbsp	instant dashi powder	15 mL
2	large eggs	2
2 1/2 cups	ice water	625 mL
	Vegetable oil	
	Green seaweed powder (*aonori*) and/or dried bonito flakes (optional)	

1. *Sauce:* In a small saucepan, combine garlic, ginger, sugar, ketchup, mirin and soy sauce. Bring to a boil over medium heat, stirring. Reduce heat and simmer, stirring, for 3 to 4 minutes or until slightly thickened. Remove from heat and let cool.

2. *Filling:* In a medium bowl, combine octopus, green onions, pickled ginger and shrimp paste. Set aside.

3. *Puffs:* In a large bowl, whisk together flour, dashi powder, eggs and ice water until smooth.

Tip

An equal amount of other cooked seafood, such as squid, crab or shrimp, may be used in place of the octopus.

4. Brush wells of pan lightly with oil. Set pan over medium heat. When oil begins to sizzle, add 1 tbsp (15 mL) batter to each well. Place 2 tsp (10 mL) filling in the center of each well and top with 1 tbsp (15 mL) batter. Cook for 2 to 4 minutes or until bottoms are golden brown. Using two skewers, flip the puffs over. Cook for 2 to 3 minutes or until bottoms are golden brown and a toothpick inserted in the center comes out with a bit of filling and a few moist crumbs attached. Remove pan from heat and transfer puffs to a plate. Let pan cool slightly.

5. Repeat with the remaining batter and filling, brushing wells with oil and reheating pan before each batch.

6. Serve the puffs warm, topped with a small spoonful of the sauce and sprinkled with seaweed powder and/or bonito flakes (if using).

Lamington Puffs (Australia)

An homage to one of
Australia's favorite
desserts, these sweet
petites provide a nice
hit of mellow vanilla to
complement the piquant
fruit filling and rich
chocolate and coconut
topping.

Tip

Raspberry jam or preserves
or strawberry jam may be
used in place of the red
currant jelly.

● **7-well ebelskiver pan**

1¼ cups	all-purpose flour	300 mL
¾ tsp	baking powder	3 mL
¼ tsp	salt	1 mL
1 tbsp	granulated sugar	15 mL
2	large eggs, separated	2
1 cup	milk	250 mL
2 tbsp	unsalted butter, melted	30 mL
1 tsp	vanilla extract	5 mL
	Vegetable oil	
½ cup	red currant jelly	125 mL
	Chocolate Sauce (page 90) or Chocolate Coconut Sauce (page 132)	
¾ cup	sweetened flaked or shredded coconut, chopped	175 mL

1. In a large bowl, whisk together flour, baking powder and salt.

2. In a medium bowl, whisk together sugar, egg yolks, milk, butter and vanilla until well blended.

3. Add the egg yolk mixture to the flour mixture and stir until just blended (the batter will appear slightly lumpy).

4. In a medium bowl, using an electric mixer on medium-high speed, beat egg whites until frothy. Increase speed to high and beat until stiff, but not dry, peaks form. Using a rubber spatula, gently mix one-third of the egg whites into the batter. Gently fold in the remaining whites.

5. Brush wells of pan lightly with oil. Set pan over medium heat. When oil begins to sizzle, add 1 tbsp (15 mL) batter to each well. Place 1 tsp (5 mL) jelly in the center of each well and top with 1 tbsp (15 mL) batter. Cook for 2 to 4 minutes or until bottoms are golden brown. Using two skewers, flip the puffs over. Cook for 2 to 3 minutes or until bottoms are golden brown and a toothpick inserted in the center comes out with a bit of filling and a few moist crumbs attached. Remove pan from heat and transfer puffs to a plate. Let pan cool slightly.

6. Repeat with the remaining batter and jelly, brushing wells with oil and reheating pan before each batch.

7. Drizzle the puffs with chocolate sauce and sprinkle with coconut. Serve warm.

Library and Archives Canada Cataloguing in Publication

Saulsbury, Camilla V.
    150 best ebelskiver recipes / Camilla V. Saulsbury.

ISBN 978-0-7788-0442-0

    1. Pancakes, waffles, etc. 2. Pastry. 3. Cookbooks. I. Title. II. Title: One hundred
fifty best ebelskiver recipes.

TX770.P34S29 2013   641.81'53   C2012-907476-4

Index

Note: The annotation "(v)" next to a recipe name indicates that it is a variation of the main recipe on that page.